WHISPERING IN THE DAYLIGHT

WHIS PER ING IN THE DAY LIGHT

The Children of
TONY ALAMO
Christian Ministries
and Their Journey
to Freedom

DEBBY SCHRIVER

THE UNIVERSITY
OF TENNESSEE PRESS
Knoxville

Unless otherwise noted, photographs were taken by the author, or donated to the project
by a former member of Tony Alamo Christian Ministries who wishes to remain anonymous.

The paper in this book meets the requirements of American National Standards Institute /
National Information Standards Organization specification Z39.48–1992 (Permanence of Paper).
It contains 30 percent post-consumer waste and is certified by the Forest Stewardship Council.

PROCEEDS FROM THIS BOOK ARE DEDICATED
TO SERVING THE NEEDS OF CULT SURVIVORS.

Library of Congress Cataloging-in-Publication Data

Names: Schriver, Debby, author.
Title: Whispering in the daylight : the children of Tony Alamo Christian Ministries
and their journey to freedom / Debby Schriver.
Description: First edition. | Knoxville : The University of Tennessee Press, 2018.
| Includes bibliographical references and index. |
Identifiers: LCCN 2017052713 (PRINT) | LCCN 2018008158 (EBOOK) | ISBN 9781621903871 (KINDLE)
| ISBN 9781621903888 (PDF) | ISBN 9781621903864 (HARDCOVER)
Subjects: LCSH: Tony Alamo Christian Ministries—History. | Cults—United States.
Classification: LCC BP605.T66 (EBOOK) | LCC BP605.T66 S37 2018 (print) | DDC 299—dc23
LC record available at https://lccn.loc.gov/2017052713

For the Children

YOU
ARE NOT
VICTIMS

YOU
ARE
CHAMPIONS

AND YOUR
COURAGE
WILL GIVE
VOICE
TO THE
SILENCE
OF
OTHERS

What you have said in the dark will be heard in the daylight,
and what you have whispered in the ear in the inner rooms
will be proclaimed from the roofs.

Luke 12:3

TELL YOUR WHISPERS
By Ruth

The voices and faces of the children that are not seen shout the loudest
Their hearts have learned to hide in shadows and cover bruises and scars
They fear to dream and bright futures do not convey in their dwellings
Personal thoughts aren't allowed, simple pleasures denied
Special secrets hold them tight, hidden darkness feels the night
Blend in, don't stand out, merge within the walls
Born to serve, learn to exist, fight your demons, bite your lip
Tell your whispers, sing your songs
Truth and freedom your heart belongs.

Contents

Illustrations

Note to the Reader

Whispering in the Daylight is the true story of children who were taken from the Tony Alamo (pronounced uh-LAH-mo) Christian Ministries in an FBI raid. Names have been changed to protect the privacy of the children. Names of the adults whose identities don't compromise the children are accurate.

The storyline of this book is based upon interviews of children taken from the cult, former adult cult members, court transcriptions, legal experts, law enforcement officials, and many others who witnessed the creation, development, and chronology of the Alamo organization. No one interview is more important than another; rather, each individual has provided a perspective that helps form a bigger picture and affirms the accuracy of the account as a whole. While memories can play tricks on us, the testimony of a large number of people in varying roles along with court records and news stories provide reliable documentation of three generations and the chronological development of the Alamo organization. Brenda and Daniel provided extensive information as first-generation cult members, beginning in California, moving to Arkansas, and participating in the prayer vigil for Susan Alamo's resurrection. Their willingness to talk with me opened many doors and provided a valuable perspective of the cult experience from their young adult days into the birth of the second generation of followers. The broad outlines of the history of the church and the progress of Tony and Susan Alamo's lives have been drawn from these interviews, confirmed, and cross-checked with other interviews, court documents, and public records. The true names of those interviewed have been withheld to protect their safety.

Sermons and content taken from Tony and Susan Alamo's written documents are Tony and Susan Alamo's own creation and are not considered to be factual. I did not seek Alamo's approval for this book.

Is Alamo's organization a cult? In the early days Tony and Susan Alamo loosely called their gathering a "church." In 1969 they filed the Articles of Incorporation for the Tony and Susan Alamo Foundation, and so members referred to it as "The Foundation." Signs for the "Tony Alamo Christian Church" appeared with expansion to Arkansas and other states. Over time terminology implied a broader scope: Music Square Church (Nashville, Tennessee); Holiness Tabernacle (Dyer, Arkansas); Alamo Christian Church Consecrated, New Jerusalem; Tony Alamo Christian Ministries, World Pastor Tony Alamo. Alamo referred to his property as a "campus" or "complex" and to his place of worship as a "church." Followers typically call it "the church."

The term "cult" is a word loaded with connotations. Traditional definitions connect the term to forms of religious worship. Over time meanings have broadened to describe nearly any group of people pulled together by the draw of a common passion such as music, pop cultures, and even literary genres. The ambiguity of definition challenges the ability to create a scientific list of qualifying traits to declare a group a cult. The International Cultic Studies Association (ICSA) promotes the scholarship of the academic and practitioner communities—sociologists, psychologists, medical physicians, anthropologists, and others—to understand cultic phenomena and the impacts on individuals and society. Experts at the 1985 ICSA/UCLA Wingspread Conference on Cultism agreed on an applicable working definition of a "totalist" type cult:

> A group or movement exhibiting a great or excessive
> devotion or dedication to some person, idea, or thing
> and employing unethically manipulative techniques
> of persuasion and control (e.g., isolation from former
> friends and family, debilitation, use of special methods
> to heighten suggestibility and subservience, powerful
> group pressures, information management, suspension
> of individuality or critical judgment, promotion of total
> dependency on the group and fear of leaving it . . .), de-
> signed to advance the goals of the group's leaders, to the

actual or possible detriment of members, their families, or the community.[1]

Law enforcement officials, psychologists, sociologists, and cultic studies academicians affirm that Tony Alamo Christian Ministries most definitely qualifies as a harmful, high-demand group. This organization fits some broad signposts of the cult definition: (1) It is exclusive, meaning if you leave the group, your salvation is in danger; (2) It is secretive; (3) It is deceptive; and (4) It is authoritarian, led by a leader who expects total loyalty and unquestioned obedience.[2] The words "cult" and "compound" trigger unfavorable visions, and such images are a perfect match for Alamo's organization.

Like many cult leaders, Tony Alamo had different faces. The public saw him as a somewhat self-important but harmless music promoter and designer of bedazzled denim jackets. He spent much time away from his compounds and always had an entourage of people (including child brides from the late 1990s until his arrest in 2008) to serve his needs. In Nashville, Tennessee, the Alamos drove a fleet of black Cadillac sedans and dressed elaborately—Tony in turtle-leather platform boots, a diamond pinky ring, and a bearskin coat with decorative bear claws and Susan in fur coats, fake eyelashes, plastic surgery, and wigs. Tony's arrivals at high-end restaurants and hotels always created a stir. His claims of grandeur seem to be missing real evidence. He boasted of having an original unpublished Beatles album in his collection, but his claim has never been substantiated. A visit to the Tony Alamo Christian Ministries website provides a comprehensive look at Alamo through his own lens.

Alamo's followers have no true picture of the outside world. In the early days they did not have access to media. Beginning in the 1990s followers saw and listened only to Alamo-approved media as it was filtered through

---

1. Louis Jolyn West, MD and Michael D. Langone, PhD, "Cultism: A Conference for Scholars and Policy Makers," Cultic Studies Journal 3, no. 1 (1986): 87.

2. Marshall Shelley, "What's a Cult?" https://www.christianitytoday.com/iyf/advice/faithqu/what-is-cult.html.

Alamo's warped worldview. Travel outside of the church property occurs only with permission and accompaniment by another church member. Tony presented himself as the World Pastor, and followers believe his teachings. His taped messages include letters read from converts in Africa, South America, and Asia. Whatever criticisms they may see and even his imprisonment underscore Tony's claims of persecution by a world doomed and slated for destruction. Tony is their only authority, a prophet of God.

Tony also had a business persona and attracted outsiders with money to donate to his ministry. In the 1990s he created a charity called Arm Full of Help and established Action Distributors, a New Jersey salvage business. Donations far exceeded the needs of the church, and unbeknownst to donors, Alamo ordered his followers to stock warehouses, repackage, price, and ship items for resale to stores and flea markets. Profits went to the church, where the treasure was totally controlled by Pastor Tony Alamo. He was greedy, shrewd, and adept at deception. He was charismatic, able to detect vulnerabilities in people and gain control of their lives. Tony's favorite recruits were not people with psychological problems or physical handicaps. He wanted people who are intelligent, productive, and able to make money for "the cause."[3]

Law enforcement, psychologists, and sociologists see Tony as a dangerous cult leader with sociopathic and psychopathic traits who did great harm to others emotionally, psychologically, spiritually, physically, and financially. Joe Navarro, twenty-five-year veteran of the FBI, lists personality traits that raise warning flags about a cult leader.[4] Tony Alamo fits every item on the list. (See Appendix 1.) To assist the reader with these varying perspectives of Tony Alamo, I have included a timeline of events selected to indicate how the outside world viewed Tony in stark contrast with his followers' limited understanding.

To learn the story, I conducted 337 interviews in person, by telephone, and over the Internet. These include interviews with Tony Alamo, the

---

3. To learn more about people who join cults, see Kelton Rhoads, Ph.D., "Cults: Questions," (1997), www.workingpsychology.com.

4. Joe Navarro, MA, "Dangerous Cult Leaders," (August 25, 2012), psychologytoday.com.

children, their foster and adoptive families, current and former cult members, the lead FBI agent on the case, prosecuting attorneys, FBI informants, forensic psychologists, sociologists, Department of Human Services staff, school counselors, teachers, and academicians who track and study cultic activities. I met with townspeople who were in the communities where Alamo had his settlements. I confirmed information through official court documents and other legal sources that are a matter of public record.

I slipped past barbed wire fences and armed guards to see the inside of one of the cult compounds in Arkansas. I witnessed gut-wrenching confrontations between the freed children and their parents who remain cult members today. I saw the fear still present in a child who went with me to Fouke, her first trip back there since the 2008 raid. As we exited the interstate, she wanted to hide on the floor of the car. She still believed Tony was telling the truth when he said that if she left the compound in Fouke, because she is African American, the people outside the cult would seize her, tie her to the end of a car, and drag her along the highway to her death. The children brought me into their world, and I saw firsthand the condemnation, rejection, and torment they experienced regularly.

Along with two of the children, a former cult member, and an adoptive parent, I attended the International Cultic Studies Association (ICSA) conferences in Washington, DC, (2014) and Dallas, Texas (2016). There I met with former members of many cults, families trying to recover loved ones who are currently in cults, and cult experts from researchers and teachers to counseling practitioners. This organization leads the work to help cult survivors with the daunting transition of becoming healthy and thriving in the outside world. ICSA now offers workshops for second-generation former cult members (SGAs). The ability to share experiences with those from different cults helps to demystify the cult experience and open the way to confident living.

And along the way, I consulted a library of insightful scholarship ranging from personal survivor stories to examinations of individual cults, features of cult leaders, intervention, and recovery issues.

What I learned opened my eyes and my heart.

Prologue
Saturday, September 20, 2008

It was an ordinary, small-town day. The sky was clear, and morning temperatures were moderate at sixty-five degrees with an afternoon high in the mid eighties. The noisy drone of lawnmowers and cheers and shouts of children playing t-ball in the neighborhood filled the air. All familiar Saturday sounds.

The sixty-third Four States Fair and Rodeo in nearby Texarkana would end with thrills of calf roping, rodeo clowns, and bucking broncos. The Miss Four States Fair and Rodeo Queen would be crowned. The final exclamation point to a week jam-packed with shows, rides, and special attractions.

As the sun began to set, amidst the songs of crickets and longer shadows of the drawing night, one could feel a tension. Looking back, people would swear that there was "something in the air."

At exactly 6:00 p.m. the mesmerizing, peaceful rhythm of the night froze in a single moment as the sound of a news helicopter hovered in the sky. The area was suddenly a vision of terror as nearly one hundred state police and the FBI converged from all directions and surrounded the property known as Tony Alamo Christian Ministries. With M4 carbines drawn, federal authorities burst into the compound. Shouts and wailing cries rang out, piercing the night, as officers broke through the doors, building by building, and emerged with six girls, ages ten to seventeen. The girls were hustled away in government-issued vans. Officers armed with Glock 40 pistols and MP5 machine guns cordoned off the property and assumed posts around the border. The lines were drawn.

News spread quickly. A small crowd gathered at the local car wash to catch a glimpse of the raid on Tony Alamo Christian Ministries. To many the events were a welcome relief and long overdue. Mayor Terry Purvis said, "I have been waiting on this for three years."

That day in Fouke was far from ordinary.

And it was Tony Alamo's birthday.

THE
EARLY
YEARS

1934

September 20—Tony Alamo is born Bernie Lazar Hoffman in Joplin, Missouri.

1964

While working as a Los Angeles music promoter, Alamo claims that God strikes him temporarily deaf and tells him to spread the word that Jesus will soon return.

1966

Alamo serves jail time for a weapons charge and then marries Susan Lipowitz, an aspiring actress. They legally change their names to Tony and Susan Alamo and start their religious work.

1969

The Tony and Susan Alamo Christian Foundation incorporates, and the Alamos begin ministering to Hollywood street kids, numbering twenty-five to thirty each night. Unable to find a church willing to share space, their home becomes filled with their newly converted charges. As numbers grow, a house on Carlos Avenue belonging to Ed Mick, Alamo's first convert, serves as a venue for services.

1970

The Alamos purchase an old restaurant sitting on 160 acres about forty-five minutes north of Los Angeles in Saugus, canyon country. They open a church and followers live in dorm-like structures and squalid conditions. Followers make meals with food donated from a supermarket. They are told that Jesus Christ is coming back to earth any day, and if they leave, they will die, go insane, end up in prison, turn into homosexuals, or become prostitutes. Followers number eight hundred. Locals in the community are curious and at times suspicious of the closed-off group.

1973

The Alamos extend their reach through the media, producing the *Tony and Susan Alamo Christian Foundation* television program, recorded in Hollywood, California (1971–72); Portsmouth, Virginia; Nashville, Tennessee (1974–75); and Dyer, Arkansas (1977, 1979). Another show, *Susan Alamo Speaks Out*, is recorded in Fort Smith, Arkansas (1981) and broadcasts nationally until 1982. Beginning in 1990–91 Tony Alamo produces a radio program that he claims to broadcast worldwide. Television and radio programs offer gospel songs, personal testimonies, and gospel messages.

Alamo's compounds attract curiosity and speculation among neighboring residents.

CHAPTER
ONE

California, 1960

TONY

The man who called himself Tony Alamo gazed into the mirror and was especially pleased by what he saw. A little bit of oil smoothed his dark, black hair over a thick mat that stood about an inch above his scalp. His shoulders were broad. He lifted his chin just a bit, tilted his head slightly to the right, halfway closed his eyes, and peering out he saw a vision of fame, glitz, money, and power.

He stepped back from the mirror and suddenly saw another image, the pathetic face of Bernie Lazar Hoffman, born on September 20, 1934 in Joplin, Missouri. His parents were immigrants from Romania and Jewish but not particularly religious. They constantly warned him and his brothers, Dan and Ricky, to say they were Romanian and not Jewish to avoid being beaten up by other children. Bernie remembered his father as a talented artist who claimed to be a one-time dance instructor for Rudolf Valentino. He thought of the family's life in Joplin and their move to Helena, Montana. A burning desire to go to California to make his fortune and to be *somebody* coursed through his body.

He quickly put on his dark, tinted glasses and snuffed out the glimmer of his former self.

Alamo smiled. Those dark tinted glasses were a perfect addition to his image. He could observe anyone without their knowing. He liked to have the upper hand. Let them think he couldn't see, all the while piercing their souls with his vision.

EDITH OPAL

Alma, Arkansas, was the epitome of a town anyone could miss. Cars traveling on Interstate 40 took exit 13 only if they were desperate for gas or needed to make a U-turn. A church steeple, a small brick school, an empty pool hall, and a canning factory resembled monopoly pieces on a flat board of five square miles of land. A small rusting sign on the two-lane highway announced Alma as the "Crossroads of America."

Were it not for the birth of Edith Opal Horn on April 25, 1925, Alma might have remained unremarkable. Edith Opal's childhood was small-town typical. While she was still a little girl, her family moved to Dyer, Arkansas, 4.3 miles in a straight line from Alma. Despite dreams of becoming a Hollywood starlet, she fell into the pattern of other girls back then. She married at fourteen, had a baby boy at fifteen, and divorced at sixteen.[1]

It was then that Edith Opal decided to take charge of her own journey to stardom and headed to California. When she reached Hollywood, Edith Opal changed her name to Susan Fleetwood. After failed attempts at a singing and acting career, she married then divorced Sol Lipowitz, and converted from her Jewish roots to evangelical Christianity. She began to preach and teach informally and in 1964 founded the short-lived Susan Lipowitz Foundation. Susan and Sol had one child, Christhiaon. Looking back on her childhood years, Christhiaon Coie describes growing up fast on the streets of Hollywood:

---

1. "Cult Leader's Kin Explains Her 'Con,'" *Sacramento Bee* (May 22, 1991).

Mama had dreams of being a star. She was beautiful in the weirdest way, not like you would look at her and go, "Wow, a striking beauty," but when she walked in a room, she had so much command that people stopped talking. We'd go from a few bucks to absolute poverty—I mean the kind of poverty that mom and I would be living in a one-room apartment with a pull-down Murphy bed and a hot plate, and we would do mystery cans, where we'd go buy cans that had no labels. You would open these cans and whatever you opened, you ate.[2]

Susan developed her evangelical skills by scamming churches under the pretense of being a missionary seeking funds. She would say to Chris, "Put on a dress. We're gonna do a church." They would go, and during the service, Susan would stand and say, "I have a message from the Lord, and I need to speak."[3]

Susan would speak, Chris would sing, church members would pass a love offering, and mother and daughter would leave with money.

And so at age thirty-four Edith Opal Horn gave birth to a new persona, Susan Lipowitz, with business acumen, powers of persuasion, and gritty determination well in place.

LOS ANGELES

From the first day he arrived in California, Bernie Hoffman hit the street running. Already he was trying out new names—Marcus Abad and Mark Hoffman—before selecting Tony Alamo, a signature he thought to be in keeping with the talented and powerful man he knew he was. He liked to think of himself as a crooner capitalizing on the popular music genre of the

---

2. Susy Buchanan, "The Daughter's Tale: Anti-Catholic Cult Leaders' Child Recounts Abuse," *Southern Poverty Law Center Intelligence Report* 129 (Spring 2008): 3.

3. Ibid. 3–4.

1950s. His performing talents were largely inflated in his mind, and fortunately he found more lucrative success as a promoter. He was gregarious,
outspoken, and seemed to have a knack for getting in on deals at the right
time with his fingers in a lot of different pots. In his own words: "I was vice-
president for a very large health studio chain. We had seventy-five studios
in the States and Canada. I ducked in and out of the motion picture and
music industries down through the years, cutting records myself to fit the
trend of music, whatever it was. I put together 'Oldie but Goodie' albums,
bought out top radio and television time, and made a fortune out of them.
. . . I would pick up complete unknowns, manage and promote them to big
stars."[4] What Tony didn't mention is that he was selling copyrighted songs
without permission, a crime that later made him the object of a lawsuit.

Tony's relationships with women were short lived. In the 1950s his marriage to Joann Dill lasted for three years and produced three children—
Corey Hoffman, Mike Hoffman, and Maureen Hoffman. He married
Helen Hagan (born Helen Alice Muller) of New York in 1961, and the
couple had a son, Mark Anthony Hoffman, on May 25, 1964.

Not long after the birth of his son, Tony along with his usual entourage
of men who served his business needs stepped into a Hollywood restaurant
for dinner. Wearing his ever-present dark, tinted glasses, Tony squinted as
his eyes adjusted to the dark and smoky room. It was then that he noticed
the platinum-blond woman sitting at the bar. She was talking loudly and
intently while flicking her cigarette ashes into a tray by her drink. A girl
appearing to be in her early teens sat next to her. Tony didn't especially
like women. By his own admission, he had no respect for them at all.[5] But
something drew him to this particular woman. Tony swaggered to a nearby
table, motioned, and instantly engaged her interest.

"I promote a lot of high-end entertainers but haven't seen you before,"
Tony remarked. Susan responded, "Well, I'm an actress, been around the
studio for years, and my daughter here is a singer."

---

4. Tony Alamo, "Signs of the Times." www.scvhistory.com/scvhistory/alamo-alamo.htm.

5. Ibid. 4.

Tony replied, "I bet she's fantastic. I can make her a big star. I promoted the Beatles and Sonny and Cher."

When Tony excused himself to go to the restroom, Chris said to her mother, "Listen to me. This guy is an absolute bum. Everyone knows that he's living with a little wannabe starlet and got her pregnant." During this time Tony also had a relationship with Judy Lee Stearns who bore him another son. Susan put her finger in her daughter's face and said, "Mind your own fucking business. When he gets back, excuse yourself from the table. And don't come home tonight."

Tony returned, and Susan looked straight into his eyes and said, "Tony, I've got to ask you a question. Did you know that Jesus Christ is coming back to earth again?" Tony looked deeply into her eyes and said, "Why, yes, Susan, I do know. But how did you know?"

TONY AND SUSAN ALAMO
IN THE EARLY 1970S.

Susan replied, "Well, let's go up to my apartment and talk about it."[6]

That day Tony Alamo found his kindred spirit in Susan Lipowitz. In a short time the two filed for divorce from their current spouses and in 1966 married in a Las Vegas ceremony, officially changing their names to Tony and Susan Alamo. Both knew their lives would never be the same. What they didn't know is how far destiny would take them from their dreams.

After Susan and Tony married, they ran a small ministry from Susan's Los Angeles apartment. They invited hippies into their apartment to pray and be saved and told them to turn over their worldly possessions. Times were hard. It seemed that Tony's claims of being a lucrative promoter were as overrated as Susan's acting career. Instructing their followers to get jobs and send them money, Tony and Susan headed back to Las Vegas, following what they said was a calling from the Lord.

Susan's daughter, Christhiaon, stayed in California and deeply missed her mother. She flew to Las Vegas, but when she was alone with Tony one afternoon, he raped her. Susan walked into the scene and accused her daughter of being a "little fucking whore" and a liar who was trying to steal her man. Chris fled back to Los Angeles with her mother's words burning in her head and betrayal breaking her heart.

Tony and Susan returned to Los Angeles on the coattails of Rouvaun, an unconventional opera singer who rode a motorcycle. As Rouvaun's promoter, Tony collected large sums of backer money and put that money to good use, buying jewels, furs, and leather jackets. But Tony's success in the music industry waned, and thus they turned to their ministry for their livelihood. Susan, the seasoned evangelist, wasted no time recruiting young people to the fold. Beginning with her daughter's boyfriend, Ed, her marks fell like dominos, kneeling on the floor and praying for salvation. She and Tony conducted nightly services, fed homeless kids food stolen from trash cans, and convinced them that they had a direct line to God. Not moving in to stay with the group and not giving to the church assured an end in hell. These young believers handed their paychecks to the church, and

---

6. Susy Buchanan, 5.

in 1969 Tony and Susan Alamo filed the Articles of Incorporation for the Tony and Susan Alamo Foundation.

Susan and Tony regularly loaded up the kids, especially the Hebrew Christians—new Jewish converts to Christianity—in cars and vans to visit big churches and display the miracle of salvation. Money came pouring in. By 1971 they had purchased property outside of Los Angeles in Saugus, California, where followers converted the old Wilson restaurant into their church. Rustic existing structures served as living quarters for the followers, and chicken coops along with a few makeshift cubicles were turned into shacks for married couples. Tony declared, "When I got saved and I met Susan, it was so exciting because when we got married, I said, God has got to love me more than anybody in the world." Susan called Tony the "eagle" because he could convert anyone he met.[7]

By this time, Christhiaon had two young children and decided that she wanted out of the foundation. Assuring her mother that she would never tell anyone about the scam she was running, Chris prepared to leave. She called a cab but before she could escape, foundation members, including Susan and Tony, stormed through her front and back doors and beat her. The cab driver called the police, and Susan Alamo told them that her daughter was a psychotic drug addict, explaining that her injuries were a result of their trying to restrain her. The police left, someone hit Chris in the head, and she blacked out. When she awakened, she couldn't find her children. The police returned and found Chris's older child hiding in the closet. They were just leaving to go to the police station to file a report when the phone rang. Chris listened to a voice saying, "If you file anything, you'll never see your daughter again. If you want your daughter, you need to leave there right now. Don't sign anything and come back to the house and get her." Chris, who had been taken into custody, fled the police station to rescue her baby.

That was the last time she saw her mother, Susan, alive.[8]

---

7. "Controversy Continues to Follow Tony Alamo." http://www.rickross.com/reference/Alamo/alamo13.html.

8. Susy Buchanan, 10.

Follow the Children

When the moon is in the seventh house
And Jupiter aligns with Mars
Then peace will guide the planets
And love will steer the stars.
This is the dawning of the Age of Aquarius.

Hair: The American Tribal Love-Rock Musical, 1968

The tapestry of the United States in 1968 displayed signs of political change, generational clashes, and social experimentation. Youth reacting to a culture punctuated by military draft, deployment to Vietnam, and civil rights issues sounded the anthem for peace, power, freedom, and happiness. This vocal and passionate generation questioned just about everything that their parents' World War II generation held "sacred." "Question authority" was the slogan of the era. Passionate and earnest voices called for the end of war and the abolishment of privileged rights, and challenged traditional symbols of family and social structure.

Physically the children of the sixties discarded their parents' coat and tie for bell-bottom blue jeans, tie-dyed t-shirts, and sandals. In response to their fathers, whose crew cuts symbolized American patriotism, males rebelled by growing long, flowing hair. Intellectually this generation was seeking a "truer" meaning of life that embraced a way of living far different from the traditional family structure of the 1950s. Experimenting with altered states brought on by meditation and drugs, this generation was looking for insights regarding life purpose and trying on their own ideas of utopia. They stepped beyond boundaries of sexuality and became vocal, critical, and eager to embrace a new kind of society.

And so emerged the "flower children" or "hippies" as the media dubbed them. Rock and roll musicians proclaimed the heart and soul of the times in their lyrics celebrating life, freedom, and the pursuit of purpose: "Where do I go? Follow the children? Is there an answer in their sweet faces that tells me why I live and die? Into the city, into the glitter where the truth lies ... Follow the neon into the city where the truth lies" (*Hair: The American Tribal Love-Rock Musical*, 1968).

The older generation reacted with dismay. Where did these children come from? Where were the values they had taught them? The American landscape has always included a spiritual element, and the occurrence of alternative religions in the 1970s was not new. As early as the late 1950s examples of religious exploration were evident among notable writers, psychologists, and philosophers. Hermann Hesse pointed to the growing fascination with Eastern mysticism as a "journey to the East," a trek that could find enhancement through mind-altering drugs. These "explorers" derived mystical meaning from their drug-induced trips, and usage became so popular that sociologists described the generation as a "drug culture."

The hippie generation stood for fundamental social and political change. The impact was impressive, including civil rights advances, student voice in education, awareness of environmental issues, lowering the voting age from twenty-one to eighteen, challenging puritanical mores of interpersonal and sexual relationships, and gender equity. Despite these positive changes, many activists remained disillusioned about the US social and political structure. Sociologist Stephen A. Kent points to a direct relationship between the turn from politics and social injustice to religion:

> Frustration, fear, and despair about the perceived failure of the Revolution provided a fertile ground for rapid transformation of the slogan chanters of the late 1960s into the mantra chanters of the 1970s.

In the very period when radicals and activists were expressing profound doubts about the efficacy of their protest actions, academics and cultural commentators began observing a new trend among young adults: a shift from radical politics to mystical religion. Religion was becoming central to the lives of thousands of people who, just a few years earlier, had been protesters in the streets. Always a strong current within the counterculture, never before the 1970s had religion been central to the lives of so many people of that generation.[1]

Alternative religious groups began popping up everywhere and making the news. Columnist Art Kunkin expresses ambivalent views in a front-page article, "The Great Guru Hunt: Where Are the Consciousness Books Taking Us?":

> There is very definitely something in the air, and it is not, as I originally thought last year, just the cycle of individualism and personal mystical search which could have been expected to fill the vacuum left by the failures of mass political activism in the 1960s.
>
> A certain cat is being let out of the bag, accidently or by design, which will either result in the creation of many socially motivated individuals of great personal energy who can stop mankind from destroying itself, or the widespread dispersal of these same energies utilized by egoistic persons will accelerate the crises.[2]

---

1. Stephen A. Kent, *From Slogans To Mantras* (New York: Syracuse University Press, 2001), 36–39. Kent's book provides an excellent study of the phenomenon of political activism and explosion of nontraditional religions in the 1960s and 1970s.

2. Art Kunkin, "The Great Guru Hunt: Where Are the Consciousness Books Taking Us?" *Los Angeles Free Press*, June 8, 1973. Source is cited from Stephen A. Kent, 39.

California in the 1960s was the destination for a new generation. The lure of freedom, counter-culture, anti-war sentiment, and anti-establishment values attracted the flower children seeking peace, love, spiritual enlightenment, and freedom to push the boundaries of American culture. Like their ancestors a few hundred years before them, the youth felt the lure of a better life and headed west. In buses painted brightly with flowers and peace symbols, on motorcycles, cars, trucks, and hitchhiking, thousands set their eyes on California. They had no money and few belongings, but they felt free, believing that rejecting the trappings they left behind them would lead them to purity, truth, and enlightenment.

Little did they know that Tony and Susan Alamo were awaiting them with open arms.

HOLLYWOOD, SATURDAY, AUGUST 6, 1971

It was a record hot day in Hollywood—113 degrees. High on the ridge the HOLLYWOOD sign served as a beacon signaling the way to ambition, glamour, and dazzling dreams. The eclectic mix of people swarming the streets and sidewalks resembled an out-of-step parade of sounds and colors. The atmosphere was charged with electric excitement and expectation.

This was the place to see and be seen. Just that week The Grateful Dead had filled the Palladium and was hailed as the band that "was at once ecstatic, sinister, joyful, dark, and simply bursting with a sense of possibility and freedom."[3]

Sunset Boulevard could easily be seen as that edge—a step into a dream world where possibilities seem to be endless.

That was the scene greeting Brenda and Daniel as they took in the activity around them on the corner of Hollywood and Vine. Brenda, eighteen years old, had just taken a break from college and hitchhiked from Ohio to California with her sixteen-year-old friend, Daniel. They were headed to San Francisco and Big Sur, but their ride stopped in Los Angeles and

---

3. https://archive.org/details/gd71-08-06.aud.bertrando.yerys.129.sbeok.shnf#reviews.

dropped them off right in the heart of Hollywood. Brenda blinked as she met the visual assault of Hollywood icons—the art deco style of the Palladium, glass triangular Luckman Plaza, and the red pagoda front of Grauman's Chinese Theatre almost lost in the myriad of wall-to-wall billboards. Adding to the sights, the sounds and smells from restaurants, bars, and clubs created an effect distinctly "Hollywood."

Wandering through Hollywood, Brenda and Daniel were awed by the mix of people on the streets—business executives, street musicians, prostitutes, preachers, panhandlers, squatters—all pushing their own special brands of salvation. In front of Grauman's Chinese Theatre while Brenda

ALAMO BUS TRANSPORTING FOLLOWERS, 1970S.

was comparing her hand with the handprint of Judy Garland, Daniel found himself face-to-face with a long-haired young man earnestly asking him, "Are you ready to meet God?" Shoving a single-page tract into Daniel's hands, the witness warned, "The world is coming to an end. We're going to perish. Repent or perish." The tract listed an address with an invitation for dinner and services with free bus transportation there and back. Eager for a good meal and anxious to hear more about what the young man had to say, Daniel ran back to Brenda with the news. Still exploring the Hollywood sights, Brenda opted to stay back with all their belongings.

Later that night, Daniel returned to Brenda and told her about the church service that moved his spirit to go down to the altar. The next night Brenda and Daniel would take all their possessions and hop on the bus that would carry them to Saugus, an hour's drive from Los Angeles and light years away from the world they had known.

CHAPTER
THREE

Dawning of a New Day

From the moment Brenda and Daniel arrived at the corner of Hollywood and Highland to catch the bus, the brothers and sisters separated them. A woman known as Sister Cynthia ushered Brenda to a seat. For the next forty-five minutes Cynthia fervently explained that all the signs of the end times written in the Bible were currently happening. She pointed out the vapors of smoke covering Los Angeles; she mentioned earthquakes and wars. Cynthia told her that God was looking for dedicated laborers to preach and save souls before Jesus returns.

The bus pulled off on Sierra Highway in Saugus, the heart of canyon country. Hundreds of people were milling about, greeting the buses and leading people about the grounds.

Brenda, Daniel, and the others were ushered into a large hall where they sat on benches and waited expectantly. The room was packed with people—standing room only. Brenda was a bit uneasy, but Cynthia assured her that she was in for a treat.

A man who called himself Brother Michael stepped up to the podium and gave a hearty welcome to the gathering: "You are as welcome as the flowers of May and the noonday sun. Praise the Lord! Amen." He continued with a few rules that included no talking during services and a ban of literature from other places. Brothers walked through the rows to collect forbidden materials. A brief prayer followed. Brother Michael's voice rang out in a strong, steady rhythm, and Brenda felt herself carried into the cadence of his prayer.

Suddenly full-band music filled the air, and everyone was standing, clapping, and singing gospel songs of praise to the Lord. The music took on a softer tone when Brother Tommy stepped forward to sing "In the Garden" followed by "Amazing Grace." Brother Michael then invited "popcorn" testimonials from the congregation. Followers rose from their seats, lined up on the right side of the sanctuary, and went to the pulpit one by one to give a short testimony:

"Thank you Lord for our Elders Tony and Susan."

"Lord God I was a lost soul filled with sin. I am now saved!"

"I was down and out, hooked on drugs and sinful living. I now have a home with Jesus. Thanks to our Elder Tony."

"Before I was saved, I had no roof over my head, no one who cared about me. Thanks to our Lord."

"I'd be in jail if it weren't for Elders Tony and Susan. Thank God for this ministry."

And so the testimonials continued. Brenda felt her head spinning as the vehemence of individual declarations grew. Then just as quickly as it had begun, the personal witnessing ended. All eyes focused on the podium, and an expectant hush fell over the assembly. Stepping up to the podium were Elders Tony Alamo and his wife, Susan. Eyeing them with interest, Brenda noticed that Tony stood slightly behind his wife with one hand around her waist. He looked protective, but Susan looked a little bit gruff and like she could take care of herself. Both had a captivating presence that commanded undivided attention. Together they were the complete package—Tony the leader of the music ministry and Susan the preacher—delivering their message of salvation. Their words were strong, challenging, and filled with foreboding.

Tony stood before the podium and in a sonorous voice said, "Praise the Lord, Amen?"

The congregation responded, "AMEN!" Tony continued:

Heavenly Father, our Lord and our God. Master, we
thank and praise your wonderful Holy name for eternal
life and the Holy Spirit. Open the windows of heaven
and pour out your Holy Spirit upon all of us. HALLE-
LUJAH! Lord and God send down thy latter rain upon
us. Open the windows of heaven. Anoint us, teach, Lord
feed us. Fill us with the manna and water our souls. Be
thou here. Touch us that are sick and afflicted. Touch us
that are weary. Lift us up as we lift our hands up unto
thee, Lord. Inhabit our praises, Lord and God, for when
you are with us we are strong and full of joy. HALLE-
LUJAH! Break down every wall and every barrier, every
mental block, open every heart, every soul, and every
mind to receive that which you have prepared for us
from before the foundation of the world. Let people be
very diligent this day to receive everything that you want
them to receive, which is every one of your laws, every
one of your precepts, everything from the Word of the
living God. Not to take favorite scriptures, but to receive
the whole word of the living God. In the mighty name of
Jesus we pray and everyone says Amen.[1]

The congregation responded with a fervent, "AMEN!"

After Tony's prayer the band began to play softly, and Susan Alamo
called the congregation to lay down their lives for Jesus Christ. As Brother
Tommy sang "Softly and Tenderly Jesus is Calling," Sister Cynthia turned
to Brenda, nodded toward the altar, and said, "Let's go pray." Caught up
in the moment, Brenda felt swept by the music and the fervor of the jam-
packed assembly. She wanted to feel the same happiness reflected in the

1. Tony Alamo recording, July 1981.

faces of all those around her. The band kept playing and playing. Feeling a sense of urgency, she went down to the altar along with about ten others who had come that day from Hollywood. Elder Tony Alamo held his palms up to the sky and said:

> To receive mercy for your condemned soul, kneel down and cry out to God in this prayer.
>
> My Lord and my God, have mercy upon my soul, a sinner. I believe that Jesus Christ is the Son of the living God. I believe that He died on the cross and shed His precious blood for the forgiveness of all my former sins. I believe that God raised Jesus from the dead by the power of the Holy Spirit, and that He sits on the right hand of God at this moment hearing my confession of sin and this prayer. I open up the door of my heart, and I invite You into my heart, Lord Jesus. Wash all of my filthy sins away in the precious blood that You shed in my place on the cross at Calvary. You will not turn me away, Lord Jesus; You will forgive my sins and save my soul. I know because Your word, the Bible, says so. Your Word says that You will turn no one away, and that includes me. Therefore, I know that You have heard me, and I know that You have answered me, and I know that I am saved. And I thank You, Lord Jesus, for saving my soul, and I will show my thankfulness by doing as You command and sin no more.[2]

The service ended, and Brenda began to follow the others out of the sanctuary. Suddenly a woman who called herself Mary tugged on Brenda's arm just as a man, Steven, grabbed Daniel's shoulder. Brenda and Daniel found themselves guided in different directions to sectioned-off cubicles

---

2. "Alamo Christian Ministries World Newsletter," 05700 (April–June 2003): 16.

they later learned were prayer rooms. Mary looked into Brenda's eyes and said, "This is where God wants you. God brought you here, and He wants you to stay. You can't make it out there on your own. If you leave here, Satan could tell you that you're not saved now, and you could go back out and take drugs, be in sin, and go to hell."

Brenda thought, "Well, I'll try this for a few days, and if it's not what I want, then I'll be on my way. What's the harm?" With Daniel no longer in sight, Brenda shrugged her shoulders, nodded, and followed Mary to a small building where she could stay. With no bed in sight, Brenda laid down on the floor. Her stomach grumbled, not satisfied by the pita bread and cheese supper following the service. As she closed her eyes, she felt a mix of excitement and apprehension. This had been a very long day, and she was far from home.

CHAPTER

FOUR

Baby Christians in the Incubator

The first few days in Saugus were instructive and tightly structured. Brenda, Daniel, and the others recently saved were called "baby Christians" and paired with an older Christian (OC) to mentor their spiritual development. No one was ever allowed to leave the premises without another member and permission. The Alamos said that these days were critical to those who have lived undisciplined, sinful lives, and they could fall prey to the smallest temptation that came along.

Mary took Brenda under her wing for prayer, Bible study, and witnessing. They took the church bus to Hollywood, passed out tracts to anyone who would take one, talked about the impending end of the world, and invited others to dinner at Saugus. Brenda felt comfort in how well the Bible seemed to answer her questions, and witnessing trips opened her eyes as if for the first time to the works of Satan. Now when they went to witness on the street in front of Grauman's Chinese Theatre, prostitutes, drug addicts, homeless panhandlers, and people simply seeking a different life overshadowed the glamour and glitter that had first caught her attention in Hollywood.

Baby Christians were carefully monitored, and Brenda and Daniel never had the opportunity to be alone together. Brenda was assigned a job peeling fruits and vegetables, cooking, and washing dishes in the kitchen, and Daniel went to the local high school during the day and kept busy working in mechanics on the weekend. The food—usually outdated—was donated from the local supermarket and consisted mostly of some fruit, vegetables, oatmeal, donuts, pita bread, moldy cheese, and potatoes. The daily schedule and rules were always changing. Followers maintained a twenty-four-hour prayer chain, and night assignments could be as demanding as those in the daytime with security watch duties and night witnessing lasting as late as 2:00 a.m. Limited dietary practices and sleep deprivation were the norm. They lived with the barest of necessities, sharing clothes, small cubicles for personal belongings, and shortages of personal hygiene products. Water could be scarce at times and plumbing less than adequate.

Brothers and sisters called "overseers" monitored the physical needs and functions of the community, such as the water supply, electricity usage, and even the distribution of toilet paper (often pages torn from telephone books). They had to seek permission from Tony and Susan for every aspect of their existence. One evening after dinner Sister Cynthia sharply reprimanded Brenda for overstepping the authority of an overseer when she turned on the lights in a building. Brenda said, "But I thought I should turn on the lights since I was the first to arrive." Cynthia retorted, "There you go *thinking* again."

The message of world doom and condemnation tethering their minds and spirits were as binding as ropes and chains. When Brenda did have an occasional doubt about making a home here, a paralyzing knot of fear stopped her in her tracks. Evening church services filled their minds with evidence of peril and sin of the outside world. That very evening a brother asked for twenty-five people to come up and give "popcorn" testimony. People readily responded, saying, "Thank God that I'm saved. I thank God for Tony and Susan. I thank God that there were people out on the streets to save me. If it weren't for Tony and Susan, I'd be dead. If I hadn't found salvation here, I'd be in hell. I'd be in jail. I'd be in a mental institution."

Then Pastor Tony told a story from the time before they moved to Saugus when the church was on Crescent Heights Boulevard in Hollywood. A guy named "Frenchy" got saved but then left the group. A few days later he was walking down Sunset Strip, and somebody pulled out a gun and shot him. He was in hell now.[1]

This story conveyed one single powerful message: if you leave, something really bad would happen to you. Brenda shuddered in fear. The more she learned about these last days, the more she knew this is where God wanted her to be. This is the only way she would find salvation for herself and her family.

Regular Bible study provided so many answers to her questions, and sacrifices were well worth it to create a community that lived bound by the common cause of winning souls before the Lord returned. Brenda, Daniel, and all the others had been searching for the truth. Jesus said, "I am the way, the truth, and the life" (John 16:6). Tony Alamo Christian Ministries seemed to be the answer. Saugus seemed like an ark of safety, just like in the time of Noah, and Tony Alamo Christian Ministries promised a haven for salvation.

They read the King James Version of the Bible, prayed, went witnessing, prepared meals, worked in the fields at Bakersfield, cleaned, constructed buildings, and did everything else needed to keep the church running smoothly. The Alamos preached their own interpretations of the Bible to underscore messages they wanted their followers to learn. To coerce church members to turn their money over to the church, Tony liked to tell of Ananias and his wife Sapphira (Acts 4–5). As the story goes, the early church in Jerusalem was formed by a group of believers so filled with the Holy Spirit that they were of one heart and one mind. So knit together were the hearts of the people that they held all their possessions loosely and willingly shared them with one another, not because they were coerced, but because they loved one another. Those who sold land and houses gave the profits to the Apostles, who distributed them to those in need. Two of the members of this group were Ananias and his wife, Sapphira, who sold a field. But the profits from this sale were kept in part by the couple, and Ananias laid only a part of his earnings at the Apostles' feet.

---

1. "Alamo Christian Ministries World Newsletter," 05700 (April–June 2003): 16.

The Apostle Peter knew instantly that Ananias was lying not only to him, but also to God, and he exposed his hypocrisy then and there. Ananias fell down and died. When Sapphira arrived, she too lied to Peter and to God, saying that they had donated the entire proceeds of the sale of the land to the church. When her lie was exposed, she fell down and died at Peter's feet. This Biblical story left no doubt in the power of the Lord, and the church considered rules just as seriously.

Punishment for violating Alamo church rules included being taken off any privileges, fasting, being kicked out of the church, separating spouses and children, hard physical labor, physical beatings, and reassignment to another living quarters within church properties. Rules were enforced through grievances filed by members against one another, even spouse against spouse, child against parent, friend against friend. Male members rotated two-hour

SUSAN ALAMO PREACHING IN A WORSHIP SERVICE WITH TONY ALAMO SITTING BEHIND HER. SAUGUS, CALIFORNIA, 1970S.

watch shifts to patrol the fenced compound every night. Brenda wondered why church grounds needed guards. Mary told Brenda, "Elder Tony is a prophet of God. No matter what you feel, what he says is true."

Tony was the prophet, but Susan Alamo was the one who drew the real profits. Susan had raised the funds to buy the Saugus property just as she had used her little girl to witness for cash during their early days in California. Each week Susan loaded the van with converts, visited well-established churches, and turned heads when she entered with her long-haired, rough-looking band of newly saved hippies. When the time came to speak, Susan stood up and told the story of how the Lord had saved these young people from drugs, prostitution, and life in sin. She left with fervent "amens" and her pockets full of love offerings.

Brenda received a little money from her parents, and she was afraid to keep it and not to give it to the church. Recently a member had received a sizable inheritance, gave it to the church, and Brenda heard that Pastor Tony spent that money on bills in about fifteen minutes. She couldn't imagine anyone spending that much so quickly. But then, there were a lot of people in need, and Brenda knew that all the money collected paid for their homes, clothing, food, and the work of the Lord. Followers were growing, numbering in the low thousands. The Alamos had purchased the 160 acres of ranch property in Saugus for a good price, and the canyon became peppered with more buildings as the congregation grew.

No one worked outside the church until spring 1972. Word came that fieldwork was available in Bakersfield, California. A handful of trusted older Christians went outside the compound to work. The work paid well, and not long after, Pastor Tony regularly sent people by busloads to hoe cotton, tie up grape vines, pick roses, and pack pears in a packing facility. Paychecks were given directly to the church. Numbers in the ministry were climbing from five hundred to eight hundred people. At any given time, three hundred people would be working in the fields, and the others would hold down the fort by building, recruiting, and mentoring baby Christians to bring into the fold.

Tony owned a number of small businesses around the compound, including a gas station. Church members worked in these businesses, and when customers came in for service, they received a gospel tract about Alamo's plan for salvation and personal witnessing. The church finances appeared to be flourishing. At the time Brenda didn't think too much about the money; she focused on her kitchen jobs and daily responsibilities. Many times she joined the field workers picking roses from early morning till night, returning home with cuts from the thorns, an aching back from bending over, and heat exhaustion. Years later, she would recall the words of one of the old-timers who had been saved from the very beginning. He said that he saw the church turn corrupt when all those paychecks from the fields came in. That was when Tony and Susan's vision seemed to change. Others looking back would say that Tony Alamo Christian Ministries was a con from the very beginning. Whatever the case, the house of the Lord was becoming the Holy Alamo Christian Church, a community guarded and cut off from the outside world.

CHAPTER

FIVE

All Work—More Pay—Ultimate Investment

The church at Saugus was growing, and Tony Alamo's pockets were getting heavy as the businesses of the church expanded. Followers were willing to work hard to support the work of God. Those who were sent to labor outside church property turned their paychecks over to the church and all monies from other sources such as families, insurance, social security, and government agencies were added to the till. Pastor Tony controlled all the money, and when they had needs, he would review all requests, approve a shopping list, and send two overseers to purchase the goods in town. No one ever left church grounds unaccompanied.

The Tony and Susan Alamo Christian Foundation was earning a reputation for its intense evangelical practices. Church members aggressively cornered people on the streets of Hollywood and handed out tracts proclaiming the end of the world. At 6:30 p.m. each day busloads of families, young folks, and middle-aged people followed the road to salvation in Saugus where they were promised a free meal along with religious services.

On November 20, 1971, Brenda and Daniel celebrated their "spiritual birthday," the end of their first three months as baby Christians, and became full-fledged Christian members of the Holy Alamo Christian Church. That evening when the bus arrived, they eagerly greeted each person with

ALAMO'S FOLLOWERS SPREADING THEIR MESSAGE IN A PARADE.
NEWHALL, CALIFORNIA, EARLY 1970S.

a fervent welcome and message: "The Lord called you here. The final days are here, and this is where you will find salvation."

Brenda and Daniel joined the other brothers and sisters as they ushered the visitors into the sanctuary. After the service, they handed out piles of tracts and free Bibles with one powerful message: "Stay for the night. If you leave, the devil will start talking to you and tell you not to come back. The world is ending, and all will perish without salvation." From across the room Brenda's and Daniel's eyes locked, and they turned and disappeared into the night with their new baby Christians.

While the faithful flock toiled within the confines of the church, Tony's dealings did not go unnoticed by the outside world. The complex displaying the name "Tony Alamo Christian Church" drew the curiosity of daily commuters driving on Sierra Highway.

One sunny September morning, firefighter Tom Adams stopped into the Halfway House Café for his usual country fried steak and eggs breakfast. The homemade cooking was enough to bring him in, but the café's proximity to the upstart church gave Tom a good view of the parcel of property used for housing. For some time he had been watching the comings and goings of the church that claimed the only path to deliverance. Tom couldn't shake the feeling that something wasn't quite right. He never did see any real movement there.

Now Tom was looking at the twinkling eyes of Mary as she poured his coffee and teased, "Tom, why don't you just knock on the door of that church? You could use a little salvation."

Tom rolled his eyes with the hint of a smile. "I know you think I'm imagining things, but something over there isn't right. How could all those people resist your burnt toast and hot grits in the morning? I have never seen anyone from that place set foot in here. What are they doing in there?"

"You need to talk to that woman over there," Mary said nodding to her right. "I hear she lets her kids play with some of theirs."

Tom's eyes turned to see a woman sipping coffee and deeply engrossed in the morning paper. He moved his chair a bit, leaned over, and asked, "Any news worth reading today?"

The woman looked up, shrugged, and stifling a yawn, said, "Nothing much to speak of."

"Hard night? Have some more of Mary's coffee. It's strong enough to wake a dead man," Tom said, motioning Mary to bring a refill.

"Sure, I guess so. I just dropped my kids at school and have a lot to do, but one more cup won't hurt."

Mary brought Tom's plate with the coffee pitcher, and casually said, "Tom, weren't you interested in that church back there? I think Lucy here might know something about it." Turning to Lucy she added, "Tom's a firefighter around here and self-appointed mayor of canyon country. He always wants to know everything about everybody. He's harmless, though."

Lucy lifted her eyes and took a real hard look at Tom. "Well, I think it is a strange outfit. My son used to play with some of the kids who lived back there. All of them were home-schooled, and I never saw any girls, only teenage boys. My kid liked them well enough, but I didn't feel comfortable letting him go over to any of their houses. And then there was that other thing."

"What other thing?" Tom asked.

"I heard from another parent that one of her older girls was riding a quad on the mountains behind her house near the back of the church property. She ran out of gas and started to walk down the mountain to get some. A man popped out of the bushes. He scared her to death—didn't hear him coming. He told her to get off the church property, because she was trespassing. It was weird how he was out there in the middle of nowhere."

Mary returned with the coffee. Lucy covered her cup and shook her head, but Tom raised his cup. As Mary refilled his cup, she nonchalantly said, "Well, we had a waitress who had a story. Claims she saw it all. It was about a year ago; a young girl 'escaped' with a man. They sat in that corner booth for about an hour to wait for a taxi. An older man showed up and tried to convince the girl to go back to say goodbye to the rest of the people at the church," Mary said. "In the middle of a heavy rainstorm the two people went outside to wait for the cab, arguing with the older man until the cab showed up. They left. Never saw them again. In fact, we never saw that waitress again, either."

Lucy shook off a sudden chill, rose to leave, and said, "Well, I don't know about all that. I'm out of here."

Mary went back to work, and Tom mulled over this new information. He had heard neighbors' reports about vans passing by the café on the drive into the complex at least once a day at about the same time. To him the property looked to be vacant with the exception of a standard-looking white Ford van and an old station wagon. Blinds in all the houses were drawn, and he never noticed movement or heard noise. Some people talked of brainwashing and polygamy. It seemed that no one really knew what was going on behind closed doors, except for the people who lived there.[1]

---

1. The dialogue in this chapter is based on a report by Hallie Cook, "Cult Leader Alamo Still Ministering from Prison, Threats, Rumors and 24-Hour Security Raises Suspicions about Local Church" (December 12, 2011). http://cougarnews.com/?p=19125.

1975
—
1982

1975

Leaving a few hundred followers to run the church and work the fields in Saugus, the Alamos move as many as seven hundred followers over time to Alma, Arkansas, where they build a church, housing, a restaurant, two gas stations, a concrete plant, a nursery, a clothing store, and other small businesses. Arkansas notables and eventual President and First Lady Bill and Hillary Clinton visit the restaurant to see Dolly Parton perform and describe Tony Alamo as "Roy Orbison on speed." The outside world sees the Alamos as enterprising and perhaps a bit quirky.

1976

The US Labor Department charges that Alamo is violating the Fair Labor Standards Act. The lawsuit alleges that the foundation exploits church followers who work twelve to fifteen hours a day, six or seven days a week at foundation-owned businesses. It was 1994 before these charges were resolved in court, but Alamo businesses are now under federal scrutiny.

1979

January 21—The *New York Times* puts a national focus on church financial practices. In addition to getting Susan Alamo on the record concerning the allegations, the *Times* suggests that the church holds people against their wishes in an interview of former church member Lane L. Petrie:

> Lane L. Petrie was an honors graduate of the University of Minnesota, traveling around the country to 'round out my education' when she joined the Alamo Foundation in 1973. 'I'd never been on drugs,' she said, but 'I believed the kids' stories—the worse sinner you are, the better testimony you have. I could have worked at my profession. I'd just finished school as an occupational therapist. They didn't want to let me. If you give it all up to God—your job, your family—that's what God demands. Time is short. The world is coming to an end. I was really eating it up. They said they had the truth, and I was looking for that. It was like quicksand—fine on the surface, but once you got into it, you couldn't get out.'
>
> Petrie's parents got her out of the foundation in 1976 under a court-ordered conservatorship and had her 'deprogrammed.' The Alamo Foundation has done battle in the last year with several sets of parents who sought unsuccessfully to remove their children from the settlement at Arkansas.
>
> 'They're jealous,' Susan Alamo said.[1]

---

1. "Foundation's Finances Stir Criticism," *The New York Times*, January 21, 1979.

1982

The US Labor Department charges filed in 1976 are brought to trial.

Followers testify that they do not expect salaries because of their religious beliefs. The case reaches the US Supreme Court, which rules unanimously that the workers are entitled to minimum wage and overtime benefits. Followers never received restitution.

April 8—Susan Alamo dies of cancer in Tulsa, Oklahoma. After she is embalmed, Tony takes her body back to Arkansas and dresses her in a white wedding dress for the funeral. Afterwards he displays her body in a closed casket in his dining room for six months and orders followers to hold a twenty-four-hour prayer vigil, taking two-hour shifts, for her resurrection.

CHAPTER

SIX

Gaining More Ground

The public didn't see behind the church walls, but Tony and Susan Alamo regularly sent messages out to the public through music and print. Hollywood gave them easy access to recording studios. Tony produced gospel songs with stars of varying celebrity, including Porter Wagoner, and J. D. Sumner and the Stamps Quartet. Every day followers vigorously distributed religious tracts on the streets, leaving papered tracts on the windshields of cars at night.

Tony and Susan became increasingly visible to the public. Wherever they went, they had an entourage of "servants" with them. Tony also continued to nurture the contacts he had in the music industry. Reflecting on Tony's connections to well-known celebrities, a former follower said, "Even if Tony had only a five-second association with a star in the music industry or in politics, in Tony's mind he became their promoter." Tony claimed to have an unreleased Beatles album in his possession. Whether he spoke truth or not, Alamo was certainly persuasive. Generous donations came in regularly to support his foundation. While Alamo's doomsday preaching and conspiracy theories regarding the Catholic Church and the US government seemed quirky and extreme to many on the outside, Alamo's false portrayal of his ministry as a rehabilitative home for drug addicts,

TONY ALAMO ON THE SET OF THE ALAMOS' TELE-
VISION SHOW, 1970S. THE ALAMOS RECORDED
TELEVISION SHOWS IN HOLLYWOOD, CALIFORNIA,
PORTSMOUTH, VIRGINIA, NASHVILLE, TENNESSEE,
AND DYER, ARKANSAS. THE SHOWS WERE NATION-
ALLY BROADCAST BETWEEN 1973 AND 1982.

prostitutes, and the homeless gave the ministry a bit of acceptability to the
general public.

Church services rarely featured both Tony and Susan. When word got
out that they were coming, anticipation grew to a high level of excitement. Tony participated in the music, sang a few songs, and led prayers.

Occasionally Tony hired people to sing with him. Then he would call to the altar "his beautiful spirit-filled wife, Susan," who delivered the message. She told interpretive stories based on the Bible while Tony read scriptures.

During the late 1970s and early 1980s, the Alamos used the media to preach their message, with Susan hosting her own television show, *Susan Alamo Speaks Out* in 1981. Shows were recorded in Hollywood; Portsmouth, Virginia; Nashville, Tennessee; and Dyer, Arkansas. Shows featured testimonies of converts, gospel music, and a straightforward message calling for salvation. Susan's sermons frequently defended aggressive church practices as necessary to fight the work of Satan. Occasionally well-known artists from the music industry appeared, Tony sang a gospel song, and the church choir and orchestra performed. The Tony and Susan Alamo Christian Foundation was establishing what they believed to be a worldwide presence.

While Tony handled the business enterprises of the foundation, Susan was clearly the one in charge. A well-practiced preacher, her sermons stirred the congregation and always left a deep impression. She had charisma, an inexplicable magnetism that drew people to her. People close to the Alamos described her as the true leader of the church. When Susan and Tony were together, she told him what to do, rebuked and corrected him. Never did they doubt who was in charge.

Followers traveled by the busload to labor in the agricultural fields of Bakersfield, and others worked within church grounds to maintain the needs of the community. With his growing fortune from his followers' labor, Tony expanded his reach, buying property in Tennessee, Florida, Arizona, Oklahoma, New Jersey, and New York. The Alamos' extravagance did not escape the eyes of federal agents. It was commonly known that Alamo followers worked hours that extended beyond a forty-hour workweek and turned all wages over to the church.

Perhaps motivated by this scrutiny of the law, the Alamos declared that California was doomed for eternal destruction. That year, 1975, they left some members behind to maintain the Saugus Canyon property and moved a sizable group of followers from Saugus Canyon to Arkansas. In 1976 the US Labor Department filed a lawsuit against the Tony and Susan Alamo Christian Foundation with the charge that their church members were employees and subject to the Fair Labor Standards Act (FLSA). The court battle that followed would not be resolved until 1985 with the Supreme Court ruling that church-related workers, even if volunteers, are subject to the FLSA.

Brenda and Daniel were among those who moved. They were an integral part of the community now, and leaving the Alamo ministry never entered their minds. By obeying Tony, they were doing the Lord's work and following His will. From California they traveled east on Interstate 40 and arrived at Dyer, Arkansas, a town 2.6 square miles with a population of 486.[1]

To Brenda and Daniel, Dyer looked like a one-time small town that had sputtered to a halt. An old military road, the railroad, and Highway 64 lay dormant without notice as the interstate traffic sped by. Except for a city hall and a library, the town seemed deserted.

Tony and Susan's vision was quite different. In this desolate area they saw the advantages of isolation. Here they would develop a hub of businesses with their labor force of followers and operate away from the scrutiny of the law. They grabbed property and purchased buildings, their holdings spreading and taking root like long tentacles throughout the landscape.

Followers traveled from California to Arkansas in waves from 1975–79, always leaving crews at Saugus to continue to recruit from the streets of Hollywood and grow the west coast ministry. After the additional Arkansas development, the population of followers in Saugus always hovered around two to three hundred. Brothers and sisters worked in the fields of Bakersfield to finance the Arkansas development and assure financial stability for the California locations. As homes were built and businesses were created, more people came from California to settle in Arkansas.

Dyer became a landscape of new buildings as nearly eight hundred Alamo followers settled there. The followers built a church directly across from Susan Alamo's childhood home, as well as printing facilities and a school. The Alamos were eager to develop income-producing businesses, so even before constructing houses, they set their followers out to build

---

1. The Encyclopedia of Arkansas History & Culture. www.encyclopediaofarkansas.net/.

SUSAN ALAMO'S CHILDHOOD HOME IN DYER, ARKANSAS,
REBUILT BY FOLLOWERS FOR SUSAN AND TONY ALAMO,
APPROXIMATELY 1975–76.

FIRST ALAMO CHAPEL IN DYER, ARKANSAS,
USED FROM AROUND 1976 TO 1978.

HOLINESS TABERNA-
CLE CHURCH (TODAY
OWNED BY LIVING
WATERS FELLOWSHIP),
BUILT BY FOLLOWERS
ACROSS THE STREET
FROM THE FIRST
CHAPEL IN DYER,
ARKANSAS, 1978.

product warehouses, the Alamo Western Wear Store and the Alamo Discount Grocery. In 1975 the Alamo Restaurant opened, instantly becoming a popular evening spot, known for superior home cooking and regular entertainment. Everyone worked. Daniel joined the men to refurbish
existing buildings and construct new ones. Girls and their mothers sorted
daily donations of food, clothing, and household goods. Brenda worked
twelve-plus hour shifts at the Alamo Restaurant.

Followers were directed to live in church property as it was purchased,
and living conditions left much to be desired. Brenda lived in the sisters'
dormitory that stood behind the chapel on a corner. With no working
plumbing, they had to walk to the kitchen in the middle of the night to use
the toilet. They showered at the few houses that belonged to the ministry.

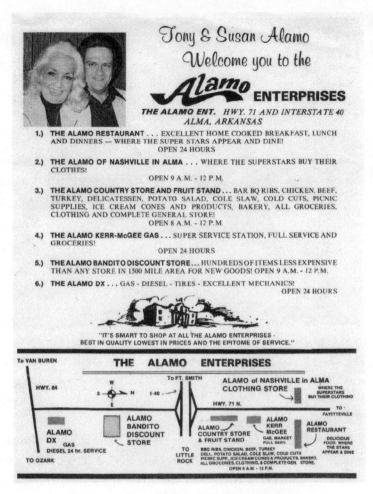

FLYER PROMOTING ALAMO ENTERPRISES INCLUDING
THE ALAMO RESTAURANT, DISCOUNT STORES, AND
A GAS STATION.

Tony and Susan did not live in squalor, however. Their followers remodeled Susan Alamo's childhood home, and they lived there until several years later when followers built them a mansion on Georgia Ridge with a beautiful view of the countryside, the Arkansas River, and the Ozark Mountains. Their home included a heart-shaped swimming pool and large

STRIP MALL AND RESTAURANT, ONE OF MANY BUSINESS
PROPERTIES ALAMO OWNED BUT LISTED IN THE NAMES OF
OTHERS TO HIDE HIS MONETARY WORTH. ALMA, ARKANSAS.

rooms for entertaining. Followers never referred to their leader's house as
a "mansion." It was called the "spec house" and the "MPB" (multi-purpose
building). Tony and Susan lived on the second floor. The downstairs served
as Tony's office, the phone room, and the tape department.

Property expanded to areas in Alma, Susan Alamo's birthplace, just 4.3
miles from Dyer. The lure of Alma may have been nostalgic, but it is more
likely that the Alamos selected the location for its strategic appeal. Alma
marked a break in Interstate 40 and provided access to Highway 71, the
continuing route to the northwest part of the state. Until the mid-1990s,
Alma served as the crossroads where travelers heading north would stop
for gas and food, offering a prime location for recruitment. Only thirteen
miles from the Oklahoma border, this location would prove to be even
more strategic to escape state law enforcement officials. Alamo businesses
flourished with additions of a grocery store, a service station, and even a

hog farm located farther away. Alamo claimed to operate a drug rehabilitation facility in Alma, but this idea was likely spun from the evangelist's method of targeting drug abusers to bring into the fold of his ministry. No accredited drug treatment center is on record as a part of the Alamo settlement. Tony's idea of drug rehabilitation was putting people to work.

For no apparent reason except to remind them of Tony's control, frequent moves were commonplace for Alamo followers, but daily living schedules remained the same. By now they had fallen into the strict routine of prayer, church, work, and church with more prayer. Children did their part, too— working fewer hours than the adults to allow time for schooling. Discipline was an everyday occurrence for adults and children alike. Everyone was expected to adhere to God's rules as interpreted by Tony. From time to time Susan and Tony would visit the school and make note of those children whose behavior required attention. Susan and Tony would see to it that the children were whipped into compliance.

DUPLEXES, LIKE ALL ALAMO STRUCTURES, WERE BUILT
BY FOLLOWERS FOR HOUSING IN DYER, ARKANSAS.

TONY AND SUSAN ALAMO'S HOUSE WAS THE FIRST
STRUCTURE FOLLOWERS BUILT ON THE GEORGIA RIDGE,
ARKANSAS, PROPERTY.

THE BACK OF TONY AND SUSAN ALAMO'S HOUSE
AT GEORGIA RIDGE, ARKANSAS.

TONY AND SUSAN'S HEART-SHAPED SWIMMING POOL
AT GEORGIA RIDGE, ARKANSAS.

THE OFFICE, PRINT SHOP, AND DORMITORY
AT GEORGIA RIDGE, ARKANSAS.

THE POND AT GEORGIA RIDGE, ARKANSAS.

A FOURPLEX RESIDENCE FOR FOLLOWERS
AT GEORGIA RIDGE, ARKANSAS.

A NINEPLEX RESIDENCE FOR FOLLOWERS
AT GEORGIA RIDGE, ARKANSAS.

THE BACK OF FOURPLEX AND DUPLEX RESIDENCES
AT GEORGIA RIDGE, ARKANSAS.

A RESIDENCE FOR FOLLOWERS AT GEORGIA RIDGE, ARKANSAS.

JUNIOR OLYMPIC POOL AT GEORGIA RIDGE, ARKANSAS.
A BATH HOUSE AND WEIGHT ROOM ARE NO LONGER STANDING.

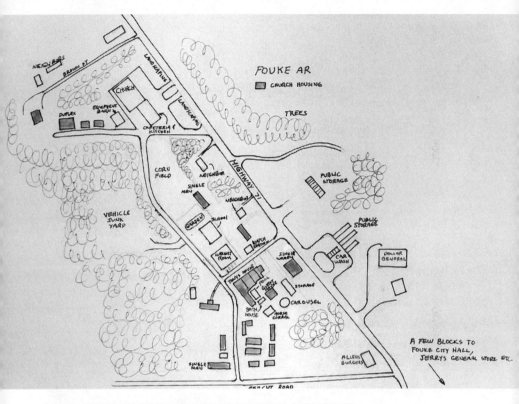

SCHEMATIC OF ARKANSAS PROPERTIES ACQUIRED
AND OWNED BY TONY ALAMO, 1975–91. DESIGNED
AND CONTRIBUTED BY FORMER MEMBER.

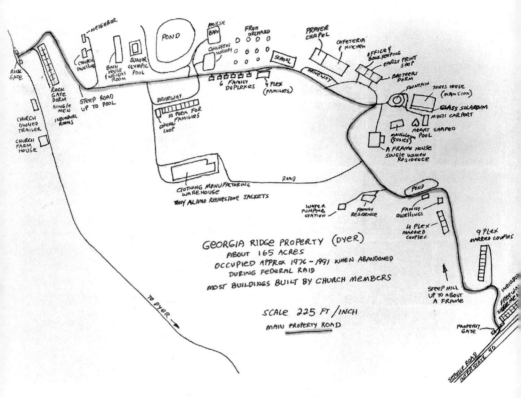

SCHEMATIC OF GEORGIA RIDGE, ARKANSAS, PROPERTY
OCCUPIED FROM APPROXIMATELY 1976 TO 1991.
DESIGNED AND CONTRIBUTED BY FORMER MEMBER.

TONY ALAMO CHRISTIAN MINISTRIES, FORT SMITH, ARKANSAS.

JEANNE ESTATES APARTMENTS OWNED BY ALAMO, PROVIDING
HOUSING FOR A SMALL NUMBER OF FOLLOWERS AND RENTALS
TO OUTSIDERS, FORT SMITH, ARKANSAS.

JOHN KOLBEK'S HOUSE, FORT SMITH, ARKANSAS.

RESIDENCE FOR FOLLOWERS, OWNED BY ALAMO,
FORT SMITH, ARKANSAS.

BUSINESS PROPERTY OWNED BY ALAMO, FORT SMITH, ARKANSAS.

ONE OF MANY WAREHOUSES WHERE FOLLOWERS WORKED
JOBS, INCLUDING SORTING AND REPACKAGING DONATIONS
FOR RESALE, AND CREATING DESIGNER JACKETS AND T-SHIRTS,
FORT SMITH, ARKANSAS.

THE MAIL ROOM USED TO PACKAGE TRACTS, CDS,
BIBLES, AND OTHER MATERIALS FOR WORLDWIDE
DISTRIBUTION, FORT SMITH, ARKANSAS.

BILLBOARD PROMOTING THE ALAMO OF NASHVILLE
CLOTHING STORE, 1976. FROM *THE TENNESSEAN*.
6 JULY © 1991. GANNETT-COMMUNITY PUBLISHING.

CHAPTER

SEVEN

Down to Business

Businesses were booming. As the ministry's workforce grew, Tony's income sources expanded. Alamo members solicited charitable donations, and their efforts brought in large donations of food, home goods, clothing, and other items that were sorted and taken to warehouses for distribution. In the warehouses women and children removed price tags and expiration labels so that items were ready for resale. Tony ran a trucking business, and his men and boys picked up the donations, loaded them in their trucks labeled with charitable contribution signs, and then replaced those signs on the trucks to read "Advantage Food Group," delivering the donated goods to stores in various states. Money from sales went into the "bookkeeper account" for use by the church. The liquidation business was lucrative. IRS records show that contributions skyrocketed from $46,000 in 1974 to $1.3 million in 1976. Little did the donors know that their gifts were lining Tony Alamo's pockets.[1]

The Alamo restaurant in Alma became known for good food and entertainment. On the weekends they featured live performances with

---

1. Susy Buchanan, "The Ravening Wolf," *Southern Poverty Law Center Intelligence Report* 127 (Fall 2007): 2–3.

notable stars such as Marty Robbins, Ronnie Milsap, Brenda Lee, Tammy Wynette, and Roy Orbison. People were impressed that Tony was able to bring celebrated talent to Alma. As many as five hundred fans filled the banquet hall on the weekends when the stars were appearing, and all of the followers worked those nights. In his autobiography President Bill Clinton recalls going to the restaurant in 1975 to hear Dolly Parton sing:

> One night we drove south down Highway 71 to Alma to hear Dolly Parton sing. . . . But the most enduring impact of the evening was that it was my first exposure to the people who brought her to Alma, Tony and Susan Alamo. At the time, the Alamos sold fancy performance outfits in Nashville to many of the biggest country music stars. That's not all they did. Tony, who looked like Roy Orbison on speed, had been a promoter of rock-and-roll concerts back in California, when he met Susan, who had grown up near Alma but had moved out west and become a television evangelist. They teamed up, and he promoted her as he had his rock and rollers. Susan had white-blond hair and often wore floor-length white dresses to preach on TV. She was pretty good at it, and he was great at marketing her. They built a small empire, including a large farming operation manned by devoted young followers as transfixed by them as the young aco- lytes of the Reverend Sun Myung Moon were by their leader. . . . When I was governor, [Tony] got into a big fight with the government over taxes and staged a brief, nonviolent standoff of sorts around his house.[2]

Continuing to cater to the music industry, in the mid-1980s Tony gained public notice for his trademark denim jackets—airbrushed, bejeweled, and

---

2. Bill Clinton, *My Life* (New York: Knopf, 2004), 232–33.

studded with sequins. On the inside of his ministry, his minions spent long hours working in warehouses to create "Tony Alamo Celebrity Designs for the Superstars and the Rich and Famous." Jackets were personalized for celebrities in the music and entertainment industry, athletes, and politicians—all well placed to give Tony prestige as the "Dean of Dazzle."[3]

Posing in an online gallery of jackets, Tony features Dolly Parton, Kenny Rogers, Mike Tyson, Elke Sommer, Porter Wagoner, Reba McEntire, Sonny and Mary Bono, Brooke Shields, Don King, Ted Nugent, Willie Nelson, Larry Hagman, Lee Greenwood, Juice Newton, Bono, Jeanie C. Riley, Burt Reynolds, Hulk Hogan, Mr. T, Ann Jillian, Stryper, Martin Milner, Rod Steiger, Take 6, Stan Freeberg, Tiny Tim, Tom Kiefer, Honky Tonk Man, T. G. Shepperd, Lou Gossett, Jr., Nicki Manaj, Roger Whittaker, Miley Cyrus, David Allen Coe, and Mayors Tom Bradley and Anthony Cucci.[4] Celebrity status increased the demand for the "Alamo of Nashville" label, and Tony placed children working side by side with their parents in the production rooms to set rhinestones until ten o'clock at night. Jackets were in high demand and sold in stores on Rodeo Drive, in New York, in the Alamo of Nashville store, and in department stores, including Nieman Marcus and Sax Fifth Avenue.

From the Alamos' beginnings on the streets of Hollywood to Saugus, they planted seeds of control in the settlements in Arkansas, property holdings in Oklahoma, Florida, Arizona, New Jersey, New York, and the Music Square Church in Nashville, Tennessee. Using the words of the Gospel the Alamos targeted people searching for a better life, condemning them as weak, sick, prostitutes, and drug addicts and giving them housing, food, and hope for a better life. In doing so, Susan and Tony Alamo robbed them of individual freedom, self-reliance, and choice for generations to come.

Many years later a former Alamo follower looks back at his life in the cult with bitterness:

---

3. http://www.alamoministries.com/Designs/index.html.

4. Tony Alamo Christian Ministries Website. www.alamoministries.com.

CUSTOM-DESIGNED TONY ALAMO JACKET.

SIGNATURE ALAMO DESIGNS LABEL.

Tony & Susan Alamo
The Holy Alamo —
Christian † Church —
Consecrated

WE'RE YOUR NEIGHBORS

Susan Alamo

Tony Alamo

TONY AND SUSAN ALAMO AND THE TONY AND SUSAN
ALAMO CHRISTIAN FOUNDATION ORCHESTRA AND CHOIR,
ON THE SET AT KCOP TV IN HOLLYWOOD, CALIFORNIA,
TAPING THEIR SYNDICATED TELEVISION PROGRAM

The Outpouring of the Holy Spirit — Music Square Church

THE "FOUNDATION" BOOK BOASTS TESTIMONIALS AND
PHOTOGRAPHS OF FOLLOWERS ENGAGED IN LEADERSHIP,
FAMILY GATHERINGS, FUN ACTIVITIES, AND COMMUNITY
INVOLVEMENT. IN REALITY, THESE PHOTOGRAPHS WERE
STAGED. THE ALAMOS WERE THE SOLE DECISION MAKERS
AND DICTATED EVERY ASPECT OF LIVING IN THE GROUP.

My wife and I were drug addicts. We were walking down the street, and someone handed me a Tony Alamo tract. We were hungry and used our last bit of money to buy drugs. I snatched the purse off the shoulder of a woman and was caught by police. I knew I was going to jail and shoved that Alamo tract into the hands of my wife. She called Alamo's church and found housing, food, and "family" there. The whole time I was in prison I thought that God had saved my family. When I got out of prison, Tony wouldn't allow me to reunite or even see my wife and kids. I lost them to his cult. It took years for me to find my children, gain custody, and my kids are still dealing with the trauma of living there.

1982
—
2000

1984

May 25—William F. Willoughby, writer for the religious column of the *Washington Times*, predicts Alamo's demise and expresses dismay at a massive nationwide poster campaign led by Tony Alamo, his personal friend:

> I speak of my dearly beloved friend, Tony Alamo. We've had some sidesplitting good times together, two quite different people on different wavelengths about a lot of things.
>
> Yes, in my heart of hearts I have rejoiced time and time again over the power of the Gospel in the lives of thousands of young people he and his late wife Susan worked their very souls out to win.
>
> But now my heart, because its love and its loyalty for a friend will not and cannot change, grieves. Tony, I ask myself, even if you do believe all that spiteful stuff about the pope and the Vatican and the Catholic Church, why do you have to turn it into a hate campaign, mistaking

it for evangelism, for attempts at winning people to the Gospel? . . .

So also, does the tract that you distribute in all your zeal, cause hurt. The one titled "All the Pope's Secrets," with a caricature photo of the pope. And even though I know you are convinced that it is so, where is the proof you present that the Vatican is responsible for the assassinations of Presidents Lincoln and Kennedy? Isn't this just as irresponsible as the news media which you so roundly attack and which did, indeed, in the past, unconscionably attack you?

. . . I asked your fellow worker if you were indeed behind the posters themselves. I had strong, but hope-it-isn't-so, suspicions.

'Tony's in agreement with them,' he said. But he stopped short of saying they were the work of your foundation. Little comfort there, since the posters and their claims are of the same genre as your tract. Even so, I hold onto a faint glimmer of hope that it ain't so.[1]

1985

The IRS revokes the tax-exempt status of Alamo's church, then incorporated as Music Square Church. Revocation is retroactive for the years 1977 to 1980. Alamo's attorneys, arguing that the businesses are exempt from federal income taxes because they are church properties, keep the issues before the courts.

---

1. William F. Willoughby, "There's no way to call off the hornets," *The Washington Times*, May 25, 1984.

1988

January—Allegations of child abuse and concerns of Alamo's undue influence over his followers heighten.

Tony Alamo orders the brutal beating of eleven-year-old Justin Miller.

February 13—Cult Awareness Network publishes a story of alleged abuses in Alamo ministries:

EX-ALAMO MEMBER CONTINUES
5½ YEAR SEARCH FOR CHILDREN

Judy joined Alamo's church in 1970 when her parents attended the church in Hollywood, California. She quit her job, moved to the Saugus compound and spent her time reading the Bible, praying, attending nightly meetings and witnessing in Hollywood. In 1972 her parents left the church but were unable to convince Judy to quit. In 1975 Judy wrote in a letter to Susan Alamo that she was in love with Daniel, another church member she hardly knew.

On September 20, 1975, though they hardly knew each other, Daniel and Judy were married because Susan Alamo believed it was God's will. The rigid lifestyle of the church allowed the couple to see each other less than 24 hours each week. They lived apart and worked 7 days a week for church-run businesses for no wages.

In August 1976, Judy gave birth to a girl. In November her husband Daniel was sent to live in Dyer, Arkansas. Judy and the baby were allowed to move to Dyer in January, but the couple still was not permitted to live together.

In December 1977, Judy gave birth to another girl. When Susan Alamo required the family to live apart,

Daniel refused. As the children grew, Judy became discouraged with life in the church. The lack of family life, control of her time and the prohibition against contact with the outside world, including her parents, caused her to question the church.

In November 1981, at the church's request, Judy left to spend time with her parents and think about her commitment. When she called her husband to tell him she wanted to return, he said she wasn't welcome back. Judy filed for divorce in 1982. Daniel brought the children to see her two times during the court proceedings.

In July 1982, Judy was awarded temporary custody of the children and permission to take them to California for 10 days. Daniel's attorney announced in court that Daniel had taken the children and supposedly fled to Kentucky. Judy is certain that Daniel is still working for Tony Alamo whose orders are for church members to raise her children. The children have not been located.[2]

March—Acting upon reports of child abuse, sheriff's deputies raid Saugus, California, compound, remove Justin, Kody, and Bobby M., and reunite the boys with their fathers, former Alamo followers who were excommunicated from the church.

Alamo is charged with child abuse for ordering followers to beat eleven-year-old Justin Miller.

May—Prosecutors drop child abuse charges, citing lack of evidence.

---

2. "Ex-Alamo Member Continues 5½ Year Search for Children," *Cult Awareness Network*, February 13, 1988.

1989

April—Eyewitnesses come forward, and Tony Alamo is again charged with felony child abuse for ordering followers to beat eleven-year-old Justin Miller.

June—Alamo goes into hiding and through the media denies any affiliation with Alamo businesses. He is charged as a fugitive for unlawful interstate flight to avoid prosecution for the crime of child abuse.

September 3—The *Los Angeles Times* reports that Alamo's businesses bring top dollars:

> FBI agents may be hot on his trail, but fundamental-
> ist cult leader Tony Alamo is still selling $600 designer
> jackets to Melrose Avenue boutiques and to upscale
> clothing stores nationwide. . . . Former cult members say
> Alamo operates with about 500 church members dou-
> bling as employees. The sequined jackets—painted with
> airbrushed images of the New York skyline, Hollywood
> and Rodeo Drive—are among the hottest items in the
> Los Angeles fashion market. Fashion industry insiders
> say annual sales of sequined jackets by "Tony Alamo of
> Nashville" total anywhere from $500,000 to $1 million.
> . . . "The clothing is so groovy, everyone wants it no mat-
> ter what they think I am," Alamo said in a telephone in-
> terview from an undisclosed location. "No matter what,
> the superstars are going to want my jackets. . . . Every-
> thing I do is a work of art. I do the designs wherever I'm
> at." Former cult members said Alamo's clothing business
> operates out of small manufacturing shops in California
> and New York, with the largest shop in Arkansas. "No-
> body gets paid," one former member said. "It's more or
> less like sweatshops."

> The Jewish Federation's Commission on Cults and
> Missionaries urges retailers to stop selling Alamo De-
> sign jackets, charging that money from jacket sales fi-
> nances cult activities. . . . Many retailers, including Sax
> Fifth Avenue drop Alamo jackets, return merchandise,
> and cancel order.[3]

Seeking to shield business profits from being tied to him and the church,
Alamo denies allegations and files a lawsuit in Los Angeles Superior Court
seeking $250 million in damages from the Jewish Federation.

Alamo says, "I make all the decisions in the business, all of them. Wherever I am is the headquarters. If you can find me, you've found the headquarters" (*Los Angeles Times*, telephone interview, August 1989). Two
months later he contradicts himself by saying that "he has nothing to do
with the Alamo Designs Company" and that he works for the clothing
manufacturer as a "freelance designer."

Alamo adds that he has severed all ties with the Holy Alamo Christian
Church in Saugus and Arkansas. "My ministry is to the five billion people
in the world, and I'm not connected to the churches what so ever," Alamo
says. "I've got thousands of witnesses who will testify on my behalf that
none of that type of stuff ever happened at my church—ever" (*The Newhall
Signal*, October 13, 1989).

Alamo becomes a fugitive until 1991. The FBI warns the public that
Alamo "is always accompanied by bodyguards who have access to numerous weapons, to include M14 rifles."

1990

August 3—The *Los Angeles Times* presents an in-depth exposé of Alamo's
church. Alamo accuses the media and US government of conspiracy.

---

3. "Fugitive Cult Leader Alamo Sells Chic Jackets on the Run," *Los Angeles Times*, September 3, 1989.

The US District Court in Fort Smith, Arkansas, Judge Morris Arnold, presiding, rules in a default judgment against Tony Alamo, who does not appear in court. Judge Arnold awards $1,466,000 to Justin Miller's family for the physical abuse Justin endured in California. Arnold is subsequently harassed and targeted for assassination.

IRS files liens for nearly eight million dollars for Alamo church-business income taxes and employee withholding.

1991

February 13—To satisfy the monetary judgment in the Miller case, federal marshals seize compound property in Georgia Ridge and Alma, Arkansas. Several days later Tony Alamo gives followers instructions to smash the mausoleum and take Susan Alamo's body so that it would not be confiscated with the property.

When questioned, Tony Alamo says that he doesn't have his dead wife Susan's body and doesn't know where it is.

After the raid Tony calls Jack Mosely, a reporter for the *Southwest Times Record*, and makes threatening remarks against Federal Judge Morris Arnold.

July—Caught using a false ID, Tony Alamo is captured in Tampa, Florida. He is charged with threatening to kidnap a federal judge, interstate flight, and felony child abuse. Denying bail, the judge orders that Alamo be returned to Arkansas to face charges that he threatened to kidnap and hang a federal judge, Morris Arnold.

September—In Fort Smith, Arkansas, Alamo is acquitted of charges that he threatened a federal judge.

For his IRS convictions Alamo is first sent to a prison in Colorado, then transferred to Texarkana, Texas, and then to Fayetteville, Arkansas. He is released in November with an agreement to pay compensation for wage violations to the Department of Labor. He never paid his debt.

1992

March—Christhiaon Coie, Susan Alamo's daughter, files a lawsuit accusing Alamo of stealing her mother's body. Alamo initially denies hiding his wife's body and then later tells the press, "I have it."

The tax-exempt status of the existing Alamo organization is stripped for good in a federal tax court.

1993

February—A Memphis, Tennessee, grand jury indicts Alamo for evading income taxes in the late 1980s.

Tony Alamo starts taking multiple wives (some underage) and cites a series of scriptural arguments defending polygamy to convince his congregation of its holiness.

1994

May–August—Alamo is tried, convicted, and sentenced to six years in federal prison for income tax evasion and for failing to pay tax on personal income. At the trial government witnesses, including several ex-wives, testify that they were beaten and raped by Alamo. When questioned about his polygamist lifestyle, Alamo pleads the Fifth Amendment ten times. Despite what prosecutors consider convincing evidence of sexual abuse by Alamo, the jury does not hear testimony on alleged violations of sex and polygamy laws because the trial is limited to tax charges.

November—Alamo is moved to federal prison in Florence, Colorado. He continues to run day-to-day operations of his cult while still in prison through phone calls, visits, and reports. He is allowed to have visits by girls as young as nine that are being groomed as his child brides. One eyewitness account describes how molestations occurred in the visiting room while Alamo was incarcerated.

1995

March—Child abuse charges against Tony Alamo are dropped because of a six-year federal prison sentence he received for tax evasion. Deputy District Attorney John Asari says that Alamo would probably have served only five months in state prison if convicted of child abuse and child endangerment charges. The cases have already been tried in civil court, and judgments were made in favor of the plaintiffs.

September—Judge orders Alamo to return Susan Alamo's stolen remains to her daughter, Christhiaon Coie.

December—Alamo is moved to federal prison in Texarkana, Arkansas, and continues to run day-to-day operations of his cult while still in prison. He is allowed to have visits by more young girls who are being groomed to be his child brides.

1997

The Arkansas Court of Appeals dismisses on a technicality Tony Alamo's appeal of an order requiring him to produce the missing body of his long-dead wife for burial.

1998

July—Alamo is told that his prison release will be in jeopardy if Susan Alamo's body is not returned. Alamo's followers bring the body in a sealed casket to a Van Buren funeral home. Medical examiners affirm the body is that of Susan Alamo, and her remains are placed in a crypt in Tulsa, Oklahoma.

December—Alamo is released from prison, moves to Fouke, Arkansas, and continues to build his church. He resumes his practice of grooming young girls, children of his followers, to become his wives. Parents allow their little girls to move into Tony Alamo's home often under the guise of having them attend school, to rehabilitate a wayward attitude, or to gain training to become secretaries. Referring to his home as the "mission school," Tony continues the practice for the next nine years until his arrest in September 2008.

2000

Former members start making complaints to the Department of Human Services, Arkansas State Police, and the FBI about the physical abuse and sex crimes occurring against children in the Tony Alamo Christian Ministries.

Over the course of the next four years Tony Alamo continues to grow his church businesses and control his followers through physical and mental abuse.

CHAPTER

EIGHT

On the Lam and a Missing Body

Edith Opal, pretty in your wedding gown,
Edith Opal, can't take it back now,
Would you if you could somehow? . . .
Even you began to believe your lies.
Your legacy lingered as you closed your eyes.
Six months dead and still in that dress—
Followers prayed and prayed and prayed
For you to resurrect . . .

Shannon Wurst, songwriter and artist

On April 8, 1982, Susan Alamo, age 56, died. Since the early 1970s she had known that she had breast cancer. Against doctor recommendations, she chose not to go to the hospital and receive medical treatment. At first she didn't even tell Tony about her illness.[1] As her cancer grew, it became apparent that she was ill, and the Alamo flock fasted and prayed regularly for her to be healed.

Shortly before she died, Susan said, "Tony, it isn't going to do any good for you to pray for me. God told me that I'm going to die no matter how

---

1. Susan Alamo, *You Damned Fool*, 19. http://www.alamoministries.com/content/english /book/youdamnedfool.html.

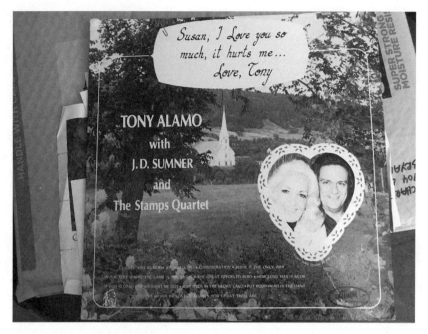

TONY ALAMO PRODUCED THIS ALBUM IN HIS NASHVILLE,
TENNESSEE, STUDIO JUST MONTHS BEFORE SUSAN ALAMO
DIED IN 1982.

much you and the kids pray for me to live. I'm going to be gone for quite a
while. Then God is going to raise me up from the dead, and you and I are
going to be the two witnesses God mentioned in the eleventh chapter of
the book of Revelation."[2]

Susan was in and out of hospitals, at one point having surgery only to
discover that cancer had claimed too much of her body to turn the disease
around. She continued to preach and travel when she could. Brenda and
Daniel last saw Susan preach at a funeral in January 1982.

When she died, Susan was in Tulsa, Oklahoma, at Oral Robert's City
of Faith Hospital near a home that she and Tony owned. At her side were

---

2. Tony Alamo, "Susan's Wedding Gown." www.alamoministries.com.

Tony and a few members of the ministry. John was one of a small group who traveled from Saugus to Tulsa that fateful day. His wife, Ellen, still feels chills when she recalls John's words when he telephoned to tell her Susan had died: "Her dying words to Tony were, 'When I die, disband the church. You'll wreck it all.'"

Devastated, Tony had Susan's body embalmed in Elmore City, Oklahoma, so that he could bring her home across state lines. Some of the older sisters dressed her, and one of the visiting Christians (people who came to Sunday church services only) who owned a wig shop in Fort Smith, Arkansas, did Susan's hair. Tony wanted to put Susan in a beautiful dress for her burial. His thoughts turned to their days together. Susan once told him that she had a vision from God of her dressed in a white wedding gown while preaching the gospel to thousands of people in a grassy meadow on a hillside. When they had decided to marry, Susan had searched for the dress she had seen in that vision. They never found that gown. The sudden memory told Tony exactly what he wanted for Susan's burial dress. He and a sister went to town and found a wedding gown that was exactly as Susan had described in her vision. While the sisters prepared Susan's body, he distinctly heard her voice saying, "I'm pretty, Daddy." Tony knew now that Susan's vision preaching to thousands of people from a hilltop was real. Susan had never preached in a wedding gown, but God had said that she would. That prophecy was going to come to pass.[3]

The funeral was in the church in Dyer, and only church members were permitted to attend. For two weeks all the Alamo businesses—now numbering twenty-nine and growing—were closed. Everyone was supposed to stay with the brothers and sisters on Georgia Ridge. Followers came from all Alamo locations and stayed to pray. Tony's grief was deep. He wondered to himself what he would do without Susan. How could he possibly continue on? What would happen to the church and all they had built together? In his desperation he looked into the mirror, saw a vision of God, and heard Him say, "Tony, you can do this!" At that moment,

---

3. Ibid.

Tony knew exactly what to do and that he would succeed. He was God's prophet, after all.

Tony declared to his followers that Susan came to him in a vision and told him that she would be gone for a while but would return once again. Tony believed that he and Susan were the two witnesses—immortal prophets—of the book of Revelation. He was certain that Susan would be raised from the dead. He laid Susan's body, clothed in the wedding gown, in the dining room of his mansion on Georgia Ridge. For the next six months, followers held a twenty-four-hour prayer vigil by her body in the closed casket to raise her to resurrection. On separate schedules Brenda and Daniel joined their brothers and sisters, signing in every day to pray their two-hour shifts. Prayer was full of emotion, sometimes with speaking in tongues and arms stretching up to the heavens. Emotionless praying was not allowed. Those who were sitting still were probably nodding off due to sleep deprivation and a lack of food.

After six months Tony called his followers together and shouted, "Because you people aren't right with God, Susan wasn't raised. Your faith isn't good enough." At an undisclosed cost he had someone build a mausoleum large enough to accommodate two caskets in front of the heart-shaped swimming pool and interred his wife there. Time would show that Susan's body would not remain peacefully at rest.

The IRS was still scrutinizing Tony's business activities first red flagged in 1975 for violations of the Fair Labor Standards Act. The government estimated that as of 1979 Tony owed at least $15.5 million in back wages, and that number would increase over time.[4] In 1985 they revoked the ministry's tax-exempt status retroactively from 1977 to 1980. The US Supreme Court ordered Alamo to pay members working in church businesses. The ruling was upheld in 1992 despite Alamo's claim that they were volunteers acting within their religious rights of expression and that church-owned enterprises were actually "churches in disguise."

---

4. Nancy Ross, "The Tony Alamo Story." www.scvhistory.com/scvhistory/alamo-alamo.htm.

Tony continued to keep his business dealings outside the eyes of the law. There is no evidence that he ever paid his employees; even church members who worked in businesses outside the church gave their paychecks to Alamo. In return they were given housing, food, and "bucks" for small allowances from time to time. A member working in Alamo's business office said, "Tony would have his people clear out files if they heard an audit or investigation was going to happen. They'd take boxes of files out, tear them apart, redo files, and bring them back."

Alamo's ruthless treatment of his followers grew right along with the expansion and diversity of business ventures. He regularly pulled people off jobs and put them on others as more opportunities developed. One time when Tony heard that the workers sewing jackets were going home early if they completed an extra-large portion of the work, he made their work

CUSTOM-DESIGNED TONY ALAMO T-SHIRT.

days even longer by sending them off at 8:00 a.m. and working them until midnight. Followers would get breaks to eat lunch and dinner and even miss church services. Two or three people would trade off watching each other's children. Sometimes they might go home to give the kids a shower and then take them to the babysitter, or maybe the babysitter would do it all. Church services took second place. Bible reading wasn't the reason for sleep deprivation; they were just trying to keep a workforce going.

The men weren't the only ones burning the candle at both ends. The women took care of household duties, and those working in the kitchen rose before the sun and worked well into the night preparing food, washing dishes, and scrubbing kitchen and dining areas. Children also worked. They adhered to a regular daily schedule of prayer, 8:00 a.m. and 3:00 p.m. worship services, and boys and girls separately went to school for four hours daily, had play period, and then had to go to work. Boys' jobs included grounds keeping, construction, and loading and unloading donated goods at the warehouses. Girls worked in the kitchen, babysat, sorted products at the warehouses, and made Alamo Design jackets in the cutting, sewing, and production rooms where they airbrushed designs and set rhinestones. Girls also were selected to work in Tony's office, a key location for operations, where followers reported rules violations to Tony. Office workers handled Tony's messages, gathered infraction reports, and passed them along to Tony, who ordered the punishments.

Violating fair labor standards and committing tax fraud weren't the only reasons Alamo was on law enforcement's radar. At the Saugus settlement in January 1988, eleven-year-old Justin Miller wore a leather scarf without permission and asked a science question in a history class. The violations were reported to Tony, who "dictated via speakerphone a punishment of 140 blows with a heavy perforated wooden paddle that Alamo had designed and named 'the board of education' while his classmates looked on. Justin testified later, 'He said I was a goat among sheep, and he was going to have to beat the devil out of me.' The boy was held down by four men and walloped until his buttocks bled. For several days after, Justin bled through his pants and had to go home from school to change, a teacher recalls. His

father, who had recently left the cult, got wind of the beating and noti-
fied California authorities. Justin was removed from the compound in late
March and reunited with his father."[5]

Felony charges were filed against Alamo in 1989, and in 1990 US Circuit
Judge Morris Arnold awarded Justin Miller's family almost $1.5 million in
Fort Smith Federal Court. When he delivered his decision, Judge Arnold
said, "No feeling person could fail to be moved by the testimony in this
case or be revolted by the cold-blooded and calculated manner in which
the punishment was carried out."[6]

With a warrant out for his arrest for felony child abuse charges in California, Tony Alamo went into hiding in 1989 and remained on the run until
1991. For a time under the assumed name of Clarence Williams, he rented
a home in Las Vegas. He always had followers with him, so he didn't miss
a beat operating the church businesses and monitoring the behaviors of his
flock. With church expansion now covering six states, Tony had plenty of
places to hide.

In 1990 the IRS filed liens of $7.9 million against church-run businesses
for taxes due in Tennessee, Arkansas, Arizona, California, Oklahoma,
and Florida. The IRS also issued a jeopardy assessment against Alamo,
claiming he owed $745,000 in personal income taxes for 1977 through 1980,
another five million in corporate income tax, and $1.6 million in unpaid
employees' withholding taxes. The jeopardy assessment allows the government to seize properties without waiting through court proceedings. This
order is issued when sufficient reason suggests that a delay will jeopardize
collection of the claim. The IRS agents, losing no time, raided the Alamo
of Nashville store and seized all property and equipment.

---

5. Susy Buchanan, "The Ravening Wolf," *Southern Poverty Law Center Intelligence Report* 127
(Fall 2007): 25.

6. Controversy Continues to Follow Tony Alamo," http://www.rickross.com/reference/Alamo
/alamo13.html.

On February 13, 1991, in an effort to satisfy the \$1.5 million judgment in the Justin Miller case, sixty US Marshals Service deputies raided the Georgia Ridge and Alma compounds. They confiscated eighty-two pews, twenty-eight mirrors, photos of Alamo with Larry Hagman, a back massager, Bibles, toys, purses, cash, sewing machines, cars, trucks, financial records, and fifteen hundred Alamo Design jackets. They did not find Susan Alamo's body.

Several days later Alamo ordered his followers to evacuate the compounds in Alma and Georgia Ridge. He commanded that his mansion be gutted. Followers removed antique furnishings, carpeting, and fixtures. Fearing that government agents would desecrate Susan Alamo's body, Tony ordered his people to take Susan's body with them. Followers broke into the marble tomb, removed her casket, and put it in a storage unit, where it remained hidden for seven years.

Still on the run, Tony not only admitted that he had his wife Susan's body. He also threatened to kidnap Judge Morris Arnold and have him stand in Alamo's own court before God. Federal agents stepped up their search and in July 1991 apprehended Tony, who was living under an assumed name in Madeira Beach near Tampa, Florida. He went to court in September 1991 and was found not guilty of threatening the judge. Followers in the courtroom that day were jubilant at the verdict. However, Tony remained in jail from July 3 until November that year because of his violations of the Fair Labor Standards Act. Alamo declared, "They'll never get ten million dollars. They'll never get ten thousand dollars, and they'll never get ten cents." And they didn't. He never paid a dime.

Even though he was out of jail, Tony's legal entanglements with the IRS and California child abuse charges continued to plague him. The legal process was slow with one delay after another; Tony used every tactic he could to perpetuate delays. He changed lawyers and hid records, and witnesses changed their stories. On June 8, 1994, he was convicted of all four charges of tax fraud and sentenced to six years in federal prison, serving time first in Florence, Colorado, and the latter portion at the facility in Texarkana, Texas. Meanwhile, California dropped all felony child abuse charges because Tony was already serving jail time. Tony seized the moment to declare, "The charges were dropped because I'm innocent." When Tony was paroled in 1998 after serving four years of his six-year sentence, the beatings on current followers were resumed.

Throughout the period of Tony's legal problems, one individual remained steadfast in her determination to claim from Alamo what was hers. Susan Alamo's daughter, Christhiaon Coie, wanted her mother's remains. She accused Alamo of stealing her mother's body and issued a plea to her stepfather to return her remains so she could bury her mother in a family plot. In a telephone interview from her Los Angeles home, Coie said, "My mother is entitled to be buried like a human being. If there was ever an inkling of love for my mother, I'm begging you to return her body."

Alamo was quoted as saying, "I stole nothing. I paid for that coffin. We were of one flesh. They were going to desecrate her body. I have it."[7]

At the end of a long custody battle between Alamo and Coie, in 1995 Alamo was ordered to return Susan's body to her daughter and pay one hundred thousand dollars in damages. He resisted and was found in contempt of court. Still acting in control, Tony buried Susan in Tulsa, Oklahoma, 124 miles from Van Buren, Arkansas, where her daughter had wanted her buried. Finally, in 1998, sixteen years after her death, Susan Alamo was put to rest.

---

7. Aaron Curtiss, "Search for Cult Leader Intensifies," *Los Angeles Times* (March 8, 1991). Articles.latimes.com.

CHAPTER NINE

"Desperately Seeking Susan"

In spite of all his arrogance and swagger, the death of Susan Alamo shook Tony's confidence. Susan had really been the one who ran the church. She preached, told Tony what to do, and had charisma. Tony's role was effective as her promoter and working the businesses of the church, but he was not a preacher. For all the bluster he spewed forth, inside he felt afraid and unsure of himself. When he gazed in the mirror, though, he saw a vision—the Lord God Himself telling him that he and Susan were the witnesses in Revelations. He knew that Susan would return. In the meantime, he would control his church followers, grow his businesses, and remain World Pastor.

In June 1984 Tony introduced Birgitta Gyllenhammer, blond and Swed-ish, as his new wife. Birgitta was forty-two years old and owned a clothing store in Beverly Hills. The marriage was not to last, ending shortly after two years. Birgitta left claiming that Tony beat her, drugged her, and forced her to have plastic surgery to look like Susan Alamo.

Two years later, in December 1985, Tony married Elizabeth Caldwell-Amrhein. Elizabeth had two children from a previous marriage, and after she married Tony, the father of her children became concerned by their changed behaviors. They were afraid and reluctant to return to their mother even to celebrate a birthday. He believed his children were brainwashed and not attending school. He filed for full custody, and Elizabeth lost the battle. Elizabeth left Tony in January 1987. Losing no time, Tony married Diana Elana Williams that July. She left him in 1989.

The list of Tony's wives is extensive. (See Appendix 3.) In September 1989, while Tony was on the run from the FBI, Sharon Ast-Kroopf became his bride. Their son, Sion, was born in the summer of 1991 while Tony was in prison. In February 1993, Lydia wed Tony and bore him another son, Tabor Raymond. That same month and year, Tony used threats and rape to acquire Jody Riley (Fryer) as his wife. The practice continued with Anne, Misheal, Carla, and Marsha—all in 1993.

When he was incarcerated in 1994, Tony continued to add to his harem. He would summon his wives to prison and request that they bring particular girls to him. At the visit the wives formed a circle around Tony to block the view of security cameras and guards. Ellen was one of the women taken as Tony's wife during this time. Born and raised in the cult, at the

HOUSING FOR FOLLOWERS IN MOFFETT, OKLAHOMA.

age of fifteen Ellen was ordered to marry an older man she barely knew. Her husband was sent to work in California, and Ellen—by then, mother of two children—stayed in Moffett, Oklahoma, but later moved to join her husband in California.

Living conditions at the California compound were inadequate at best. They had no running water or electricity, and the duplexes were infested with roaches, mice, and rats. "Out of the blue" Ellen's husband was accused of having pornography and making a 900 call months earlier when they were living in Moffett. He was kicked out of the church. Ellen was given the choice of moving back to Arkansas or Colorado Springs with Tony's wives. Before she could move to Moffett, her choice, she received a message from Tony that God wanted her to live in Colorado Springs.

When she arrived, she was surprised to see one of her sisters, age eleven, living there with the other wives. Her sister told her that she was married to Tony. Tony requested photographs of Ellen. At this time, Ellen's nine-month-old baby became ill and was hospitalized for several days. Tony sent a message to Ellen saying that the Lord had told him that she was to become one of his wives. She responded that marrying a sister's husband is against God's wishes. Tony replied that if she didn't become his wife, her daughter would die. Ellen agreed to remain in Colorado and live with his wives.

She couldn't help comparing their beautiful house, loaded with amenities, to the substandard conditions of the housing in California. Ellen visited the prison with the other wives and took her place next to Tony. Fondling the wife sitting on his other side, he was getting an erection and being aroused while telling her all the things he was going to do to her when he got out of prison. He said he would spend four straight nights with her and told her in detail how the first night with each of his wives had been. The man who called himself God's prophet sickened Ellen. Finally she sent him a note saying that it was not in her heart to marry him and begged him to let her go. She was given five hundred dollars and sent to California where she found her husband and freedom from Tony Alamo.

As Tony grew older, so did his appetite for younger girls. He selected a girl, told her parents that God wanted her to be his spiritual bride, and they turned her over to him. Parents were taught that this was an honor, and if they were at all reluctant, fear of displeasing Tony quelled any second thoughts. Tony would take the girl into his bedroom, perform sex on her, and the girl would emerge wearing a wedding band as his new bride. Underage girls included sixteen-year-old Andrea (January 1994), who bore Tony's child, Bella, in 2001; fifteen-year-old Gail (late 1993 or early 1994); fifteen-year-old Lynn, who "married" Tony after his release from prison in 1998; twelve-year-old Allison (1999); eleven-year-old Avril; fourteen-year-old Nora; eight-year-old Monique; and eleven-year-old Shadow. To the critics outside the ministry, Tony continued to be bold and absolute in his claims that the Bible supports polygamy and taking child brides once the girls have started menstruation. Tony's network of brides remaining in the cult continued to defend him, visited him in prison, and carried out his bidding.

2001

Former follower, Brenda, contacts Arkansas State Police with information regarding Tony's coerced "marriages" with underage children.

2003

Brenda again contacts Arkansas State Police with more information on Alamo's crimes. This time, individuals with Arkansas State Police and Crimes Against Children interview her. More interviews are conducted of other former followers over the next several years, but no legal action is begun.

2005

Former members come together on FACTnet, an Internet discussion group, to expose the abuses occurring in the Alamo ministry.

2006

February—Fouke town officials present a Certificate of Appreciation to Alamo and his ministry for his acts of "Christian love and kindness" in helping those in need.

April—Alamoministrieswatch.com, a watchdog site exposing the evil crimes of Tony Alamo, becomes available on the Internet.

August—Fouke locals become incensed when Alamo posts armed guards along the road to his compound.

Some citizens in Fouke organize a group known as PACA (Partnered Against Cult Activity) to inform the community and local authorities of the true nature of the group.

2007

February—Tempur-Pedic International brings suit in federal court against several individuals including long-time Alamo member Tommy Scarcello for stealing eight thousand mattresses that were donated to Hurricane Katrina Victims. Two Alamo wives are also implicated because the mattresses were stored in a warehouse they own.

July—Alamo's lawyers use intimidation and threats to have the website alamoministrieswatch.com removed.

October—Southern Poverty Law Center lists Tony Alamo Christian Ministries as a hate group for its anti-Catholic statements and publishes an in-depth article about Alamo entitled "The Ravening Wolf." This article prompts more media attention and widens the door for scrutiny.

Tonyalamonews.com debuts as a new watchdog site exposing Alamo's crimes.

Alamo follower Leslie Ray "Buster" White pleads innocent to federal charges of trafficking counterfeit merchandise.

2008

September 2—In a plea bargain Leslie Ray "Buster" White enters a guilty plea to one count of trafficking counterfeit musical CDs before US District Judge David Folsom in the Eastern District of Texas, Texarkana division. White requests an exception to the rule restricting him from associating with a convicted felon so that he may consult with his minister, Tony Alamo, and attend services at Alamo's church.

September 20—Federal and state authorities, prompted by allegations of child pornography, conduct a search at the Fouke location of Tony Alamo Christian Ministries. Child welfare workers take custody of six girls, ages ten to seventeen, believed to be in immediate danger.

September 25—The FBI arrests Tony Alamo in a hotel in Flagstaff, Arizona. The federal charging document accuses Alamo of taking a thirteen-year-old girl across state lines for sex in 2004 and of aiding and abetting her transport across state lines for sex in 2005.

October 16—Authorities in Fort Smith, Arkansas, issue a warrant for John Kolbek, an Alamo associate, who allegedly beat adult and juvenile followers with a wooden board when they didn't follow Alamo's rules.

October 22—At Alamo's bail hearing, a judge rules that Alamo must stay in jail until his trial because he is a flight risk and a danger to the community.

November 17—Circuit judges sign removal orders for more than 125 children of Alamo loyalists in Texarkana and Fort Smith, Arkansas.

November 18—The FBI seizes seventeen children ages one to seventeen in church vans heading from Arkansas to the Texas state line. Three boys who were just sworn in to testify as witnesses are ushered into state care from the courtroom. The whereabouts of more than ninety children remains unknown.

November 24—During custody hearings, Tony Alamo admits to sharing a house with multiple women but contends that he was only married to one at a time.

December 2—Six children of Tony Alamo Christian Ministries are found in Indiana and will be united with their father, who hasn't had contact with them in years.

December 4—FBI affidavit reveals that three girls who lived at Alamo's Fouke, Arkansas, compound said that Alamo had sexually abused them, and one said he had threatened to have "someone take care of you" if she talked.

December 12—Four children of Tony Alamo followers are found in Arkansas and placed in state care.

CHAPTER TEN

All for One, Tony Alamo's New Jerusalem

I have not found a new religion,
I have returned to the faith of my fathers,
Abraham, Isaac, and Jacob,
and I am preaching and teaching
the same gospel another Jew lived and died for,
my Messiah and Savior, Jesus Christ.

Tony Alamo

FOUKE

The church was hot, and twelve-year-old Audrey fought the urge to fidget while the brother preached from the podium. She knew she was displeasing God by not listening more closely, so she scooted her back flat against the pew and focused her eyes on Brother Michael. Now he was closing his Bible. As he invited prayers to the Lord God, Audrey closed her eyes tightly. She prayed for her sisters and brothers; then prayed for her mother and father; then said a prayer of gratitude for Pastor Tony. Without him, who knows where she would be? Her mind wandered again to just last week when she first came to stay at Tony Alamo's house.

Recently her dad was kicked out of the church at Fort Smith, so Audrey moved to Fouke so she could be with her sister who was living in Tony's house. She was eating breakfast in the kitchen with the sisters. Everyone was chatting and looking at the newspaper when all of a sudden they all got up at once and began to look very busy putting away the dishes. That left Audrey at the table where she was reading the comics. Pastor Tony walked in, and Audrey casually looked up. Tony then pointed to her and yelled for someone to take the papers away from her, saying those were his personal papers. When he did this, he kicked Audrey's legs a few times in anger.

She was surprised and confused. What had she done wrong? She was only looking at the comics. She soon came to realize the reason for his outrage. The newspaper was from "the outside world," and he didn't want someone new to his house learning something about him or learning anything that might contradict him. Audrey quietly got up and began to walk into the next room, Tony's office. He began to yell that the girls who came to Fouke from Fort Smith were all fakes and phonies.

Audrey had just entered the office when Tony continued to rant. To show respect to this man of God, Audrey politely stopped and turned around to listen to what he had to say. Tony then entered the room and did some kind of martial arts move on her. All she saw was his black shirt as her head turned in a very uncomfortable way while his leg hit hers. It all happened so fast. Audrey just stood there much more confused and hurt. What had she done that was so wrong to deserve this treatment from this person she looked up to with so much respect? Pastor Tony then pointed to the back of the house and yelled at Audrey to go there. Audrey, fighting back tears, rushed into her room where her sister Tatum was. Sobbing, she said, "I was only looking at some comics. What did I do wrong?" Tatum quickly told Audrey to get into the mirror room (where they kept all their toiletries) before Tony could hear her, because if he did, it would not be good. Tatum knew how it was to live in his house because she'd been living there for several years. Audrey listened, and crying, she ran into the dark room where she stayed until there were no more tears in her eyes.

Audrey opened her eyes. The choir was singing now, and shaking off the sudden chill she felt, Audrey rose and joined the others in song. The memory stuck in her head. She had experienced how scary this man of God could be.

THE EXPANSE OF LAND
AND PROXIMITY TO
TEXAS AND OKLAHOMA
DREW ALAMO TO FOUKE,
ARKANSAS.

In 1994 Tony was convicted and sentenced to a six-year prison term for tax evasion. After serving four years Tony was released in December 1998, and he settled his ministry in Fouke, Arkansas, about fifteen miles southeast of Texarkana. Followers had already begun occupying property in Fouke before Alamo's release so they could be near the prison facility in Texarkana. It took little time to build a compound including the church, housing, and multi-purpose buildings. The relatively short driving distance to Texas and Oklahoma assured quick evacuation across state lines in the event of another government raid. With its finely landscaped gardens and lawn, the church might catch the eye of an occasional passerby on Highway 71, but the compound appeared unremarkable and oddly desolate. "No trespassing" signs seemed ominous and out of place when one thought of a church. Tony Alamo's house was located across the drive from a guardhouse, and a large green house stood directly across from it. Several outbuildings dotted the landscape, as did a swimming pool and a carnival-size merry-go-round. A building on the other side of the pool served as a recreation and multi-purpose area. Single to multifamily dwellings were positioned among larger structures for general use including a school, cafeteria, and workspace. No one knew exactly how many people lived in the compound, but estimates were two to three hundred.

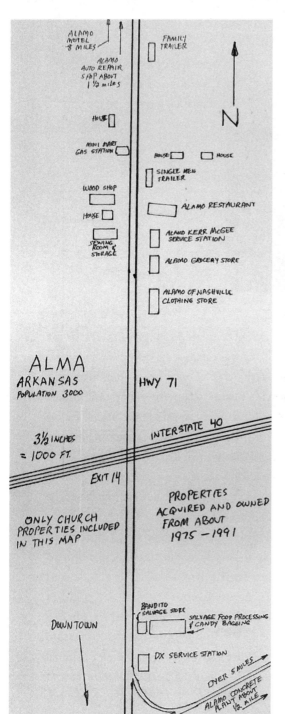

ALAMO MOTEL -8 MILES

FAMILY TRAILER

ALAMO AUTO REPAIR SHOP ABOUT 1 1/2 MILES

N

HOUSE

MINI MART GAS STATION

HOUSE

HOUSE

SINGLE MEN TRAILER

WOOD SHOP

HOUSE

ALAMO RESTAURANT

SEWING ROOM & STORAGE

ALAMO KERR McGEE SERVICE STATION

ALAMO GROCERY STORE

ALAMO OF NASHVILLE CLOTHING STORE

ALMA
ARKANSAS
POPULATION 3000

HWY 71

3 1/2 INCHES
= 1000 FT.

INTERSTATE 40

EXIT 14

ONLY CHURCH PROPERTIES INCLUDED IN THIS MAP

PROPERTIES ACQUIRED AND OWNED FROM ABOUT 1975 — 1991

DOWNTOWN

BANDITO SALVAGE STORE

SALVAGE FOOD PROCESSING & CANDY BAGGING

DX SERVICE STATION

OVER 5 MILES

ALAMO CONCRETE PLANT ABOUT 1/2 MILE

SCHEMATIC OF ALAMO'S FOUKE, ARKANSAS, PROPERTY FRONTED HIGHWAY 71 AND WAS BOUNDED BY BROWN AND REDCUT ROADS. A SMALL PARCEL OF LAND AT THE CORNER OF REDCUT ROAD AND HIGHWAY 71 IS PRIVATELY OWNED (ALLEN'S BURGERS). TWO PRIVATE LOTS WITH RESIDENTIAL HOMES ARE AT THE FRONT OF ALAMO'S PROPERTY FACING HIGHWAY 71. DESIGNED AND CONTRIBUTED BY FORMER MEMBER.

TONY ALAMO'S HOUSE, FOUKE, ARKANSAS.

GUARDHOUSE USED BY ALAMO MEN AND BOYS TO
MAINTAIN AN AROUND-THE-CLOCK WATCH ON THE
ROAD TO TONY ALAMO'S HOUSE, FOUKE, ARKANSAS.

THE "HOUSE OF SCORN," FOUKE, ARKANSAS.

Tony did not open as many businesses in Fouke as he had in Alma, but he did attract the notice of the town's people. After he donated sixty thousand dollars—about thirty percent of Fouke's total general fund—to the town to build a park, Mayor Cecil Smith authorized a town fire truck to water a piece of Alamo's property without telling the fire department. Tony Alamo's close relationship with the mayor troubled residents. He seemed to have special privileges.

In December 2006, just before city elections were held, controversy arose concerning a street that ran alongside Alamo's property. The street had been accessible to the public, and Fouke residents lived on one side of it. The church began restricting its use, and a homeowner reported that when she ventured up the street to her home, a church member stopped her with a gun. The dispute became a key election issue: Mayor Cecil Smith accommodated all of Alamo's wishes. It was time for a change.

A large constituency convinced Terry Purvis, a town council member, to run against Cecil Smith. A record number of voters turned out that day. Purvis supporters, Wilma and Drucker, were working the polls and keeping track of the votes as they came in. Near the end of the day, they

ONE OF FOUR DUPLEXES FOR FOLLOWERS BEHIND
THE CHURCH BUILDING, FOUKE, ARKANSAS.

GYMNASIUM, FOUKE, ARKANSAS.

grew concerned that Smith's votes were outnumbering Purvis's, so they
quickly called everyone they knew in town to get to the polls to vote for a
new mayor. Terry Purvis won the election by sixty-five votes, and he won
the next term as well. After losing two elections, Cecil Smith, no longer
of value to Alamo and publicly disgraced, went into hiding.

POOL AND GUEST HOUSE, FOUKE, ARKANSAS.

CAFETERIA INSIDE THE CHURCH BUILDING, FOUKE, ARKANSAS.

Tony Alamo continued to wield political influence when his own church member, Ben Edwards, ran unopposed to fill an empty seat on the town council. Edwards influenced a number of council members to vote with him on various issues, and the council voted to drop the street right-of-way issue. Alamo added opposing town council members to his "hit" list, announcing on his radio broadcasts that "God will strike down certain members of the Fouke town council."[1]

People actively against Alamo were targets for public smear campaigns, harassment, threats of vengeance, and economic ruin. Alamo's henchmen regularly threatened lawsuits for accusing church members of having weapons or calling Tony a pedophile. No one really knew what was going on behind the gates of that compound. A heavy shroud of uneasiness settled over the town of Fouke.

ONE OF THE MANY TRACTS SPREADING ALAMO'S MESSAGES OF SALVATION, DOOM, AND WORLDWIDE CONSPIRACIES.

1. "Tony Alamo Ministry Resurrected" (December 1, 2007). Religionnewsblog.com.

CHAPTER

ELEVEN

Just a Little Girl

Families in Alamo's ministry moved frequently, and family structure was fluid. When mothers and fathers fell out of Tony's grace, they could be kicked out of the church. Occasionally family members ran away, leaving behind spouses and children to be farmed out among church members. When men were sent to transport goods throughout the US, they could be gone for months at a time. Their family members might be moved and separated to stay with other families.

By the time she was seven, Irene had lived in five different places. She was born in Fort Smith, Arkansas. When she was two years old, her family moved to Chicago for a short time and then back to Fort Smith. In Fort Smith they were kicked out of the church, moved to another house there, and then returned to Alamo's property in Fort Smith when they were accepted back into the church.

In early 2000 Irene's family moved to Fouke. Irene was especially excited because her sister lived in Tony's house, and she loved the idea of being close to her. For the next three years, Irene moved back and forth among Tony Alamo's house, her parents' house, and The House of Scorn. The green House of Scorn was a residence for sisters and girls who fell out of grace with Tony. Vicki, one of the sisters, ruled it with an iron fist. When Irene was at Tony's house, she would grow to miss her parents and go home. After a while she missed her sister, friends, and the privileges of living in Tony's house and asked to go back. Tony allowed her to do this for about two years before deciding that he didn't like her shuttling back and forth and told her to pick one place to live. Irene chose his house.

One particular day Irene was finishing her work in the kitchen. She and five other girls made fruit salad in the mornings right after church and before school. As Irene picked up one of the bowls filled with salad, she felt it slip through her hands and crash to the floor. The loud noise startled everyone, and one of the sisters, Anna, quickly ran to help her. Irene's eyes filled with tears, and she tried not to blink so they wouldn't cover her face and give her away. Anna glanced at her and said, "Irene, what's wrong with you? You haven't said a word all morning. And now look at this mess!" Apologizing, Irene picked up the spilt salad, cleaned the floor, and, grabbing her books, ran off to school. Irene was carrying a lot of worry in her head that morning.

Before church, Irene's mom had told her that she had given Pastor Tony a report describing the disrespectful remark she and some other girls had made in school that week. At first Irene hadn't been worried about it, because her mother was always submitting reports on the kids' misbehavior. But it did make her uneasy.

When she got to class, her agitation turned into absolute fear. She saw that her friends, Shadow, Alisha, and Monique, were having trouble sitting on their wooden school seats. That could only mean one thing—they had been beaten. They told Irene that the report was reviewed the night before and that Tony had already summoned John Kolbek to come from Fort Smith to discipline some other people who had offended him, so he was going to have John deal with them as well. Shadow was Tony's wife, and she managed to talk him out of letting another man beat her, so instead one of the sisters did the job. Since Alisha and Monique were there, they went ahead and took their beatings too. The sister used a two-by-four board resembling an oar that was crafted just for this purpose to beat them. The beatings hurt, but they were lucky.

Irene knew she was in serious trouble. John Kolbek was Tony's "dirty-work" man; he got his hands "bloodied" (literally sometimes) with the beatings while Tony sat back and watched. Of course, Tony would have enjoyed doing the beating. He made sure he was careful so that he did not personally physically abuse anyone in case the law got involved. John was well known and feared by anyone who was in trouble, and he beat ruthlessly and seemed to enjoy it.

Irene knew that with every passing minute, John Kolbek was a minute closer to coming to town and she would endure the worst beating of her life. She tried to do her schoolwork, but all she could think about was how her entire digestive system felt jumbled into a huge knot and that she had a strong urge to pee. She could feel the heavy thumping of her heart as if it were pounding audibly for everyone to hear. She was terrified. And what made it worse was that she had to wait all day to meet her fate.

The hours passed slowly until Kolbek finally arrived. Before they walked to the gym where the beatings would take place, Tony asked Irene what she did wrong. Then he asked her mother why she would ever ask for Irene to be punished by John Kolbek when she knew it was the worst beating anyone could get. Irene's mother replied that she didn't want Tony to accuse her of not disciplining her children. Tony then asked some of the sisters in the room for their opinions, and Irene was touched to hear some of the sisters say that she didn't deserve to be punished at all. They were disgusted that Irene's own mother would bring such a punishment upon her. For the first time, a tiny part of her actually believed that she might escape her fate that day. But Tony rarely got a request from a parent to discipline her own child, and he would not turn this one down. He liked the idea that he could use Irene as an example of his power for others to see.

They all filed into the gym. First would be two boys who were being punished for playing with window cleaner solution, and then Irene, followed by a middle-aged man who was accused of questioning the authority of someone Tony had left in charge. A small crowd had gathered on command to view their punishment as an example of the consequences of misbehavior. Finally, the beatings began. Tony made sure everyone watched. John started beating the boys with his fists, sending blow after blow, which they took silently. Tony told John to be careful not to get blood on the carpet, which could be used as evidence in the future should these brutal beatings be known to outsiders. He then declared that the boys had taken enough punches and announced that it was time to use the board. Irene cringed with every loud smack that sounded from the board making contact with each boy's backside. She lost track of the number of board hits each endured. After what seemed like an eternity, they were finished. The boys left so bruised and battered that Tony ordered them not to go to church services for about a week until the bruises became less noticeable.

Irene's turn was next. She was so scared that she wasn't sure if she had walked to where John was standing on her own or if Kolbek had called out for her to come. Either way, she had apparently not come far enough, because John suddenly grabbed a handful of her ponytail down to the roots and pulled her to where he wanted her to stand.

Somewhere in the distance she heard Tony say to be easy on her and to make sure she was beaten across the legs, not on the backside. Tony's warning caught her off guard. Why would he say that? Because she's a girl? Because it's her first time being beaten by John? Later Irene learned that apparently Tony was aware that heavy beatings could injure a girl's reproductive system.

Irene quickly snapped out of her musings when John barked at her to stand with her feet spread about three feet apart with her hands on her knees. As soon as the board hit her legs, the pain exploded in her backside, and the force from the blow threw her about five feet forward onto her face. She cried out from the pain but shed no tears. John yelled at her to get back into position so he could beat her again. Once more, Irene flew forward. This happened about eight times before Tony declared it was enough. Irene left as soon as the ordeal was over. She knew she would have horrible bruises the next day, and at this point all she wanted was to be alone and recover.

She returned to Tony's house and went through the maze-like building until she found a room where she could be alone. To her surprise when she walked in, she found her friend Monique, weeping and huddled in a corner. Irene was shocked. Why was she weeping? She had already received her punishment last night, and it was not nearly as bad as what Irene had just undergone. Irene asked her what was the matter, and when her friend looked up to see Irene, between sobs she immediately asked if Irene was okay. Irene told her she was fine. The beating hurt, but she would be okay. Again Irene asked her friend why she was crying. Monique blurted out that as John Kolbek's daughter, she knew exactly what kind of beating Irene got, because she had endured them before. She was heartbroken that Irene had to go through that abuse at the hand of her father. At that point Irene assured her that she should not feel guilty for the actions of her father. Irene was touched that she cared so much about the unfair punishment she received. Then she sat down next to her, embraced her, and broke down crying with her, allowing all of her emotions to flow wordlessly into a friend who understood.

This took place in 2004. Irene was only twelve years old.

CHAPTER TWELVE

Tony's Conversion Story

Tony Alamo did not preach from the pulpit as Susan did. After her death, he rarely if ever appeared at worship services. He recorded his messages to be played at church and during the day for prayer and Bible study times. One of his personal favorites was his conversion story, played so often that followers could recite it verbatim.

> I know Jesus Christ is real. I know He is the Messiah. I know He is coming back to earth again. I know it because God told me so. Jesus was so far removed from my life; my sins were as the sands of the sea . . .
>
> It was on or during one of my big promotional extravaganzas that I met Jesus of Nazareth, my Lord. My mind was so far removed from anything concerning God the day He turned my whole world upside down. I had picked up a boy singer, a complete unknown, and did a gigantic promotion on him. I had him booked to all the top television shows.

I was driving around town in a chauffeur-driven lim-
ousine with a police escort and an entourage of seventeen people, putting the world on a trip. I had a barber, a
bodyguard, a nurse, and all sorts of "yes" men. If I went
to a hot dog stand, or a motion picture premiere, I went
with the limousines, chauffeurs, cops, and the whole re-
galia. The bodyguard would open the door, throw down
a big velvet pillow; we would step onto the velvet pillow.
The barber would comb our hair, the nurse would take
our pulse. One of the fellows would spray us with co-
logne, another strew flowers in our path, and the cops
would stand at attention. Where did I get the cops, the
chauffeurs, and the limousines? I rented them from a funeral parlor for a hundred bucks a day.

I had spent so much money on promotional ads and
on keeping the entourage of seventeen people that my
expenses were running into thousands of dollars a day,
and I needed money. My attorney told me some of the
superstars had invested money in a holding firm, and
they were interested in investing money in my campaign.
Would I meet with them and their attorneys? At first
I said no. "I have a hit record. The record distributors
owe me money. Within thirty to forty-five days I will
have all the money I need." My attorney said, "Tony, the
way you spend money, there is no way you can survive
thirty to forty-five days." I ranted and raved. "Sure they
will put up the dough. I have the star made. I've done all
the work. Why wouldn't they take the frosted cake for
a million bucks?" "Well, Tony," he reasoned, "don't sell
half of him." I agreed to see them and offer five percent
for fifty thousand. Little did I know what was waiting
for me that day.

The black limousines lined up, the police escort went
into formation, and we cruised down the streets with mo-

torists and pedestrians gaping, wondering who the dignitaries were. We cruised over to the attorney's office. The police lined up the limousines, the chauffeurs opened the doors, and we got out of the limos and went up the flight of stairs to the attorney's offices in Beverly Hills. The offices were packed. The motion pictures stars were there, their attorneys, and, of course, my seventeen people.

The attorney representing the investment firm was a little Jewish man. He came forward rubbing his hands and smiling. "Tony Alamo," he said, "I have been wanting to meet you. This is the greatest promotion I have ever seen in all my years in the industry. It is an extravaganza," he exclaimed, sweeping the wall with a gesture, and I saw he had the whole promotion laid out on his wall, still rubbing his hands and smiling as we sat down. "Now," he said, "I understand you boys need money." I was getting ready to haggle with him, and I thought to myself, "I have one up on him. He thinks I am Italian, and I know he is Jewish." I answered him with, "Well, I don't need as much money as you had originally offered."

Suddenly my ears went completely deaf. I could not hear any noise from the crowd in the room. We were only one floor up, yet I could not hear any noise from the street. I looked at the people in the room. Some of their mouths were moving, but I could not hear anything they were saying. Suddenly I heard a voice; a voice that came from every direction. It was all around me. It was going through every fiber of my being. The voice said, "I AM THE LORD THY GOD. STAND UP ON YOUR FEET AND TELL THE PEOPLE IN THIS ROOM THAT JESUS CHRIST IS COMING BACK TO EARTH, OR THOU SHALT SURELY DIE."

I looked around the room to see if someone was putting me on some kind of a trip, and they were all looking at me. I felt as if I were sealed into some sort of gigantic vacuum. I thought, "I am going crazy. I'm losing my mind. Yes, that's it; I'm cracking up." People had told me I was a genius, and geniuses often cracked up, so that was it. So I would get out of here before I made a fool of myself.

I stood to my feet and said, "I am ill." The giant pressure that was upon me forced me back into my seat, and the voice as many waters flooded all around and through me again. "I AM THE LORD THY GOD. STAND UP ON YOUR FEET AND TELL THE PEOPLE IN THIS ROOM THAT JESUS CHRIST IS COMING BACK TO EARTH AGAIN OR THOU SHALT SURELY DIE."

I struggled to my feet again, and took one step. As I did, God started playing with my soul like a yo-yo. He would pull it half out of me and then put it back. My heart was palpitating so hard it felt as if it was going to jump out of my body, and suddenly a revelation came to me, so real I was astounded that I had not always known it. I knew there was a heaven and a hell! I started screaming to the top of my lungs, "No, God, No! Please don't kill me. I'll tell them! I'll tell them! I'll tell them!" The breath went back into my body, and my heart stopped jumping.

I said, "God, You don't know these people like I do. They won't believe me. But I'll tell them. I'll call them all on the phone, send them telegrams, anything. But please don't make me do it here; they will think I'm crazy." Again he started pulling the soul out of me. My heart was jumping out of my body. I was gasping for breath. "No, God, no—please," I began screaming, "I'll do it. I'll do it. I'll tell them." Again my breath went back in my body; my heart stopped thumping.

I looked at the people in the room. They were all staring at me with eyes as big as owls. "I know you won't believe me," I said. "But God is telling me to tell you that Jesus Christ is coming back to earth." Now, I said to myself, I said it. Oops, again my soul started going in and out, again, gasping for breath. "What's the matter, God? I said it. I told them." Suddenly every promotion I had done in my life was laid out before me in block form. The enthusiasm I had built and sold a star or a product with. And the Lord said, "NOW THAT YOU KNOW I AM HERE, IS THAT THE BEST YOU CAN DO FOR ME?"

"I know you won't believe me, but Jesus Christ is coming back to earth again." This time when I looked at the group of people, they all looked so small to me, and I really wound up with all enthusiasm. "Repent," I screamed. "Jesus is coming!" I had never read a Bible scripture in my life. I had seen the picture, "*Elmer Gantry*," and I commanded everyone in the room to get down on their knees and repent immediately, the Lord Jesus was coming. I thought that if I did not do a good job, they would all disintegrate before my eyes, and I would disintegrate for not doing a good enough job.

The vacuum around me began to lift, and my hearing was returning, and the Lord said, "THAT'S ENOUGH." My attorney grabbed one of my swinging arms and said, "Tony, Tony, what's the matter with you?" The little Jewish attorney was almost backed out of the window. Papers were flying all over the room. (I had knocked his spindle off the desk.) "Get him out of here," he screamed, "He's nuts!" I thought for a moment, how can I blame him? If someone had come into my office and done the same thing I had just done, I possibly would have thrown them out of the window.

I walked out of the office with all my entourage following me. My bodyguard (who later went with Sonny and Cher) was laughing so hard he was falling down the hall. "Tony," he said, "what's the matter? Didn't you dig the cat? Man, he'll wind up in a straight jacket over that scene." The more I tried to explain to them that God had talked to me the more they laughed. "Come on, Tony, put them on a trip but man, don't try to put us on it." As I got to the foot of the stairs, there [were] the funeral limousines lined up. "Oh, my God," I thought, "the last thing I want to see is this mess." I made them all get in the cars.

I wanted to walk. I wanted to be alone. As I walked alone, I looked up into the sky. "Dear God," I said, "now that I know you are there, just tell me what you want me to do. I will do anything you say." No answers. I thought, "Maybe God wants me to go to church. Yes, that's it. I will go to church."

I picked the biggest one. I thought the biggest one should know the most. I went in and talked to the priest. I told him what happened to me. The priest said to just keep it in my heart to be baptized. This infuriated me. To think that God had told me that Jesus was coming, and here is a man of God telling me to keep it in my heart to be baptized. "Look," I said, "I am a promoter. I know my business. If you ask me how to promote a product, I will give you a positive way to promote it. You are supposed to be a man of God. You tell me about God." This priest was later filled with the Spirit and is now preaching the Gospel, but he had no answers for me then.

I went from one church to another, but found no one preaching the powerful message that God had given to me. One by one I left each church, more depressed than I had been before. I felt that I was the only person in the world that knew the truth—that Jesus was really coming.

I had left all my business; I was broke. I took what money that came in and paid off debts. I couldn't work. I was afraid that God would come down on me again in front of people. I was desperate, and I was confused. I did not know what to do. I went to my room. There was an old Gideon Bible laying [there]. I opened it and read, "Blessed are they who hunger and thirst for righteousness, for they shall be filled." "Oh, God," I cried, "that's me. I am hungry for truth." "Blessed are the meek, for they shall inherit the earth." "Oh, God," I cried, "I have never been meek, but now I am broke. Now I am in this shabby room. Maybe I qualify now." As I read the words of the Bible, I knew every word of it was truth. I felt the same Spirit I felt that day in the office, and I knew that God had come down on the prophets, the disciples, the apostles, in the same way. He had come down on me in that office that day, by the power of the Holy Spirit, and told them what to write.

I felt the power of the Holy Spirit deep in my heart and soul. I found the plan of Salvation. How we must ask God for forgiveness of our sins and ask Jesus to come into our hearts. I cried out to God to forgive me of my sins. My life had been so filled with sin. I asked Jesus to come into my heart and make me a new creature. God gave me a vision of hell. I cried out, "God, don't let me go there." Then He gave me a vision of heaven. I saw myself little, naked, kneeling before God. I was so peaceful I never wanted to leave. There I was, at His feet; I was afraid to open my eyes. I know if I did, I would be looking into the face of Jesus, and I was afraid to look Him in the face. Then I saw a large illuminated cross and stars bursting, thousands of them, and angels singing. The spirit of God entered into my body, and I knew beyond any shadow of doubt I passed from death into life. God broke my heart into a million pieces, and I lay on the floor with tears streaming down my face, and my body rocking in sobs, but I knew I was saved. Bernie Lazar Hoffman, a.k.a. Tony Alamo, was a changed creature. I took a shower, changed my clothes, and walked out into the rain.[1]

1. Tony Alamo, "Signs of the Times." www.scvhistory.com/scvhistory/alamo-alamo.htm.

CHAPTER THIRTEEN

Living on Quicksand

The rain was pounding on the roof of the trailer, but Victoria was sobbing so hard that she didn't even notice. She was usually quiet and tried to keep her feelings to herself, but this time she was beside herself with hurt and anger. Her father, Glen, had been gone for months. He was in town for just one night, and the church sister, Sonia, who was taking care of her wouldn't let Victoria and her brother see him because they didn't finish their homework. Ever since her father had moved them from the compound in California to Fort Smith, Arkansas, life was so different. When Tony came to California, he mostly met with business people and stayed in hotels. He rarely spent time at the settlement in Saugus, so life in California felt more laid back. Victoria buried her face in her pillow. She just didn't understand why her father had changed. She wanted to turn back the clock.

Glen came from Bakersfield and grew up in a typical, financially sound, all-American family. His parents were happy to give their children the best opportunities, and they played sports, had lots of friends, and celebrated their sixteenth birthdays with sports cars. While his two brothers went to college, attended graduate school, and pursued professional careers, Glen had difficulty deciding what to do with his life. He enrolled in a community college and worked at a bakery, but he didn't quite measure up to his

parents' expectations. He further shocked them when he joined Tony
Alamo Christian Ministries in 1977 and moved to Saugus at the age of
nineteen. Glen's choice was a mystery to his brothers, but already with an
edge over the members who were prostitutes, drug addicts, and panhandlers, Glen had found a place where he could truly be successful.

Tony Alamo recognized intelligence when he saw it. He also knew how
to spot vulnerabilities. He knew that Glen felt estranged from his family
of wealth and prestige, so he placed him in the office where he could keep
an eye on him. Glen began to thrive. He worked day and night; at times
he even slept at the office. Becoming Tony's right-hand man, Glen took on
elements of Tony's personality. He believed in the teachings of the church,
and his charisma commanded respect from all the members.

Glen worked alongside Tony for the next sixteen years. At the age of
thirty-five, he married Quinn, a fifteen-year-old girl who had been born
in the cult. Over the next six years, Quinn gave birth to Glen's four children—Paige, Victoria, Ian, and Stefan. Never afraid to tell his children
about his life before the cult, Glen shared boyhood stories and took his
children to visit his parents. Victoria was especially close to Glen's mother,
and this connection gave her a sense of family and the belief that despite
Tony's teachings, there was something good in the world outside the cult.

Too young to be a mother, Quinn was unhappy. Her childhood in the
cult had been torturous, and the abuse continued even now. Her father had
escaped Alamo's grip some years ago and now lived in Vermont. Though
she knew only what Tony had preached about life on the outside, Quinn
couldn't bear to continue living under such abject conditions. She and
Glen decided to leave the church. Glen took Quinn with her baby, Stefan,
dropped them off at a local hotel, and told her to call her father for airfare.
Glen vowed that he would follow with the rest of the children.

Believing Glen's promise, Quinn fled to Vermont. Days passed, and she
heard nothing from Glen. When she finally reached him, he said that he
couldn't leave. Learning of Glen's plan, Tony had preached hell to him for
three hours. Glen had changed his mind; he was keeping the kids. In her
heart Quinn knew what Tony Alamo was capable of when wanting to keep
children from the parent who left.

From that day forward Tony regularly publicly condemned Quinn to his followers, drawing a picture of a mother that was far different from who she really was. Quinn loved all her children. Now for the first time in her life she was on her own with a little baby, separated from her other children, the only family she had ever known, and with no knowledge of how to survive in the outside world.

For the next year and a half, Glen relied on the church members to help with his children. As time went by, his responsibilities working for Tony required more and more time. Someone always had to come over to watch the children and clean the house while Glen continued to work long hours. Tony sent Glen on work details away from the compound, sometimes for weeks and even months at a time. When a babysitter wasn't available, the children were farmed out to other households. Victoria sometimes felt that they were a burden to families who had enough to do caring for their own children. Glen's protective nature with his children was obvious and drew some resentment from other church members. Their children were managed just fine; what was so special about his? If he has a family, they thought, he should take care of them just like everyone else.

The man that Tony had plucked from the outside was now becoming a problem, and Tony ejected Glen from the church. The action was not uncommon; for reasons known only to Tony, followers were kicked out of the church to face eternal condemnation. Some returned, and others were forever gone. To give himself time to get settled and find a job, Glen took the children to Vermont to live with their mother, Quinn. Victoria, six years old by now, barely remembered her. Papa Tony had taught her that Quinn never wanted her and that she was a drug addict and a whore. Victoria felt afraid.

Victoria and Paige became protectors and caregivers for their younger brothers. Sadly, just children themselves, they needed someone to protect them. When one of Quinn's friends saw that Victoria was frightened by a movie on TV, he tried to comfort her. Afraid and angry, she demanded, "Where is daddy?" Glen had always kept them clean and fed. He had always taken good care of them. He sent them so many gifts for Christmas when they were in Vermont. Why couldn't they live with him? Why had he left them with this mother who didn't seem to want them?

One day Glen suddenly showed up, took all of the children, and returned to California. It would be eight years before Quinn would find her children again. For weeks Stefan, holding his blanket, stood at the door and called for Quinn by name. Unlike his three siblings, his mother was the only parent he really knew. Stefan was always aggressive, breaking all his toys, writing on walls with crayons—Glen said Stefan needed extra loving. They all took it on as their responsibility to be extra good to Stefan and to love him.

Those days in California were fun. Even though Glen worked a lot, he always saw that they were safe. Sometimes he took them to work with him. Victoria and Paige used to put on their dresses and hats, and telling them how pretty they were, Glen would take pictures of them. They ran through the sprinklers, laughed, and played. One day Quinn's mother called. Grandma wanted them to go back home to Arkansas. "It would be better for the children," she said. So Glen and the children went to Fort Smith.

The rain was coming down harder now. All out of tears, Victoria bunched up her pillow and hugged it close to her. She hated Fort Smith. Why did they come back there? Tony was always sending her father on the worst jobs, away from home. They weren't even allowed to talk to Glen when he was gone for months at a time. Before he left, Glen said he would take them to the lake and do fun things when he returned. Victoria doubted that would ever happen. He just said that to distract them from crying when he left. Tony would never let them be a real family again. Victoria shuddered. Last week some of the sisters had talked badly about her mother. They called her a whore and a stinking weasel. Victoria got so angry, and screaming for her mother, she refused to eat. Pastor Tony stepped in, made a list of food she had to eat, and ordered that Victoria be forced to eat until she threw up. Whatever Pastor Tony said was the final word.

Not even her father crossed that line. Today he continues to live in the cult and remain faithful to the laws of Alamo.

CHAPTER

FOURTEEN

The Alamo Brand of Discipline

Tony Alamo loved children—or so it seemed. The compound at Fouke had a swimming pool, a full-size merry-go-round, a rec room, and even a petting zoo. His house resembled a dorm with rambling room additions for the children—girls—who lived in Papa Tony's house. He had big-screen televisions (permitted for no one else), biblical movies, and a card table always loaded with candy in his personal spa bathroom.

The special privileges of living in Tony's house extended only to females. The only boys living there were Tony's sons, Sion and Tabor, and his stepson, George, whose mothers also lived with Tony. At any given time, as many as twenty-five sisters and young girls stayed in Tony's house. They were assigned duties there —cooking, cleaning, babysitting, and doing office work. The kitchen was a gathering place for the few visitors who came to the house to see Tony. Just off the kitchen was the office that connected to Tony's bedroom, but visitors and male members almost never entered a room other than the kitchen. If they did happen to venture into the office or Tony's bedroom, it would have been by invitation only. Tony did record spiritual messages in the office, and at times a young boy might be asked to offer his testimony.

Tony wanted the children to grow up loving the Lord. His teaching method was clear: children adhered to a rigid schedule of Bible study, prayer, school, and work duties. Girls and boys did not co-mingle, and rules were taken seriously. Violations were handled with standard punishments known as "proverbs" (beatings), "fasts," and "diesel therapy" (months of traveling with his truckers on the road), as well as ejection from the church. While some might consider his methods extreme and abusive, Pastor Tony knew that his instructions came directly from God. Church members enforced the disciplinary system by reporting violations in writing to Tony's office. Regardless of their ages or relationships—children, parents, and siblings—all members were expected to report misconduct to Tony.

Members believed that Tony could read their minds, so failure to report a violation could result in punishment for them. The accused was asked to respond to the charge, and Tony arbitrarily determined the truth and issued the penalty. Punishments were intended to keep followers from backsliding and falling into ultimate disfavor from God, and so the accused was expected to feel grateful and thank the one administering the punishment. Tony had a special brand of discipline for the girls living in his house: he sent them to live in a green house across the yard from his home. Tony referred to this house as the "House of Scorn."

Vicki, one of the sisters, managed the house, and banishment could last for just a few days or for periods lasting months at a time. Tony had the sisters print out scriptures from Proverbs about scornful women and how they need to be punished. They taped these scriptures on the walls throughout Tony's house. Whenever a girl would upset him, he would point to the scriptures on the wall, call the accused "scornful," and send her to The House of Scorn for an indefinite amount of time.

When beatings were called for, Tony commanded an adult to carry out the punishment. Sometimes sisters held the guilty child face down on a bed while the mother or father beat the child—sometimes as many as forty strokes. Each family had a paddle resembling a boat oar uniformly made from a two-by-four piece of lumber, narrowed on the end to form a handle similar to that of a baseball bat. Tony referred to this weapon as the "board of education." Other times beatings took place in the gymnasium for wider public viewing.

On these occasions Tony's friend, John Kolbek, later dubbed "the Enforcer" by the FBI, did the beatings. Kolbek was large, strong, and ruthless. Kolbek's appearance always generated fear. Tony took special delight in presenting Kolbek with a rousing, "Here's Johnny!" Because of their limited knowledge of the outside world, cult members failed to understand the private joke between Tony and Kolbek, comparing Kolbek's entrance with Jack Nicholson's use of the line in *The Shining*.[1]

Fasting was also an option for punishment. When charged to fast, the accused could consume only limited sips of coffee, and fasting periods varied from a day or two to weeks. By the time they could eat, children especially were so hungry that they gorged themselves on food only to become sick.

Sentences to "diesel therapy" were limited to boys. Accused children were ordered to ride with one of the men on his interstate route to receive and transport donated goods to distribution centers for resale. These trips lasted from weeks to months at a time, essentially putting the accused in isolation. When the violation called for both beating and "diesel therapy," the ride was especially uncomfortable with bruised and bloodied buttocks.

Tony effectively controlled the adults with even stiffer sentences. He mandated work assignments that took parents away from families, men away from wives, and ejected members from the church. His methods corrupted the family unit and established Tony Alamo as the one and only authority. He displaced the men, leaving women and children particularly dependent on him for every aspect of their existence. Tony approved shopping lists, authorized the driver and the rider who would go to town (always in pairs), and dictated acceptable books they could read, music they could listen to, clothing they could wear, and food they could eat.

All this Tony Alamo did in the name of the Lord.

---

1. In *The Shining*, a film based on the Stephen King novel, actor Jack Nicholson plays a character that has clearly gone mad and is chopping down the bathroom door with an axe to get to his wife. Nicholson ad libbed the line, "Here's Johnny!" imitating the introduction that Ed McMahan used to introduce late-night television host Johnny Carson's humorous monologues.

CHAPTER FIFTEEN

Behind Closed Doors

Resting on pillows against the headboard, Tony Alamo breathed a deep sigh of satisfaction. His girls surrounded him on the bed. Two were tenderly massaging his feet. The music of JD Sumner and the Stamps Quartet—just one of many musicians that Tony claimed he promoted to stardom—was pumping through the speakers. Peering through his dark glasses, Tony studied the scene before him and marveled at how far he had come.

For a moment he felt a pang of sadness. Susan had been dead for more than twenty years, and many wives later, he still missed her. Susan always handled things so well. She could preach to anyone and move souls to salvation. Until Susan came along, Tony had only one use for women: to pleasure him in the bedroom. But Susan was different; she took charge. She knew how to attract people, stir their spirits, and get them to give their lives to the Lord. Remembering the busloads of hippies she brought into the fold, Tony almost laughed out loud. At first he didn't know what she saw in those "losers," but she put them to work, converted them to Christianity, and before long, Tony and Susan were dripping in furs and diamonds and driving fancy cars.

The music suddenly stopped, and Tony's attention turned to the girls who were now rubbing his neck and arms. Shoving them aside, he swung his legs to the floor and growled, "What are you girls looking at? You are a bunch of ugly weasels. All you ever do is eat, sleep, and go to the bathroom. Get out of my sight. You're disgusting." As the girls scrambled to their feet, ten-year-old Sissy caught her foot on the bedpost. Grabbing her by the arm, Tony grinned and said, "Hey, not so fast. Stay here a bit longer. I have something special in mind for you."

Hours later, Sissy walked quickly down the hall to her room. She closed the door, climbed into bed, and pulled the covers up to her chin. She clutched her well-worn teddy bear, shut her eyes, and willed herself to sleep. Later that night one of the sisters quietly opened the bedroom door and found Sissy sleeping with her covers tangled in a heap and her bear on the floor. As the sister picked up the bear and straightened the covers over the little girl, the light of the moon caught the shine of a plain gold marriage band on Sissy's left hand. The sister turned, quietly closed the bedroom door, and walked down the hall to finish her evening chores.

The hallway extending from Tony's bedroom led through a maze-like pattern of bedrooms for girls, sisters, wives, and Tony's three sons, Sion, Tabor, and George. Next to Tony's room was a large spa with a stand-up shower, a toilet, a bathtub, an in-ground hot tub, two tanning beds, a Roman table, exercise equipment, and a card table covered with bulk boxes of candy. In one area Tony kept papers and notes.

A door from the spa opened into the mirror room, the area where the girls had all their toiletries and dressed. The door had a sliding bolt on the girls' side. Younger wives usually entered the spa room through the girls' door. One day when Irene and Sissy put on their swimsuits to play in the hot tub, they found some of the little girls posing on the bathtub trying to look pretty for Tony. Irene didn't know why, but she suddenly felt a knot in her stomach.

When Irene first moved into Tony's house, everything was special and fun. She didn't have to work much, and she had fun playing with the other girls. A year later, when she turned nine, things changed. Her sister, Avril, was fifteen then and spent most of her time with Tony. Irene had moved into the house because she wanted to be with her sister. Now she didn't understand why Avril was more serious and secluded in Tony's bedroom for long periods. Avril was always gone. Sometimes from the mirror room Irene could hear Tony's booming voice reading scripture to Avril. At other times she heard one of the sisters reading scripture while Avril and Tony made noises in the bedroom. When Tony presented Godiva chocolates and flowers to Avril on Valentine's Day, Irene knew that they were married. That was his trademark gift to all of his wives.

And then there was Tony's other wife, Sharon. Irene never knew what to expect from her. Sharon seemed passive about the other wives, but she was left with having to look after all the little girls that came along. She lived in a closet with just enough room for a bed, until finally, she got her own room at the back of the house. Sharon slept during the day and worked at night—all the sisters had varying sleeping schedules, and anyone who woke up a sister would get beaten. The girls learned to tiptoe around the house and be quiet.

Tony always had someone sleeping with him.

Work became more demanding. At first the duty lists changed every week, but then they extended to monthly assignments. The sisters made the lists, and all duties had to be done three times each day (e.g., clean bathrooms three times). They got in trouble for not doing things right; when someone knocked over a plant when vacuuming in Tony's room, Tony was furious. Even though she didn't do it, Irene was terrified that she would be punished.

Tony wouldn't let the girls leave his house to go to church, and they remained secluded in his house for weeks on end. To some it felt like forever. When the girls did get back to church, the boys wondered where they had been. Tony didn't want his girls to be around other boys or men. Men would ask to marry them, and Tony would say, "No, they are already taken." When a visiting Christian inquired about Avril, Tony made Avril pretend someone else was her husband instead of Tony.

Children didn't always know what information was deemed to be Alamo family secrets. When a few kids from Fort Smith came to Fouke for a visit,

Tony's little girl, Bella, charmed them. They asked if Tony was Bella's father, and Irene innocently confirmed that he was. Irene's close friend and Tony's wife Shadow whispered to Irene, "This is a trouble conversation, and I don't want to be a part of it."

A kid from Fort Smith furrowed her brow and wondered aloud, "But she's not Sharon's daughter? Andrea's her mom?"

Irene continued, "Yeah, you've seen her call Andrea 'Mom,' but Sharon is Tony's wife." Irene didn't know how to handle the "family" secret that Bella is both Andrea's and Tony's daughter while Sharon is Tony's wife. They were still teaching Bella to say that Sharon was her mom. Shadow became scared, and even though no one else was there, she said, "Irene, that's bad. You can't tell that." Shadow reported Irene, who was subsequently sent to The House of Scorn for being a big mouth. Apparently sometimes they were supposed to lie. Irene put her stuff in her laundry basket and carried it over to the green house. After three days, she had completed her penance, returned to Tony's house, and from that day on remembered Tony's rule: "Everything that happens in his house stays in his house."

CHAPTER

SIXTEEN

Birthdays and Holidays

The day before Victoria's eighth birthday, Tony called her a "gluttonous pig." So when she opened her birthday present, Victoria felt fat. Everyone had an Easy-Bake Oven—all the girls got them for their birthdays. But she got shoes instead. Seeing the disappointment in her sister's face, Paige ran to her room and gathered all the toys she could carry to give to Victoria. Everyone wanted toys. Shoes were for school.

The previous year, when Victoria turned seven, her father celebrated with a princess party. It was her best birthday ever. She got lots of toys, and her friends all came to their apartment, which had been decorated elaborately to match the theme. Her dad had snapped pictures of Victoria wearing her pink birthday dress and a sparkling crown. Victoria's eyes filled with tears. She thought, "This is shit." She missed her dad. Everyone else had family, but Victoria and Paige had no one there with them. Irene's mom did bake Victoria a cake. That was a little consolation.

Victoria forgot her birthday the following year. Mostly birthdays weren't that special. All the kids got the same gifts. Tony would throw a pool party for all the birthday kids, the sisters would make a cake, and that would be that. Birthday celebrations could be fun times with friends, but they weren't really designed to make a birthday girl or boy feel special.

Birthdays coinciding with a punishment period were especially difficult. Irene was frequently banished to The House of Scorn, and one time when she was already serving time there for a minor offense, she was punished for not sweeping the floor thoroughly. She was taken off swimming for the entire summer and placed on a three-day fast. Hungry and hot, Irene had a miserable tenth birthday.

That year all the kids with summer birthdays came to Fouke from Fort Smith to celebrate with a pool party. Sister Lydia made a beautiful cake with their names on it. Victoria even got sneakers that lit up, and she loved them. That was the only special birthday party they ever had there. Irene was so upset that she had to miss it. And no one even remembered that she wasn't there.

That fall one of the sisters, Jennifer Kolbek, prepared a special gift from the congregation to give to Tony for his birthday: a letter-sized book of photographs of all the children in the ministry, even including members in California and New Jersey. Each child's picture had its own page, along with a special birthday message to Papa Tony. This gift would seem particularly twisted in the future when Tony was convicted of sex crimes against children.

Christmas was another time for gifts. Children routinely sorted donated goods in the warehouses. Just before the holidays, they were directed to take goods and wrap them for Christmas. Victoria had wrapped some of her gifts at the warehouse and knew what she was getting. They wrapped all the kids' toys for Christmas. It was just another way to be sure kids didn't feel special. All age groups were given the same things, and the gifts weren't necessarily well matched to ages. Everyone knew that there was no Santa; everything was from Papa Tony. Irene, though eleven years old, found a set of building blocks under the tree.

One Christmas little Victoria opened her gift to find an end table. When her uncle called to wish her a Merry Christmas and asked her what she got, she wasn't sure what to say—it was the same gift that all the other kids in church had received, but she didn't want to tell him that. In the past her father had always worked really hard to give all the kids nice gifts.

One year Victoria got a collectable porcelain doll. It wasn't a toy she could really play with, but she found it to be of great use. The box was a perfect place to hide contraband. Victoria had begun to lift small items from stores when she was allowed to go into town as a rider with a shopper. When a sister found Spice Girls, Brittany Spears, and News Boys CDs in her closet, the sisters held Victoria spread-eagle down on the bed and beat her with a two-by-four.

Victoria loved to read. She had read a book about a girl who was left by her parents. The girl had to steal just to stay alive, and she knew how to hide stuff. The story ended with the father's return and the girl's happy life restored. Victoria identified with the story, and like the girl in her book, she found more inventive ways to hide her stolen treasures, tucked away in the box with her porcelain doll.

Victoria carefully rolled a little locket into the folds of her doll's dress, closed the box, and pushed it to the back of her closet shelf. She stepped back and looked through the window.

CHAPTER SEVENTEEN

Broken Family Ties

In Muldrow, Oklahoma, the bunch of trailers rested on nice foundations. There was a pool in the middle of the grounds. One day Victoria was staring out her window when she caught a glimpse of Janet, who just that morning had made fun of her speech impediment and called her "Dumbo" because of her big ears. Putting her arm around Victoria, her big sister, Paige, had guided her from the kitchen and comforted her. "Victoria, pay no attention to Janet. It's time to go to Sonia's house and play with her children. You are the most beautiful and sweetest sister ever." Victoria had tightened her hold on Paige's hand and blinked her tears away. She could always count on her sister to protect her.

Victoria put on her Barbie t-shirt, blue-jean mini skirt, and light-up Scooby-Doo sneakers. She was ready to go to Sister Sonia's house. Sonia was always fun—of course, they had their chores to do, but later Sonia would have fun group activities for the girls. They played games outside, baked cookies, and acted out Bible stories. Victoria and Sonia's daughter, Susan, had just finished reading *Anne of Green Gables*. They would pretend they were Anne and Diana, writing notes to each other.

Finding childcare had been difficult for Victoria's father. He ran into problems when Tony changed his work assignments to jobs that kept him out of town for months at a time. On the Arkansas properties, when children turned seven or eight years old, they would go to a same age group for daycare. In Oklahoma, Glen's children were forgotten. When she was seven, Victoria started working in the kitchen, cooking macaroni and cheese. Victoria's younger brothers were farmed out to different families every day. They always felt like an inconvenience for everyone else who needed to take care of their own children.

Finally, Glen placed the children with Sonia in Muldrow, Oklahoma. Sonia and her husband had two boys, one Ian's age and another a little older than Stefan, and a daughter, who was Victoria's age. Sonia's husband was a trucker for Tony and often away from home. The girls' room was tiny for the three girls, and the boys had a big room. For a while an older woman lived with them and helped in the household. When she married and left, the children had to go by her home regularly to receive their job assignments that came from Fouke by way of her fax machine. Victoria usually had to sweep and mop—if the sisters didn't like your mother, they would give you bad jobs. Following Tony's lead, the Alamo adults demonized Victoria's mother, Quinn, to the children.

Sonia was the closest person to a mother that the children had, though several family members on their mother's side still lived in the cult. Quinn's mother, a fireball, was a fierce, strong woman and was known as one of the "crazies" in the cult. She would fight anyone to stand up for what she believed in. Before moving to Arkansas, she lived in California.

When the children went to their grandmother's house, she always asked each one what they wanted for breakfast, and she would cook it. She was determined to take care of her grandbabies with pure grandmotherly love. One night, though, the children were sent back to live with Sonia because they got caught nibbling on chocolate chip cookies in the kitchen at night. Their grandmother moved to Paris, Arkansas, to run a warehouse.

For a brief period of time, Victoria was sent to take care of her aunt, her mother's sister. Too much responsibility for a little girl, Victoria lost her temper and shouted, "I am not your slave!" As taught by Tony, Sonia disciplined Victoria just as she did her own children, with a switch and fasting.

Victoria regularly threw fits until she was about ten years old. Like her sister and brothers, she was holding a lot of emotion inside. Sometimes she thought she would explode. At the end of each day, Victoria coped by remembering the time when Glen was a good dad. He had been the hero of their world. They used to get spankings that were typical of parents' discipline—never beatings. Victoria rarely got in trouble when Glen was caring for them. When she was little, she was sweet, always making sure that everybody was happy. She would give her toys and candy to other people. Back then Victoria was happy.

Glen's children lived with Sister Sonia for nearly four years. But, the older they grew, the weirder things got. Now when their father came home, he was always met with a long list of complaints about the kids, so then he had to punish them. It got so that they dreaded his coming home because he would beat them. It seemed like Tony was deliberately punishing Glen. Glen was powerful and everyone liked him. He would have done anything for his children. Tony wanted to break him, and the first step to succeeding was to shatter his family ties.

CHAPTER EIGHTEEN

The Power of Tony

Tony Alamo was a demigod. At least that's what his followers were taught
to believe. They believed he could summon fire from the heavens if he
wanted to. He had supernatural powers, the ability to know their thoughts
almost before they had them. Tony was ever present in their lives and bred
a combination of awe and fear even on the most mundane level. At times
Tony's erratic behavior raised doubts among the adults, and some may
have quietly shared their concerns with others, but they remained obedient, firm in their belief that they were saved and that Tony's church was
a work of God.

Tony saw himself as a great singer and likened himself to Elvis Presley.
Afraid to disrespect him, church members always put Tony at the top of
their lists of favorite singers. Tony was a person who could cause mountains to crumble and the earth to quake. He would never take second place.
True to the model of cult leaders, Tony demanded complete obedience,
told his followers that his powers came from God, and punished anyone
who crossed him.[1]

---

1. See Appendix 1 for a listing of traits of cult leaders.

When people first came to Tony's church, they saw nice, energetic people. Everyone was amazing, and being there felt like a great experience. Church members showed nice behavior on the outside—and so new members continued to come. There were rules, but after newcomers got used to a few rules, one more rule wouldn't kill them. As long as baby Christians were eased in like that, before they knew it, they were drawn permanently into the fold.

Tony Alamo's plan for salvation required complete submission to the church. Members lived on his property, gave all money to the church, followed every instruction Tony directed, and lived cut off from the outside world. Their survival became completely dependent on Tony Alamo. Lest they forget, Tony regularly reminded his followers that they came to him because they couldn't make it on their own. The adults knew of others who had been successful outside the church; in fact, after the 1991 raid on Georgia Ridge, almost everyone went out, worked, and paid their bills. Later Tony demanded that they resubmit to the church and his authority. He was a master of blotting out history and teaching his own version of truth.

Men that Tony knew in the Fouke/Texarkana community occasionally visited worship services to attest to the powerful influence Tony had on the world outside the cult. Buster, a man with one arm, sang the praises of Tony with his stories and his wallet. Buster was one of many slick business operators who supported the ministry. When he came to church, followers loved to share their witness of Tony's messages from God. "You'll never amount to anything in life outside of this church," Tony reminded them. And certainly, by turning all income over to Tony and relying on him for total sustenance, that message seemed true enough.

Tony would expound on the messages from God, even stopping to cock his head as if he were listening to the Lord Himself. Then in his resounding voice he would declare what God had just told him. Tony used the King James Version of the Bible as the only authority. He liked to show his followers that God revealed truths to him as a prophet, and church members, eager to learn God's messages, held onto every word. When Tony was teaching from the book of Revelation, he demonstrated his special pipeline to God.

And when the seven thunders had uttered their voices,
I was about to write: and I heard a voice from heaven
Saying unto me, Seal up those things which the seven
Thunders uttered, and write them not. (10:4)

Tony suddenly stopped, listened, and said, "The Lord just told me what the seven thunders uttered. But you are ignorant like sheep. You can't comprehend all that God has told me. I can't share with you what God has revealed to me."

The message of salvation varied. Depending on Tony's mood, his followers might or might not be God's chosen people who would be saved at the time of mass destruction. Worshippers were encouraged to "seek the spirit" and shook, danced, and spoke in tongues at a high, furious pitch. Ian and Stefan would watch in fascination, waiting to be so moved. Victoria suspected that followers were doing this themselves; she didn't believe that angels spoke in such weird chanting. No one dared to express what he or she really thought, given that their inability to find the spirit likely signified their disfavor with God. So they all continued to try to be good Christians. Victoria had been baptized in the Pacific Ocean when she was four years old, and at age twelve Irene was baptized in Tony's hot tub. Irene prayed long and hard until she fell asleep one day in the pew. They understood the meaning of commitment to the Lord, but for some reason they just couldn't figure out how to be overtaken by the Holy Spirit.

CHAPTER NINETEEN

Breaking Out

She was standing at a distance and saw a kid get flung by his backpack into a ditch. Frank caught her face from the corner of his eye, and turning to the boys fighting, he shouted, "Oh, my God—we're all in trouble! You guys, stop it!" He pulled the boy up from the ditch, and they all got quiet. That's when Melissa called out, "Come over here. You're all in trouble." Sure enough, she had reported it to Tony. It got back to him that they were all fighting each other. John Kolbek was on his way. All of a sudden, they got the message: "All the boys are invited to the gym." Trembling, they all knew what was coming. Even the people not close to the fighting knew that something wasn't right.

In the gym, parents and other kids were lined up on either side. Frank was called out to the middle, and Brother Charlie began asking him what happened. Frank tried to tell him how he had been trying to stop the fight, and Charlie just kept saying, "You're lying. You're getting beat."

John Kolbek, a muscular man who stood at six feet four inches, stepped up and punched Frank, a young but well-built teenager, in the face with his fist until his face was bleeding. His teeth went right through his gums. The force of Kolbek's blows knocked Frank over three times, and when he didn't think he could get up again, Kolbek ordered him to stand and grab his ankles. Kolbek picked up a three-foot-long board two inches thick and four inches wide and beat Frank's backside forty times. Even with his head ringing Frank could hear Tony saying, "Keep going." Kolbek would occasionally shout, "You made me come all the way down here to do this. You think I like doing this? No! I love it!"

All the girls were crying because Tony made them watch. Frank tried not to cry because he had been beaten before and knew it didn't do any good to cry. Then Kolbek shouted, "You're real tough, aren't you? You're just trying to show off for the girls." At that point, Frank started screaming. But that didn't help. Kolbek just kept on going. Frank tried to block him with his hands and Kolbek shouted, "Move your hands!" Before Frank could move his hands, Kolbek beat him on his hands three times. The board hit on his arm and bruised the whole length of it. Then Kolbek shouted, "My daughter handles this better than you. I beat her."

That night Frank still played the piano for church. His hands were swollen, and it took a week before he could even try to sit down. An accomplished, self-taught musician, his hands were permanently injured from this one beating. It wasn't the first time he was beaten, but Frank determined it would be the last. It was 2007, and he was only one year away from his eighteenth birthday.

Frank was thoughtful, smart, and logical. The past few months he had been rethinking the ways of life. Frank grew up as a well-behaved child, believing what he was taught. He knew the rules, and when he didn't understand them, his mother told him not to question, saying that Papa Tony taught the true word of God.

As a growing teen, Frank wondered about women. Tony often degraded women. He heard that Tony had humiliated Anne by calling her a pig. That time Tony said that he couldn't rape her and had to have her cervix surgically opened so he could penetrate her. Why would Papa Tony say something like that? Frank saw women as good people. He thought, "Well maybe some women can be pigs, but guys can be pigs too." Boys weren't allowed to look at girls. The one time Frank tried to talk with a girl, he was sent out on diesel therapy for three months. Then there was the troubling thought of his eleven-year-old sister, Avril. She had moved into Tony's house and simply disappeared. He had a bad feeling that something was going on there. He knew that Tony preached polygamy and said that girls were of the age to marry when they reached puberty. He didn't want to believe what he thought was happening.

Frank was thinking about all the rules. At first they sort of didn't matter. Then more and more rules were added without explanation. He felt confused. The reporting system generated fear and assured extreme punishments. He didn't know whom he could trust, even in his own family. His mother and father clearly supported every tenet of Alamo's teachings. The schedule now was rudimentary. Men and boys had breakfast at 9:00 a.m., worked all day, showered at 7:00 p.m., and went to church at 8:00 p.m. Then working in pairs, the men and boys took two-hour shifts as night watchmen. Frank was sleep deprived all the time. Even the younger children had no more scheduled play times. Frank was uncertain of all that he had been taught. He was exhausted. He was unhappy. It was time for him to test the principles he had been taught. He had to find out for himself what was really true.

Over the next three months, at seventeen years old, Frank planned his escape. Even risking discovery, he decided to confide in his close friend, Brady. Brady immediately bought into his plan. Frank sneaked a telephone from one of the men working construction, was able to get a message to his brother who had left the cult years earlier, and patiently waited for the right time to leave. As luck would have it, the night watch schedule provided the best opportunity for leaving. Frank and Brady were assigned to the duty schedule for the same night. They packed two duffel bags, backpacks, and left on their 4:00–6:00 a.m. shift. They ran to the highway and looked frantically up and down the road. Former members had arranged to have a ride waiting for them. In a few short minutes the headlights of an approaching car blinked, and their hearts were beating wildly. They jumped into the back seat and headed for the Little Rock airport. In a few hours Frank was flying to Washington to meet his brother. There was a problem with Brady's ticket, so they drove him to Memphis instead, where he boarded a bus for Virginia to meet with his mom, aunt, uncle, and many cousins, all former members.

The boys were afraid of the world outside the cult, but they were free. They had left the house of God and had a new life ahead of them. If they were now entering the kingdom of hell, as Tony so often warned, they were certain it could be no worse than where they had lived.

CHAPTER TWENTY

Left Behind

Irene was fifteen years old and loved singing in the choir. Lifting her voice in song, she almost forgot the news of the morning. Her brother Frank was gone. Pastor Tony said that he would become a drug-addicted homosexual and should be rebuked. She felt everyone's eyes examining her closely as if she might instantly turn into a weasel and become a backslider and reprobate. Irene was afraid. She loved her brother and didn't know where he would go. Her mother had held her in her lap that morning and crying, begged Irene never to abandon the church. She had hugged her mother and assured her that she would never leave her.

Irene's mind wandered to the days when they all were together as a family. They had lived in a duplex in Moffett, Oklahoma, when she was really young. Then they moved to Fort Smith, and Irene had the impression that they had been kicked out of the church. Happy little memories popped into her head—going to Chuck E. Cheese's Pizza, meeting a cousin and her grandmother on her mother's side. Their mom first let the boys and then Irene watch movies on a hidden TV set. Her mom said that if anyone knocked on the door to turn off the TV and hide it. They had enough money to get by then. Her dad cleaned windows, and her mom stayed home with the kids. They continued to tithe to the church. Then as quickly as they had stopped, they were again members of the church.

And the family moved to Fouke. The church community provided great support for members' needs. When her brother needed to have surgery, Irene and her sister, Avril, stayed at Tony's house. Irene was six years old, and Avril had just turned eleven. Tony's wife, Sharon, took good care of them. They played with Barbie dolls and had fun, but Irene missed their mom. She couldn't wait to get back with the family. But when they returned home, Avril said that she was going back to live at Tony's house. That was when Tony gave her parents a new minivan. Irene had ached for her sister; only boys were left in her house. Soon after, Irene moved to Tony's house to be with her sister.

The first time Irene met Tony Alamo, she thought, "Wow—that's Papa Tony!" Then she decided that she was too old to call him "Papa." From the very beginning, his presence was frightening. Irene had lightly knocked on the door, opened it, and was heading quietly to the candy table in Tony's bathroom. She jumped when Tony greeted her with a boisterous, "Well, where are you going?" He was lying on a bed with six women sitting around him. Two of the girls were massaging him. He wore his usual black, thin, slick lounging pants, and Irene noticed with surprise that he wore a toupee.

Irene's sister, Avril, would stay in Tony's room for days at a time. Irene thought Tony was reading scriptures to her and didn't think anyone else was there. Shadow said that Tony would read scriptures or have someone else read scriptures while he did sexual things with the girls like touching and fondling breasts and rubbing his penis. Tony used pornographic movies to show the girls what he wanted to do. Irene was aware that everyone who stayed in Tony's room was considered married.

Irene didn't know what it meant to be married, but she knew that it changed her sister. They used to have fun playing and laughing together. The first time she noticed her sister was different was soon after she moved into Tony's house. They were playing, and Irene, then seven years old, squirted hand sanitizer on Avril, who was eleven at the time. Avril told Tony, and Irene was beaten.

Irene had hardly ever misbehaved as a child, but in Tony's house, she always seemed to get in trouble. She was beaten, forced to fast, and frequently banished to The House of Scorn. One time, tired of being sent to the green house, Irene just moved out of Tony's house and back to her parents'. Tony said that she would have to be beaten before she could return. Eventually, missing her sister, Irene went back. She took the beating but didn't remember what rule she had broken.

Tony's house family consisted of a growing number of wives and people who, like Irene, seemed to come and go. Tony married Sharon in 1989, and then beginning in 1993 more brides were brought into the fold: Lydia, Jody, Misheal, Marsha, Anne, child brides Gail and Andrea, and Carla. In 1994, while Tony was imprisoned in Colorado, he married Ellen and child brides Patsy and Christine. These prison marriages were never consummated but likely "groped" and "fondled" during visitations.

Tony had some children other than those he took as brides. His wife Sharon's daughter from a previous marriage, Rebecca, lived there for a time. Three boys also lived in the household: Tony and Sharon's son, Sion; Lydia and Tony's son, Tabor; and George, the son of Misheal and her first husband. In 2001 Andrea gave birth to Bella, of whom the sisters were always protective. Tony built a new upstairs section of the house for his little girl, and she was allowed to pick Avril to live with her.

Relationships could be complicated, and Tony always controlled them. This was especially apparent in the story of Tony's acquisition of his wife, Misheal. One of Tony's wives from the late 1980s had a son, Jared, from a previous marriage. Jared fell in love with a young woman, Misheal, and they married. Just before Misheal gave birth to a little boy, George, Tony decided he wanted Misheal for his own bride. Tony kicked Jared out of the church, took Misheal as his wife, and raised George. Jared, the little baby's father, was never able to see his son.

Tony's house was filled with an underlying tension. Tony's boys were not allowed to go anywhere the girls were, which meant the freedom in the house was only for girls. The boys resented the girls and routinely got them into trouble. All the girls would then be called into Tony's office as a group. They were subject to rules 24/7 and could even be awakened at 3:00 in the morning to report for an infraction. They would all be scolded, sometimes forced to fast, and beaten. The older wives were jealous of little girls being there and resented having to watch over them. The sisters and boys had an unspoken alliance to report the girls for punishment at every opportunity.

Not every boy was seen as an enemy, though. In her early teens, Irene was starting to get curious about boys and had a slight crush on Sion. Maybe this was why Sharon seemed to pay special attention to Irene. Irene became scared of Sharon. Every time Sharon came in the kitchen, Irene always hid her food and covered her tracks. One time Sharon told her, "You don't need to be hiding." Irene felt the cold knot in her stomach and thought to herself, "Oh yes, I do."

A sharp elbow poking into her side jolted Irene from her thoughts. Audrey was carefully studying her face. Irene met her eyes for a moment and then joined the voices in the choir. They were singing "Shout to the Lord," one of her favorite gospel songs. As she sang her heart out, she couldn't help wondering if she would ever see her brother again.

CHAPTER
TWENTY-ONE

Paige Turned

It was the final straw. Brady was gone. She had been beaten too many times. If she wanted to survive, she had to leave. Paige pressed her lips together and marveled at the fact that her decision was propelled by her love for a boy. She had so many other reasons to leave.

Paige had the reputation of being a troublemaker. She spoke her mind, and even the beatings didn't teach her a lesson. If anything, they made her more determined to be tough. Back when she was ten, Paige told one of the sisters that she was rude. The sister reported her behavior, and Tony said, "She's a bad kid. She's just like her mother, going to hell. She has to get spanked." Later that day Paige was working in the rhinestone room of the Alamo line of designer denim jackets when Jennifer Kolbek found her and told her that she was going to get into trouble. Paige shrugged her shoulders and thought, "Whatever—my dad does that to me all the time. I don't even care." She thought one of the sisters was probably going to beat her.

A few minutes later, Jennifer returned and said, "Paige, it's time." Paige saw the look on her face and said, "I'm not going to John. And if you think you're going to take me to John, you're very mistaken." Jennifer said, "Paige, you have to come with me." And Paige said, "No, I'm not." So then three large women grabbed her, and John Kolbek joined in to drag Paige to the back of the warehouse, away from the rhinestone room and behind the mailroom. Waiting there were the brothers, sisters, boys, and girls. She recognized her friend, Audrey, among the girls who were there. John Kolbek dragged Paige kicking and screaming, "I'm not going with you!" Out of the corner of her eye, Paige spotted her ten-year-old little sister, Victoria, and her heart sank. Victoria was crying and didn't know what to do. Wanting to help her sister, Victoria stepped up and said, "I'm the big sister!" At that moment Paige felt so proud of her little sister, and her heart broke in two.

There were wooden pallets everywhere, and Paige grabbed onto one of them. Kolbek kept dragging her across the floor, and she felt the splinters tear into her hand as she fought to hold onto the pallet. Bleeding, she let go. Kolbek continued to drag the twelve-year-old kicking and screaming to the table where he was going to position her for a beating. Paige continued to scream, and Kolbek punched her in the face. He shouted, "I almost killed my daughter! You think I won't do the same thing to you?"

Paige looked him in the eye and said, "No, I don't!"

Kolbek bent Paige over the table, and while three sisters held her, Paige looked back at Jennifer Kolbek and said, "Jennifer, please, please, please help me!"

Jennifer responded, "I am helping you."

Paige called out to John Kolbek, "How many are you going to give me?"

He snarled, "I'm not telling you." Using a large two-by-four, he beat her four times.

Paige squirmed and slid under the table. Kolbek was furious. He shouted to the sisters, "Get her out from under that table!" Paige thought he was about to kill her. They pulled her out, put her back face down on the table. He said, "Do you want me to call the brothers?"

Paige said, "No. I don't want you to do that." So she let him beat her some more, and when she couldn't take it any longer, she slid under the table again. They hauled her on top of the table for more beatings. Eventually, everyone was tired. Kolbek said, "I have never, ever had to deal with anything like this before you came along."

When they dragged Paige away, they slammed the door. The other girls could not see in the room, but they could hear her screams from where they stood. Audrey and the other girls started crying, and Victoria began stuttering that she wanted to go home. When Paige walked out, her face was pale and she didn't say one word. She had to go back to work, so she went into the other room and continued working. Audrey could imagine how huge her bruises must be. They were all crying silently. They didn't want to cry out loud because Kolbek and the others would come and ask, "Do you want to be next?"

Paige went back to the rhinestone room and fell asleep. One of the sisters looked at her and quietly crying said, "I can't believe that just happened to you." Word of the beating spread throughout the church. Everyone knew Paige was the only kid who wouldn't take a beating. Memories of that day left indelible marks even after the hand marks on her face and the bruises disappeared. After the beating, Paige never had a regular period.

From that point on, Tony saw Paige as a bad kid who needed to be beaten. Just a couple of months after the legendary beating, another opportunity to test Paige's endurance presented itself. Paige and the other children were playing in the swimming pool at the church property in Moffett, Oklahoma. Paige noticed the sisters talking quietly among themselves and glancing nervously in her direction. Pretending not to listen, Paige heard them say, "We can't tell her. We're going to have to do this in secret, and she can't know what's happening."

The sisters called out, "Girls, we all have to go back to the church. We have something that's going to happen."

Paige knew that she was in trouble for something. She got out of the pool, changed her clothes, and took off into the cornfields that surrounded the property. The sisters chased after her in vain. They called the police to report Paige as missing. The police found her, thirsty and sweaty, dressed in the requisite baggy pants and shirt that suited boys more than girls.

The officer asked, "Why are you running away?"

One of the girls chimed in, "Yeah, Paige, why are you running away?"

Paige snapped, "You know exactly why I'm running away! Don't act like you're stupid."

The officer asked again, "What are you talking about? Are you sure you don't want to tell me?"

Knowing that she was in enough trouble already, Paige was afraid to say anything further. The sisters were standing apart from the police and looked worried.

One of the sisters held up her phone and called out, "Paige, Tony wants to talk to you."

Paige retorted, "I don't want to talk to him!"

The sister heard Tony's voice roaring through the telephone, "Put her on the phone!" She shoved the phone into Paige's hand, and Paige answered, "What?"

Tony said, "Why did you just run away?"

Paige said, "You know why! Because I don't want to get beat. I'm not going to get beat."

Tony replied, "Are you going to simmer down?"

"Am I not going to get beat? I will keep my forked tongue."

Tony barked, "No you're not."

"Do you promise? Do you swear to God that I am not going to get beat?"

"Yes, I swear to God. You are not going to get beat."

Then Paige agreed. "Okay. I won't run away again."

So Paige wasn't going to run away—then. Not because of the beatings. Now she had another reason. She was in love with Brady. In the church boys and girls were not permitted to talk or interact in any way. Their schedules were deliberately planned so that they wouldn't co-mingle. The boys ate their meals an hour before the girls did, and they did everything else separately, too—school, Bible lessons, prayer, and work. The only place they were together was in the church worship service, though they sat apart, and in the choir. For the preteen and teenage set, it was only natural that they would steal glances at each other. If a boy and girl wanted to talk with each other, they first needed Tony's permission. Then the meetings took place with both sets of parents present.

Paige knew that her friend, Irene, and Tony's son, Sion, were talking. So Paige asked Tony for permission to talk with Brady and obtained approval.

At first they met in the nursery, chaperoned by Tony, Sharon, and Paige's father, Glen. After that, Brady and Paige continued to meet and talk.

One night she got home a little bit late, and Tony asked, "Where have you been?"

Paige told him that she had been talking with Brady.

Tony replied, "I only meant for you to do that one time!" Tony called their fathers, who yelled at Paige for hours on the telephone.

Then all the girls in Tony's house were called into the office, and Tony made each one tattle on Paige. They knew if they didn't tell on her, they would be punished. With every accusation, Tony sneered, "Say something to me," and he then punched Paige in the face.

Not long after that, Brady ran away. It was the final straw. Paige had been thinking about running for the past two years. She had never really felt brave enough, and she worried about her sister, Victoria. Paige was more like a mother than a sister to her. If she were to tell Victoria of her plan to leave, Victoria would probably tell on her. She would be afraid for Paige and say that she's a backslider. Paige thought, "She is too little. I don't want her to have to deal with this."

She thought about her brothers and her dad and realized that she didn't know anyone on the outside except for her mom. And she didn't know where her mother was or if she was even alive. Paige closed her eyes and tried to picture the last time she saw her mom—eight years ago when she left them in California. Tony said she didn't care about them. He said that she was a stripper and a drug addict. Driven by the devil, she just left her kids on the doorstep. Paige thought, "What if she doesn't want me? Then I'll be out there by myself, and I have no idea what I need to do in real life." Then she opened her eyes and decided. It was time to go. If her mom didn't want her, she could just come back. One way or the other, she had to know.

On the day Paige decided to leave, her sister, her brothers, and her dad were in Fort Smith. She thought, "They all have each other. They're going to be fine. I'm just going to go." She and her friend, Pamela, had often talked about running away. Paige told Pamela, "I'm ready to leave. I want to find my mom."

So they made a plan. Pamela's sister, Lynn, used to be one of Tony's wives and had left the church. They would contact her for help, but it would be tricky. Tony never allowed anyone to use the telephone without supervision. Every night all the phones were gathered and locked in his office. That night Paige and Pamela slipped into Tony's office to find a telephone. As luck would have it, one of the phones had been left out on the desk. They went into the bathroom, found Pamela's sister's phone number, and called her. They asked if she could meet them at the Walmart in Texarkana at noon on the following Saturday.

Lynn said, "I can't even leave Oklahoma City. My car is broken down."

Paige and Pamela replied, "Well, we're just going to leave anyway."

The girls were at least twenty miles from Texarkana with no transportation and no plan, but they decided to go. It was 1:00 p.m.—lunchtime for the girls. They knew that everybody would be in the front of the house in the kitchen eating lunch. Paige and Pamela were at the back of the house in the rec room by the pool. They counted on the fact that no one would be looking at the security cameras. They went out the sliding door at the back, crept quietly behind Tony's house, and slipped between the trees shielding them from the security guards. When they got to a big open field, they began to run. Panting, they reached the other side of the street where a Dollar General Store stood. Desperate to stay out of sight, the girls ran toward the store. Unbeknownst to them, a man and a woman had been watching them. Now the man was stepping out of his car and heading toward the girls. He blocked their path into the store. He said, "What are you girls doing? Are you from the place across the street?"

Paige stuttered, "No . . . no we aren't from there. We are just going to use the phone."

Giving her a hard, steady look, the man said, "It's okay. You can tell me. I'm not going to make you go back or anything. I just want to know. I'm not going to tell anybody."

Paige said, "We're not . . . I mean, I don't know what you're talking about." As the man continued to talk, Paige and Pamela began making steps toward the store. Just as they reached for the door, a woman came out and said, "Drucker, I found those balloons for the party." She eyed the girls sharply and asked, "Where are you girls trying to go?"

Scared and realizing that they needed to say something, Paige blurted out, "Well, I'm trying to find my mom."

The woman who called herself Wilma said, "Get in the car. We'll take you to her." The girls got in the back seat, and the car took off down Highway 71. Then suddenly the car slowed down, made a sharp right turn, and kicking up dust on a winding country road, it disappeared into the hills.

>>>><<<<

The sun was barely up, but Victoria was already dressed and looking out the window. She had been to a wedding in Fort Smith with her father and brothers during the past week, and when they returned to Fouke, they learned that Paige was gone. Tony said that she never was anything but trouble, and she would be a whore and addict just like their mother was in the outside world. He said the devil got her.

Victoria wondered, though. She was remembering that last morning she saw Paige. As usual, at 6:30 a.m. her sister woke her and told her to get dressed. Every night Paige helped Victoria lay out her clothes for the next day. Paige hated to get up early, and Victoria usually just put on the clothes that were there without thinking.

On that morning, though, she wanted to wear her pink butterfly shirt with a green plaid skirt. The minute Paige saw her, she had exclaimed, "Victoria, go back and put on the clothes we picked out. That shirt and skirt don't go together at all. It's too early in the morning for all your antics."

Victoria had thrown herself on the floor and refused to return to her room. She had shouted, "You aren't my mother! I'm tired of you ordering me around all the time!"

Now big tears began to roll down Victoria's cheeks. She knew the devil hadn't taken Paige; she was the reason her sister had left. What would she do now? Whenever Paige went somewhere, Victoria was with her. Who would take care of her now? Who would protect her? Now she felt mad. Why didn't Paige tell her she was leaving? Why didn't she take Victoria too?

A Boy's Life

The hot morning sun was filtering into the boys' room, and Ian squinted at the brightness. A quick glance at the empty bed next to his told him that his little brother Stefan was already up. Scrambling, Ian knew that if he didn't get up quickly, he would be in trouble.

Ian was born in Fort Smith, Arkansas. He really didn't have a clear understanding of the moves that put him living sometimes with his father, Glen, and sometimes with his mother, Quinn. He saw his mother for the last time when he was almost five. His father had come to Vermont and taken them back to California. Then Ian, his brother, sisters, and father moved to a trailer park owned by Tony in Muldrow, Oklahoma. When he turned ten, they moved to Fouke, where Ian and Stefan lived in the brothers' dorm that housed all the men who had no wives or family. His dad was driving trucks for Tony and absent for months at a time, so the task of raising his brother, Stefan, often fell to Ian. His sisters, Victoria and Paige, lived in Tony's house. For most of the children, that was considered to be a great honor. The fact that only females were allowed to live in Tony's house did not cross Ian's mind.

On this morning Ian dressed, went to the kitchen for breakfast, then to a morning Bible study group, and on to school for a few hours of lessons.

At noon he returned to the kitchen for lunch and then was ready to go to work. All this week he was assigned to stuff tracts.

The workroom had high stacks of pages that Tony wrote to spread the word of his teachings. The children inserted one piece of paper into another to complete the eight-page "Tony Alamo Christian Ministries World Newsletter." Sometimes the pastor addressed issues that required even more inserts. The work was monotonous and never ending; thousands of issues were compiled and distributed throughout the world. "World Pastor" Tony Alamo spread the news of the government's interference with God's work. He warned of the conspiracy at play between the United States President and the Vatican. Tony wrote how the government persecuted him, a prophet of God. There were letters from believers throughout the world sending prayers for Tony's ministry and requests for more Bibles, literature, and taped messages. The back page of every tract listed a prayer and true plan of salvation with locations of churches and worship times. The mission clearly stated that salvation Alamo style required total life immersion: "Tony Alamo Christian Ministries Worldwide provides a place to live with all the things necessary for life to all those who truly want to serve the Lord with all their heart, soul, mind, and strength."

As Ian was stuffing tracts, he saw the letters from New York, Virginia, and Texas, along with notes from India, Peru, Pakistan, and Zambia. Pastor Tony was always reminding them that his ministry reached the world. Ian felt a mixture of awe and undefined fear. They were doing God's work and the reward would be salvation.

This would be a long day and sleepless night for Ian. He was on the watch schedule for tonight from 10:00 p.m. until 2:00 a.m. He wasn't sure who his partner would be. He really didn't care. They would stay alert and guard the grounds from outside infiltrators, including church members who weren't where they were supposed to be. All the boys started pulling this duty when they were eight years old, and all of Alamo's properties were secured by guards and surveillance cameras twenty-four hours a day.

Ian stifled a yawn and kept stuffing tracts. All he really wanted was a good night's sleep. He didn't always have to be on tract stuffing duty, though. Many times he went out on construction sites—sometimes with his dad. He really loved that. There was always a lot of junk to play with, and he could help his dad frame a house, put up a roof, or landscape. Ian smiled to himself as he thought about his dad, Glen. His dad was his number-one hero. People admired him, and when he preached short sermons in church, he really got the congregation going, shouting "amens." Dad could play the guitar, and many times he was on stage playing the music for worship. Ian loved sitting in his dad's lap and listening to him tell stories. He always talked about the evils of the outside world and the paradise they had within the confines of the church.

Over the years his dad was changing, though. Tony made fun of him for reading children's books to his kids. Even more unsettling, Tony had lashed out at him when he preached at church the past few months. Tony said that he was a soft weasel soon to be a backslider if he didn't toughen up. Then Tony moved Glen from working on local construction sites to driving trucks across state lines for weeks and even months at a time.

With his dad gone, Ian had become like a father to his younger brother, Stefan. Stefan was always getting into some kind of trouble, and Ian tried his best to keep him from getting beaten. On work sites Stefan was always getting hurt—stepping on rusty nails and getting splinters in his fingers. The boys could hardly carry the lumber and dry wall, and they often slipped and fell. Sitting high up on the roof to help install shingles, Stefan struggled not to look down for fear that he would fall. But his greater fear was of making his father angry. Glen would go into a rage and beat them all soundly with the two-by-four that was the staple of every household. Many occasions left Stefan bruised and bleeding. Ian could hardly stand seeing his brother hurting like that. He would gladly take a beating in Stefan's place if he could. Lately his dad was never home. And when he was, the kids always knew they were in for a beating because the sisters were armed with stories and ready to greet him with reports of bad behavior.

CHAPTER
TWENTY-THREE

Tracting across America for God

They had been riding in the van for hours. The sandwiches the sisters packed for the trip had been eaten, and tired of the long ride, Audrey, Irene, and Victoria fidgeted in their seats. This was going to be a long road trip, and they were excited. Tony always selected the adults to drive and the children who would go with them. Brothers and sisters never intermingled, so this was an all-girls trip.

Sisters Martha, Kate, and Connie were driving three vans, one being a large Expedition pulling a trailer loaded with clothes, food, and tracts. They were going to St. Louis, Indianapolis, and Pittsburgh, ending up in New York City before returning home. They hoped they would get to sleep in hotels along the way. They stayed for free in hotels.

Sisters and brothers representing Tony's charity, Arm Full of Help, would call around and get complimentary hotels and restaurants to aid needy families. After doing this for so many years, Tony established contacts across the country, and it was easy to get donations almost every time. Tony had no compunction about using these gifts for his own benefit; after all, he was doing God's work.

After eight hours with only short stops in rest areas, they could see the lights of St. Louis. The girls stared out the windows to get a glimpse of a city far different from Fouke, Arkansas. They were there to work, not to sightsee, but it was still fun to sneak peeks at the unfamiliar landscape.

The vans made a sharp turn into a parking lot. The sisters gathered the children and put them into teams of three. Audrey, Irene, and Victoria stuck together and jumped in to help unload tracts from the trailer. They moved the heavy bundles to each of the vans, and then climbed back into a van to be driven to a distribution point. The sister drove just a few miles and then pulled into a large parking lot by the stadium. As the girls grabbed large bundles of tracts, Sister Martha said, "I will place bundles at points throughout this lot. Be sure you put a tract on every car. I will come back around to pick you up in two hours. Work fast. People will be going to their cars as soon as the game is over. I don't want to see you until your arms are empty."

The girls heaved their bundles into their backpacks and spread out. They were fast and careful to avoid being detected. One time a police car cruised by, and they hid on the ground between the cars. To a man who asked what they were doing, they explained that they were saving souls. The man scoffed, "Don't be putting this trash on my car," crumpled the tract in his hands, and threw it on the ground. After he drove off, Irene picked up the pamphlet and stashed it in her pocket. The girls worked quickly and efficiently. They were running out of tracts. Audrey ran ahead, and sure enough, she found a stack that the sister had placed to replenish their supply. The girls were getting tired and hungry, but they loved the excitement of being in the outside world and hiding from the police. In a little over two hours they reached the other side of the parking lot and were empty-handed.

They only had to wait a short time before spotting their van. All the way to the hotel they shared their stories and talked about how many tracts they had given out. When they arrived at the hotel and crammed into one room for the night, Sister Kate called Tony to report the numbers. They had distributed 20,000 tracts that night! They knew that he would be proud of them. They listened expectantly while the sister announced their accomplishment to Tony. She paused, listened, and said, "Yes, Pastor Tony, I will tell them. We will do even better tomorrow." The sister hung up the phone, wearily turned to the girls, and said, "The other group handed out 70,000 tracts in Phoenix today." With that, deflated and exhausted, the girls spread out on the bed, chairs, and floor where they would sleep.

Morning came with a jolt when Sister Martha pulled open the curtains and hustled the girls to get dressed. They were ready for their next stop, Indianapolis, a short four and a half hours away. They piled into the vans and were off. The girls promptly fell asleep to the rhythm of the drive and so were surprised to reach their destination so quickly. It was just after one in the afternoon and they were hungry. As if she were reading their minds, Sister Martha pulled into a fast food restaurant, ordered burgers, fries, and water at the drive-through window, and paid for the food with gift vouchers supplied by Tony's donors. The girls devoured the lunch, a special treat they savored when on tracting expeditions.

The caravan pulled into the parking lot of a sprawling shopping mall. The girls jumped out of the vans and filled their backpacks with tracts, their groups of three swiftly moving to different parts of the lot. By now they knew the drill. They worked quickly, placing a tract under the windshield wiper of every parked vehicle. When they ran out of pamphlets, they found boxes placed at strategic points throughout the parking lot. During the day it was especially challenging to accomplish their goal without being chased away by mall security officials.

The shoppers they encountered in the parking lot sometimes looked at them as if they didn't even exist. Some tore off the tract and threw it on the ground, and others actually stopped to ask about what they were doing. Victoria, Audrey, and Irene loved talking with people about Tony's message. Tracting trips presented the only opportunities to talk with strangers, especially boys, on the outside. They knew what to say and stuck to the script, but all the while they thought about every nuance of these people who were condemned to destruction unless they followed Tony's steps to salvation.

After three hours, every car in the parking lot had a flyer on its windshield. The girls were hot and tired, but they knew their work was far from over. Sister Connie was calling for them to stop dawdling and get back into the vans. Audrey muttered under her breath, and Victoria and Irene exchanged looks. They were all glad that Sister Martha was their driver instead of Sister Connie. Martha was kind to them. They knew she would have cold water bottles waiting in the van.

The next stop was a Walmart. Following the same drill, the girls set to work. Shoppers were always more prevalent in single-store parking lots, so they had to be prepared for anything to happen. A woman with a little baby shoved her cart, almost hitting Irene. Irene decided it was unintentional until the woman shouted to her, "You people need to stop littering. I'm sick and tired of finding this junk on my car!" Irene moved away. Her back was hurting, and she just wanted to sit down. She glanced around, and seeing the other girls working, she kept going.

Back in the vans, they drove through heavy rush hour traffic across town to another shopping mall. As the girls armed themselves with full backpacks, Sister Kate said that she would get some food and have it ready for them after they completed their work. The thought of burgers, fries, and maybe even dessert pies gave the girls a lift, and though tired, they worked diligently. Fortunately, probably because of the dinner hour, not as many shoppers were at the mall, and that meant not as many cars to tract. Motivated to finish the job before the evening shoppers arrived, the girls felt a spurt of energy and finished their job.

They piled into the vans and began eating the promised food. Sister Martha glanced at them and said, "After you eat, close your eyes and get some sleep. Pittsburgh is about six hours away, and Tony wants us to drive through the night to get a good early start. The other group just finished in Denver, and they handed out their entire supply of tracts. It's up to us to finish the job."

It was nearly two in the morning when the sisters pulled into a twenty-four-hour travel stop. They were weary and needed a break. They roused the girls, and everyone went into the stop for a restroom break. Sister Kate was pumping quarters into a vending machine and got coffee for everyone. A man and woman studying a map on the wall stared as the girls eagerly grabbed for their coffee. The woman sniffed with disapproval and spoke up sharply, "You are all too young to be drinking coffee. You should be home in bed."

Audrey looked at her with interest and said, "We all drink coffee regularly. All of us kids do."

Sister Connie walked over, motioned to the girls, and said, "Come on everyone. Let's be on our way now."

They drove for a short distance on I-79 north and then took the exit to I-376 east. Sister Martha was in front and took leading very seriously. Leaning forward a bit and squinting her eyes, she said, "Would everyone please look for exit 81 toward Penn Hills? And then we need to make a quick left."

As soon as she said it, the exit appeared. Victoria spotted Duff Road on the left and said, "Turn!"

As the sister made a sharp turn, they all fell left into each other and laughed but suddenly fell silent as they entered a huge tunnel with tiles glistening on the walls. Emerging from the Fort Pitt Tunnel they were astounded by the dazzling lights of the cityscape. "Well, hello, Pittsburgh!" declared Sister Martha. "We have arrived."

Sister Martha drove easily through the city streets, still empty in the early morning hours. She turned and headed west toward the airport. After driving about fifteen miles, they spotted a line of "park and fly" lots filled with cars. The sisters pulled to a street between two lots, and the girls climbed out and filled their backpacks. It was too early for people to be about, so their only concern would be security officers. The parked cars cast long shadows in the well-lit lots, and the girls giggled as they darted to and fro. The lone night watch officer was in his booth and seemed oblivious to the sister who was keeping careful watch over him. It was exciting to be out at night on this single mission for God when everyone else was sleeping.

The girls emptied their packs and refilled them many times until they came to the other side of the parking area. The sun was starting to come up, and people were arriving to catch their morning flights. They fell into the vans and continued to chatter, boosted with extra adrenaline from the night. Even Sister Martha was smiling and chiming in about the ways they had avoided being seen.

As the morning commuters started pouring into the city, the vans moved stealthily out of the city. In no time at all they were speeding on I-81 north toward Harrisburg, where they would find a hotel to catch some much-needed rest. From there they would have only a three-hour drive to their final destination, New York City.

Audrey, Victoria, and Irene were standing on Broadway. They looked around with wonder, taking in the sights and sounds of the crowded sidewalks and streets. Irene pointed to a billboard picture of Mariah Carey and wondered who she was. They definitely weren't in Arkansas and were getting a full dose of the outside world. The sisters urged them on, and Victoria nearly tripped over a man sitting against a building with his dog. The man had a hat with a few coins and crumpled dollar bills in it. Victoria thought of a brother who had testified about his life on the streets before being found by Tony. These were the people Tony wanted them to save. She dropped a tract into the hat.

The sisters gathered all the girls together and told them about the plan. They would work in groups of three. Two girls would carry a large box of tracts and the other girl would hand them out. There was no place to leave boxes to be replenished with supplies on the streets of New York. When the box grew heavy, they could switch positions, but the best way to lighten the box was to work quickly and hand out all the pamphlets. They were to meet back at this corner on Broadway only when their boxes were empty. They were told to remember to stick to their script of salvation.

The task wasn't easy. Most people walked so fast that they couldn't offer the tract to them before they were gone. Others glanced down and just shook their heads. The girls moved faster and fell into the city step. They found a new pace and doggedly pushed the tracts into the hands of every person they met. People took the pamphlets if only to get the girls to move out of the way. Some threw them on the sidewalk, and others crumpled them into their pockets. But that box was getting lighter, and Tony's message was sure to reach some of these people. They stopped only to eat hotdogs with drinks that the sisters brought to them after a few hours. The sisters had also brought more boxes with tracts, so their work continued on into the late afternoon. The city blocks felt longer and longer as the girls labored. Finally, they turned back to find their meeting place. They were nearly twenty-four hours away from home, but their job was accomplished, and the long drive back to Arkansas would allow for some much-needed sleep.

CHAPTER
TWENTY-FOUR

Brothers Bonded

Stefan had just made a big mess, and Ian was about to lose his temper. They had spent hours pulling weeds, and the hot sun was taking a toll on his energy. They had gathered big piles of weeds and dried brush that needed to be hauled away. Ian watched as his brother turned over the bushel basket and the contents were scattered by the wind. Tony insisted that the grounds around the church be kept perfectly manicured to reflect the respect they have for God's creation. If they didn't get this job done quickly, they would have hell to pay. Tony would be more than happy to order a beating or fasting, and just the thought of being deprived of food for a week made Ian's stomach hurt. As soon as he shouted for Stefan to stop playing around, Ian regretted it. Stefan was just a little kid, and his eyes filled with tears when he saw that his big brother was angry. Ian took a big breath and said, "It's okay, little brother. Let's just scoop all this up one more time."

As they finished the landscaping, Ian thought about their father and felt a pang of sadness mixed with anger. He had been so happy when their dad had moved them from Fort Smith to Fouke. Tony's properties were scattered throughout the country, but everyone wanted to live in Fouke. Tony's house was located there. To a child the trees, pool, and carousel looked like paradise. But since the move, their dad had been more absent.

Tony sent him to jobs that kept him away for months, and when he did return, he was distant and short-tempered with the kids. Stefan didn't even remember fun times with their dad. Now Ian was more of a father to Stefan than a brother.

And the boys were always getting in trouble. If they even looked at a female, punishment was sure to follow. Ian and Stefan got beaten all the time, and they really didn't know why. Mostly they were just messing around, tussling with other boys and not hurting each other. The previous week Ian had been roughhousing with another kid. When his dad heard about it, he accused him of doing a homosexual thing and beat the living hell out of him. He still didn't understand exactly what he had done wrong, but whatever it was, he wouldn't forget that beating.

It was getting close to suppertime for the boys. Ian and Stefan noted the time and automatically turned and headed toward the eating area. As they got closer, they caught a glimpse of a girl dashing into Tony's house and heard the door slamming behind her. They stopped just for a moment and Ian felt an odd, sick feeling in his stomach. Why did only girls live in Tony's house? It was not the first time the thought nibbled at the edge of his mind.

CHAPTER
TWENTY-FIVE

Tony's Bounty

Irene ran so quickly into Tony's house that the back door nearly caught the tail of her shirt as it slammed behind her. She had taken just a moment to sit outside, and as usual, her mind was wandering when suddenly she saw the boys walking toward her. She leaped to her feet and ran into the house. Tony did not allow the girls living in his house to go outside when the boys were present. If she were caught, she would face a punishment that would likely include banishment to the green House of Scorn. Irene had spent enough time in that house and wasn't eager to return. The sister in charge of girls living there was strict, and the seclusion was more than Irene could stand.

The girls who lived in Tony's house had privileges. Tony had a shelf of movies and lots of books. They had Internet access and were permitted to order from different restaurants. All the other kids had movie nights—the girls on Fridays and boys on Saturdays—and everyone got to have one bag of M&M's. But in Tony's house, the girls had more access to movies. Even though the collection was limited to Bible stories, *Ben Hur*, *The Ten Commandments*, and Elvis Presley movies, the girls felt privileged to have these movies available whenever they wanted them. That isn't to say that they could watch movies whenever they wanted to, but just knowing that they were there made the girls feel special. Tony had a large-screen, projection television set in his bedroom, big reclining chairs, and a limitless supply of bottled water. And there was always plenty of candy on the table in his spa bathroom.

Irene stifled a yawn. She hadn't gotten much sleep. Tony was taping his messages, and at 2:00 a.m., Sister Sharon woke all the girls so they could respond and make it appear he was addressing an audience. The format for each message was always the same: Tony welcomed the radio listeners to his broadcast. Then he asked Sharon to read letters that had been received from followers all over the world. As Sharon read each letter, Tony would interrupt to give special emphasis to something the writer had said or to insert praise and prayer of thanksgiving. He expected the girls to respond every time with a rousing "AMEN." The previous night they hadn't been loud and enthusiastic enough, and Tony made them re-record the segment a dozen times. By the time they had finished, the girls were almost too tired to walk to their beds. Morning came much too early, and now they all were walking around in sleepy stupors.

From the kitchen Irene could see Victoria working in Tony's office. Victoria's job was important. She sorted the behavior reports into stacks for Tony's review. She answered the telephone, took messages, and answered the volumes of mail they received daily. Most were requests for tracts, Bibles, and CDs or tapes of Tony's recorded messages. All were free for the asking, and Victoria was always careful to accurately document the requests for Tony's records.

Irene watched Victoria for a while, thinking that most everyone believed that Victoria was the next girl Tony would choose to be his wife. Tony entrusted to Victoria the keys to the gym. He would regularly refer to Victoria as his wife or mistake her for another wife. When he did so, Sister Misheal would step up and correct him. All the girls appreciated Misheal's willingness to defend them. Tony had his favorites and always chose who would sleep with him at night. An air of tension was ever-present in the house. The older wives didn't like the younger and prettier girls. They resented having to take care of the young girls as if they were their own children. These girls threatened their connections to Tony, and anyone could fall from grace for no apparent reason.

In Tony's house, Misheal, Lydia, and Sharon administered the beatings. A two-by-four plank kept behind Tony's desk served as the paddle. Four people held the culprit down spread-eagle on Tony's bed. Everyone in the house had to watch. If she didn't cry, Tony said, "It's not good enough— she's not crying. Hit her more." All the girls learned to cry. Beatings hurt, and they were humiliating. Tony wanted the kids to cry. He did slap and punch them, but he did not beat them with the board.

Beatings didn't happen every day. Tony had plenty of other punishments to impose—extended fasts, banishments from group activities such as swimming, and verbal abuse. Tony spent much of his time holed up in his room. When he was angry, he could be heard yelling, "You stinking bitch, I'm going to get you!" He would burst out of his room and chase his target through the house. Never knowing what might get a girl in trouble made everyone scared. He punished a sister because her baby had a diaper rash. He accused girls of being lesbians. Tony regularly told the girls that they weren't beautiful and that they didn't compare to movie stars and models. The girls never saw movie stars or models, so they believed Tony when he said they were ugly. They also believed him when he said their mothers who had left the church were pigs, stinking weasels, whores, and backsliders. And if their own mothers were such reprobates, how could they expect to be any better? Tony had ways of humiliating the wives. He snorted and called Anne *marrano* ("filthy pig"), and then he told stories about how he tried to rape her but couldn't get through her, so he had her surgically fixed so he could penetrate her.

The girls in Tony's house shared common experiences even though they were too frightened to talk about them. They all were at the mercy of their pastor. At twelve years old, Jade was taking a shower in the girls' bathroom. The light went off, the door opened, and she felt a hand over her mouth. Tony, naked, began touching her breasts and vaginal area. Suddenly a girl knocked sharply on the door and said to hurry up. Tony warned Jade not to tell anyone about the incident or he would have John Kolbek beat her. Jade knew that no one would ever believe her anyway because Tony was the prophet. Not long after, Alamo ordered Jade and other girls to participate in a recorded radio program to say that he had never touched them.

Victoria had always envisioned Tony as being larger than life. With his strong, fit body he could do anything, and his position in the music industry made him even more amazing. He claimed to know every important performer in the business. He was as iconic as Elvis and even had an unpublished Beatles album. Tony would emerge from his bedroom and walk with his king-like stance into the office area. Sitting in a chair, he would beckon the girls to rub his neck and feet. Although he claimed failing vision, looking around the room through piercing eyes and tinted glasses, Tony would single someone out and snarl, "What are you looking at, you dirty pig? I know what you are thinking." In those moments Victoria felt sheer terror. But as frightened as she was, she noticed chinks in his armor that made him more human and less godlike.

Tony always thought he looked so fabulous. He bragged about working out, saying that his stomach was rock hard and that he could bench press more than anybody. One time when he came out of his room, though, his bushy black hair was replaced by a purple bandana, and Victoria could see his bald head peaking out underneath the kerchief. He was wearing magnifying glasses so large that his eyes looked like the compound eyes of a grasshopper. She wondered, "If he is so perfect, why is he so old and look so human? Why does he wear a toupee?"

Tony traveled regularly, especially to Los Angeles. Except for a few wives perhaps, no one knew what he did there. He usually took Sister Allison and some of the child brides with him. Sanford White would drive Tony's Class A Motorhome bus, another trusted member would accompany them in a van, and they stayed in fancy hotels and ate in top-rated restaurants. These trips would come under future scrutiny in Tony's trial regarding his forcing sex on underage girls.

When Tony was gone, life remained the same inside his house. The reporting system was so effective that no one trusted another person to bend the rules. After all, Pastor Tony could read their minds, and a person not reporting a violation would be considered as guilty as the rule breaker. One time Victoria walked in on a sister watching *Little House on the Prairie* on the computer, and Victoria didn't report her. She worried about that but valued the opportunities to watch videos and movies on the sly in Tony's house and wasn't about to jeopardize a sister's chance to do so.

CHAPTER TWENTY-SIX

"There's Something Happening Here"

It was a gray day in Texarkana, Arkansas, and FBI Special Agent Randall Harris stared out the window at the city street below. He had been transferred to this post in December 1998, coincidentally the same time that Tony Alamo was released from the halfway house after completing a stint for tax evasion.

Texarkana was a unique office for the FBI because of the state lines. Two agents worked on the Arkansas side, answering to Little Rock, and three agents worked on the Texas side, reporting to Dallas. Seven counties in southwest Arkansas were Harris's territory. This was a new post, and Harris wanted to get a feel for what was going on in the community. He hadn't been there long when someone mentioned that he might want to keep an eye out for a guy calling himself Tony Alamo. Harris had been vaguely familiar with Alamo when he was a fugitive, but he hadn't known what was going on with Tony Alamo Christian Ministries.

In 1994 evidence of sexual abuse of minors had been brought out in Alamo's trial for tax evasion, and even though the prosecutor had turned this information over to Arkansas, it was not pursued. Beginning in 2000 many former members and concerned parents contacted law enforcement in Fort Smith and Texarkana, and underage sexual assaults were reported by Wellspring Retreat Counseling Center, where former members were seeking help with cult-related trauma. In 2005 and 2006 the Alamo organization began attracting more attention. Former Alamo followers were posting disturbing information on an anti-cult website called "FACTnet." Accusations focused on Alamo's sexual abuse of children and underage marriages. Other charges drew a grim picture of Alamo's children working long-hour stretches in hot, rat-infested conditions with beatings for those who did not follow orders. It hadn't taken long for the postings to become emotion-packed pleas to save the children from sexual slavery and physical abuse. There had been many occasions in the past when former members had contacted the Arkansas State Police. In fact, Harris had been contacted one time, but the FBI didn't have jurisdiction over the reported crimes. Until now.

Randall Harris had a nagging suspicion about Tony Alamo and his so-called church. He couldn't shake the idea that the workplace abuse of children and tax-evasion issues were indicative of larger and more insidious crimes. So when John Bishop, a criminal investigator for the Arkansas State Police, contacted him saying that they had something going on with the Alamo group, Harris agreed to join forces. Bishop had started looking into the Alamo group in 2003 after former members came forward with information about Alamo's crimes.

This time Bishop had received a phone call from a man living in Colorado who claimed that his granddaughter wanted to escape from Tony Alamo Christian Ministries. He was going to drive down to Fouke. She was going leave the compound and run across the street to the Dollar Store. The grandfather was calling the state police because he knew how the group worked and was afraid there would be trouble. What would he do if Alamo's guys were chasing her or if they confronted him?

Harris and Bishop went to the Miller County Court and found a judge to sign a temporary custody order so that if the grandfather came, and his granddaughter made it to his vehicle, then he legally had custody of her in Arkansas. As it turned out, the girl's escape plan changed, and her grandfather did not drive to Fouke that day. A little more investigation revealed a history of child abuse allegations against the parents of the girl, and state officials from the Crimes Against Children (CAC), a civilian division of law enforcement, wanted to confront the parents with the facts of those allegations. State rules dictated a small window of time in which the allegations were to be addressed.

Harris and Bishop worried that they might tip their hand by acting on this one incident, thus jeopardizing a more expansive investigation. Randall sighed in frustration. He and Bishop had tried to explain that the CAC couldn't just show up and knock on the door; if they went out there, they were going to be confronted by guards who would probably just lie and say that the people in question didn't live there. But they insisted on going despite these warnings.

Randall closed his eyes, remembering that Friday afternoon. He and Bishop told them, "Okay, if you insist on going, then you can go. But we're going to have law enforcement personnel out there to kind of keep an eye on things." So Randall, John Bishop, and another four or five investigators set up to surround the compound to watch what would happen. Two women with the CAC pulled up to the compound, the guards stopped them, and they told the guards that they were there to meet with the girl's father about a complaint that was filed. They stayed in the driveway on the circle drive, clicking their heels for a long time. Harris and Bishop positioned themselves at the back entrance on Red Cut Road, watching the south side of the compound. All of a sudden the back doors to all these houses flew open. All these kids came running out, huddling around the trees, where a van pulled up. They loaded up the van and took off. As suspected, the CAC investigators were eventually informed that the girl and her family no longer lived there. It was later learned the girl and her family were, in fact, at the compound that day. That night, however, Alamo moved them to California.

This incident opened the door for a full-fledged law enforcement investigation. Even before this time Harris had "unofficially" been watching Alamo's operation. Over time, residents in Fouke had called him complaining about the bullying manner of Alamo's men and their encroachments on the town. Wilma and Drucker, a couple who were community advocates, had even come in person to Randall's office to appeal to him for help. They had given Randall an earful that day, with stories of Alamo's attempt to control city council, the ousting of Alamo's henchman, Cecil Smith, from the mayor's office, guards brandishing guns at the property lines, SUVs, and eighteen-wheelers coming and going at odd times throughout the night. Still with no real evidence to warrant an FBI investigation, Randall's hands were tied, but he did enlist the couple to keep watch over the Alamo compound and report any unusual activity to him.

Wilma and Drucker took their job seriously. Every day they drove the perimeter of the Fouke compound. They would park at the Dollar Store, directly across the street from the entrance, and watch out for individuals bullying other people. They regularly saw white Expedition vans, SUVs, and various cars. Whenever vehicles approached, a guard would stop them at the gate before signaling them through. Rarely did they observe women anywhere. When they saw boys working in the beautifully landscaped garden in front of the church, Wilma would shake her head and wish they could get some water for them. They were always out there working, even on the hottest days. She worried about them and wondered what kind of parents would approve of their children doing such long, arduous tasks without breaks.

CHAPTER TWENTY-SEVEN

Wilma and Drucker:
The Eyes and Ears

Wilma had known about Tony Alamo for some time. Her parents lived in Fort Smith when Alamo's group was in Alma, Arkansas. She was familiar with his antics, so when she saw the Tony Alamo Christian Ministries sign appear on the church in Fouke, she was horrified. Wilma started an Internet search and found postings from former members on FACTnet. There she connected to Sally, who had left the ministry after being a member since its beginnings in California. Sally and Wilma visited with John Bishop and Randall Harris a number of times to discuss their concerns. Wilma and her husband Drucker, informants to the FBI, owned a business in Fouke. They genuinely cared about the people in their tiny town. They recounted the nasty business about water rights and the dispute about public access on the road that ran alongside Alamo's property. They also told Randall about the town elections and Alamo's constant efforts to control the city council.

Wilma got a call one day from a former member who asked if she would be willing to help her nephew escape from the cult. Wilma and Drucker agreed at once and called Harris and Bishop to alert them of the plan in case anything went awry. At 5:30 a.m. on the designated day, with Harris and Bishop nearby, Wilma and Drucker parked on the road that ran behind the compound. Silent, they both stared at the trees lining the property.

Suddenly the boys appeared, Brady from one direction and Frank from another. They were carrying their backpacks and running wildly. Drucker signaled to the boys by flashing his headlights. The boys jumped into the car. Wilma took Frank to the airport in Little Rock where he got on a plane to join his brother in Washington. Brady couldn't get on a flight, so Wilma drove him to Memphis, where he boarded a bus to join family and friends in Virginia.

A couple of months later Wilma and Drucker were preparing to host a high school class reunion at their home. They needed to go by their church to get some extra tables and chairs and get some things at the Dollar Store. They were driving on Highway 71 when Wilma spotted two girls with backpacks walking along the road.

"Drucker, those two girls are from the compound."

"Oh, probably not. They wouldn't be just out here."

Wilma insisted, "Yes, they are! Those girls are from the compound." She just felt it, had cold chills and knew they needed help. Drucker pulled the car into the Dollar Store parking lot and said, "You go on inside. I'll watch to see what they are doing."

After Wilma entered the store, Drucker got out of his car and casually started to wipe the windshield, all the time watching the girls from the corner of his eye. The girls had stopped in front of the store and seemed unsure of themselves as they kept glancing behind them. They took a few steps closer to the parking lot, and Drucker called out, "Hey, what are y'all doing?"

The girls jumped at the sound of his voice, and the taller one said, "Oh, we just need to use the telephone in the store."

Drucker asked, "Are you girls from that place across the way?"

They both began to shake their heads and the same girl replied, "Oh no, sir, we are not from there!"

Drucker knew they were lying, but he was determined to stall them there until Wilma came out of the store. Just then Wilma did emerge, and Drucker said, "Wilma, these girls here are looking for a telephone."

Wilma asked, "Are you all from the Alamo compound? We aren't going to hurt you or send you back. We just want to help you."

The girls then looked at each other for a moment and the tall girl, Paige, acknowledged that yes, they were from the church and that they were going to Walmart where their sister planned to meet them.

Drucker said, "Do you know that Walmart is twenty miles away? You can't walk twenty miles. I'm not going to let you walk that far. Is your sister there already?"

Pamela, who hadn't yet talked, spoke up and said, "No, we haven't called her yet. She lives in Oklahoma City."

Wilma said, "So you're going to sit at Walmart for a day and a half while your sister comes to pick y'all up? No, girls. You're going home with us."

Surprisingly, the girls agreed. And Paige and Pamela found safety in the care of Wilma and Drucker who took them to their home and helped them call Pamela's sister, Lynn. Wilma called Sally, her contacts from FACTnet, and found the telephone number for Paige's mother, Quinn. They drove the girls to Fort Smith where they would meet Lynn and Quinn. On the way they told the girls that they knew Brady and Frank. Overwhelmed, Paige nearly cried for joy. Wilma handed Paige her cell phone and she called Brady, and they chatted the whole way to Fort Smith. Both had found freedom.

CHAPTER
TWENTY-EIGHT

Friday, September 19, 2008

Tony Alamo had done enough things, many immoral or illegal, that a case could now be built against him. Harris and Bishop had convincing evidence that Alamo moved underage children across state lines for illegal purposes. They knew that Tony conducted a number of unlawful activities, but this was the crime that could put Alamo in prison for life. They had an October target date, and that meant Randall would be working long hours to ensure they had dotted their i's and crossed their t's. He had seen too many cases thrown out of court because of procedural mistakes. That couldn't happen this time.

Alamo had a record of moving children and disappearing. Before his 1991 arrest for threatening a federal judge, Alamo had been missing for nearly two years. He owned property in many states, and his followers were willing to do anything for him. Reflecting on his time in the cult, a former member said, "We all believed everything Tony told us. We would have done anything for him. I would have killed for Tony." When law enforcement finally arrested Tony in Florida, he had been living in rented property and using a false name.

Just like every Friday evening, Randall had taken work home. When his telephone started ringing, he glanced at the clock and saw that it was

6:00 p.m. He shook his head. He had been hoping to finish the stack of papers on his desk without interruption. Randall's boss was on the line, and he informed him that someone from the US Attorney's Office had accidentally sent an email that included information about plans to raid the Alamo compound. The email had gone to every media outlet in the state of Arkansas. The cat was out of the bag.

Randall thought about the recent raid that Texas had made on the Fundamental Latter Day Saints compound. That event dominated the news for a long time. He suspected that Tony was already paranoid by that having taken place. So Randall's initial reaction was not to worry about the leak and to act hastily, because Tony was always paranoid.

Randall spoke to his boss, "Let's just wait and see what happens. Before acting too quickly, I want to read the email. I want to see what information was sent out."

His boss insisted, "We've seen it. It's bad."

Randall replied, "Well, just send it to me. Let me read it."

His boss responded, "I'll get in touch with the US Attorney's Office, and you can talk directly to them. But we may need to think about doing this raid as soon as we can. How soon do you think we can do it?"

Having a general idea of how many people the raid would need, Randall said, "Good grief. It's probably going to be next week before we can gather enough law enforcement people and get a plan put together." They hadn't even started typing affidavits for warrants at this point.

Again his boss urged, "Well, you might want to consider doing it quicker than that."

Taking a deep breath, Randall asked, "Well, how soon were you thinking?"

His boss replied, "We think that we may have to do it in the next few days."

Randall responded, "I'm going to say Sunday at the earliest. That gives me at least forty-eight hours to get ready."

But Randall still hadn't seen the email. So finally one of the assistant US attorneys called him, apologizing because it was his office's fault that the errant email was sent.

Randall told him the same thing, "Let me read the email. It may not be that bad." And then the attorney said, "Oh, it's bad."

So finally they sent Randall the email, and sure enough, it was bad. Randall had contacted the prosecutor assigned to the Alamo case to request that they send their victim services coordinator to attend the next meeting to plan the raid. The prosecutor had written a lengthy, detailed synopsis of the case to justify the coordinator's expense for travel and lodging for the trip to Little Rock. She sent the email to her boss, who approved the request. But instead of sending her approval via email to "All Management," her boss hit the wrong button on her Blackberry and sent the email to "All Media." And of course, once you shoot the gun, you can't get the bullet back. So now both the US Attorney's Office and the FBI were scrambling around and calling every television station in the state, newspapers—everyone who received the email. They were begging them to keep this news confidential. The media responded, "Well, we don't mind cooperating with you, but the first hint we get that somebody else is going to publish the story, then we're going to have to tell it as well."

Randall called his partner, told him what was going on, and they agreed to meet at Randall's house where they set up a mini-command post. They decided to start getting the troops together, so they called John Bishop with the state police. John was wanting to complain about the leak, but Randall cut him off, saying, "John, there'll be a time for griping about it later. Right now, we've got to get this done, so we just have to focus on that." They agreed to meet at the FBI office in Texarkana. Randall called his secretary, who would be needed to type the affidavits. They knew that they would be working all night and set the raid for Sunday.

It was about nine o'clock that evening, and Randall was backing out of his driveway when his phone rang again. Drucker was on the phone. "Randall, what is going on?"

Randall snapped, "What do you mean—what's going on?"

Drucker said, "Well there are trucks from all the news stations just driving up and down the road."

Cursing under his breath, Randall said, "Are you kidding me?"

Drucker replied, "No. We've seen about two or three of them just driving up and down the road. On a Friday night! Do you know of any reason why they'd be doing that?"

Randall answered, "I don't have a clue."

So as soon as he hung up, Randall called his boss, the US Attorney's Office, and John Bishop to say, "We can't wait until Sunday. We've got to do this tomorrow, as soon as we can."

And so they worked all through the night, and assistant US attorneys were going to be driving in on Saturday morning so they could review the affidavits and warrants. At this point, they just had to go with the information they had collected from members who had left the cult. In fact, Harris and Bishop had just returned earlier in the week from a trip to Virginia, where one of Alamo's teenage victims was interviewed. They prepared a federal search warrant affidavit related to allegations of child pornography and the interstate transportation of minors, and they rendered a state search warrant affidavit related to the other child abuse allegations based on state violations. And then they wrote an arrest warrant affidavit for Tony Alamo.

They set up a conference meeting room at a business office in Texarkana for the briefing to accommodate about one hundred people involved at the state and federal levels—the FBI, the state police, and the Department of Human Services. They decided not to include local law enforcement.

At this point, they didn't know what they were going to find. Plain clothes state police investigators were dispatched to Fouke to maintain surveillance on Alamo's compound throughout the night and the next day. The sudden lack of preparation time limited the locations they would have probable cause to search. They knew they would be searching Alamo's house, the gymnasium or recreation room, the tape department, and a small supply building standing next to the gym. Randall gritted his teeth and hoped they would hit pay dirt.

CHAPTER
TWENTY-NINE

Saturday, September 20, 2008

7:00 A.M.

The plan was just about ready. They had worked all night to be sure their strategy was solid. By Saturday morning, they had learned that Alamo was not in Fouke; he was out in California. So Randall had been in contact with his counterparts in California, briefed them on what was happening, and told them that right before they headed down to Fouke, he would fax them the arrest warrant so they could go into the California compound and arrest Alamo.

Randall went home, took a shower, changed clothes, and headed back to the office. While most of the assembled personnel could only watch and wait, Randall and John Bishop were busy throughout the day finalizing the warrants, appearing before federal and state judges to sign them, and putting the finishing touches on the raid plan.

4:00 P.M.

They gathered at the briefing location at 4:00 p.m. They could meet one last time to make final assignments and do a meticulous run-through.

Then they could make the twenty-three-minute drive to Fouke to take down Alamo. Sitting in his car, Randall took in the array of state police and federal agents maneuvering their vehicles into their caravan positions. Randall looked at his watch. It was 5:30 p.m. It was unbelievable that they were able to pull this plan together in fewer than twenty-four hours. Lining up first were the state police cars that were going to block off streets so no one could leave. Then the FBI SWAT team would move in to take control of Alamo's house and nearby buildings. Evidence technicians, computer technicians, and DHS personnel to deal with the children followed in their SUVs and white vans. Altogether they were about one hundred people strong.

6:00 P.M.

As they approached Fouke, Randall immediately saw the news media lying in wait. A helicopter was flying around, and as soon as the law enforcement team pulled up, the media came out of the woods. Randall cursed and pulled quickly into the Dollar Store parking lot. He pushed a speed dialed number on his phone and said, "It's fixing to happen." Drucker and Wilma

THE DOLLAR GENERAL STORE AND CARWASH ACROSS
THE HIGHWAY FROM THE COMPOUND, FOUKE, ARKANSAS.

JERRY'S GENERAL STORE LOCATED NEAR THE BOUNDARY
OF ALAMO'S PROPERTY, FOUKE, ARKANSAS.

immediately pulled up, and rolling down his window, Randall said, "Go
to the car wash." So Drucker and Wilma pulled into the car wash where
a small crowd was gathering.

Marked state police units blocked off all the roadways, and the state police SWAT team surrounded the outer perimeter along the woods to make
sure nobody ran out from that direction. The FBI SWAT team maintained
access to and around Alamo's house. Randall remained out on the street
to wait for SWAT to give the all-clear signal. The weapons were necessary
because no one knew what they would face inside the compound. It was
not uncommon for cult followers to martyr themselves for the cause, and
it was well known that Alamo had armed private security guards. Strain-
ing to see beyond his powers, Randall stared into the guardhouse at the
gate. Alamo had the whole place wired with video security, so they needed
to be quick. They wouldn't be able to nonchalantly roll up and knock on
the door. Alamo's people could see what was happening from inside the

house. The agents clipped as many feed wires as they could find. As far as they knew, Alamo himself could be watching their approach from his compound in California.

INSIDE THE COMPOUND

It was an ordinary day. The kids had finished supper and now were doing evening chores. The girls were stuffing tracts in the recreation room. Three days ago, Tony had allowed some of them to go to the fair. Irene was chatting about the animals, her ride on the Ferris wheel, and the other kids from Fort Smith who had gone with them. This had been the day when Irene usually went with her mother to work in Tony's thrift store, Junkin' for Joy. Irene hated working there, and she had talked her mother into letting her stay home this time. Because no one was allowed to go alone outside church property, her mother had found someone else willing to go with her.

In the backyard some sisters were watching girls playing with Tony's daughter, Bella. They heard the helicopter overhead but didn't think anything of it, because people sometimes take helicopter rides in Fouke. Suddenly Irene's sister, Avril, came running into the room and shouted, "There are people outside trying to get in. They have guns!" The girls quickly got down on the floor, sneaked out the door, opened a gate by the swimming pool, and began to run toward the trees. They ran right into a big, tall man with a gun who said, "Go back. This area is blocked." The girls returned to the recreation room where they met four SWAT team members who pointed their guns and said, "Freeze! Put your hands up!" The girls were terrified. They thought the FBI agents were going to kill them. That's what they had been taught. "Why are you doing this? We're just girls," they cried trying to hold back tears.

"You're going to be all right," an agent said. "We just have to make sure that no one's here with guns."

Irene wondered, "That's crazy. Why would anyone even think that?"

The agents herded the girls through the house and asked about the function of each room they passed. When they came to Tony's office, the girls were horrified to see the officers going through files and records. Irene thought, "Oh my God. This is sacred. Why are you doing this?" She knew that some people thought that Tony did bad things, but she did not believe that he was a bad person. The officers took the girls to the sunroom and kept them there under guard. Clearly, they really didn't want the girls to talk to each other. They just sat there silently taking it all in. Avril saw a portable phone in the chair, quickly grabbed it, and held it behind her back. "Give that to me," One of the officers said. Reluctantly she handed him the phone.

A woman with a Department of Human Services name badge came in and said, "I'm going to interview you kids." She took each girl individually to a room and asked for names, parents' names, and ages. While the girls sat in the sunroom, images of other government takeovers flashed in their minds. Tony had taught them about Waco, and not too long ago they had watched in horror as the children of Warren Jeffs's FLDS community were taken from their mothers and disappeared in government-issued white vans. Papa Tony had told them that the same would happen to them, and now it seemed that their day had come.

An agent asked Andrea her age. He didn't believe that she was thirty. She did look young, and all the girls insisted that she was telling the truth. Victoria suspected that the agents were trying to catch Andrea in a trap to force her to say she had Bella before she was eighteen. Andrea's little girl did seem older than she really was. All the girls came to Andrea's defense.

Then the DHS person who had been conducting the interviews came back into the sunroom and said, "We are taking all the minors." Some of the girls started to cry, "Where are you taking us? No! Not me! You can't take me! I'm sixteen. My sister's here!"

The DHS woman grabbed Bella, who started to scream and kick.

Andrea cried, "Don't take my baby from me!" Bella was all that she had.

Tony had always treated Andrea horribly. Her daughter was everything to her. In truth, Tony used Bella to control Andrea with the threat that he would take her daughter away from her if she "misbehaved." All the girls loved Bella, and seeing her being removed was more than they could bear. They pleaded with the agents, "Don't take her! If you're going to take us, fine. But don't take the little girl away from her mommy!"

Finally, Randall said, "Okay, you're her mother and you're not underage. We'll let her stay because her mom is with her."

All the girls breathed easier and walked out with the agents to the white vans. That is when the girls realized that they really were being taken away.

The procession of vans moved down the street and then turned onto Highway 71 where a line of at least fifty police cars waited. It was getting dark. As they passed the church, the shining lights signaled that nightly services had begun. Irene cried out, "My mom is in there right now. She's right there. Stop! I'll show you where she is. You're going to let me stay with her. Right?" The DHS woman just shook her head. Irene thought in despair, "If I had just listened to my mom and gone with her to Junkin' for Joy as usual, I would be safe right now. I'd be with her." And at that moment she was consumed with sadness knowing that her mother was so close and didn't know what was happening to her. Irene desperately wanted her mom to save her.

Audrey stared out the window and tried to quiet her nerves. Tony had said the government would get them someday, burn their houses, and kill them all. She was pretty sure that would happen. The DHS woman with short hair said that they were going to go get some pizza, and then they would come back.

Audrey knew they were taking them away. She didn't believe anything they said. If only they could have gotten away through the woods! Instead the FBI agent had taken them to the sunroom in Tony's house. They kept asking where their moms, dads, and other members of the church were. Audrey wasn't about to tell them.

They asked where the pornographic pictures were. She thought about all the papers and glass on the floor in Tony's office. She wondered if they had been looking for drugs. Tony wasn't even there. He was on a trip in Los Angeles. All the girls were crying. Then Victoria started singing, and they all tried to sing something cheerful. They sang gospel songs and shared encouraging looks. They weren't going to let these people get them down. If they really were taking them somewhere, then they probably weren't going to kill them.

The vans slowed and turned into a parking lot. The DHS workers told the girls to go into a large National Guard armory. They had bought pizza for them, but most of the girls, compliant with Tony's dietary restrictions, refused to eat it. They took showers in a large bathroom and bedded down on cots. Victoria led the girls in prayer. They all murmured to each other, "Be quiet, keep the faith." One of the girls was holding a picture of her mother, who had left the church. Irene grabbed the photograph, tore it up into little pieces, and said, "No, you can't have that. People who leave the Church are fornicators. Be strong in your faith." They all agreed not to talk. They couldn't trust anyone from the outside. They knew that they would be separated. On the other side of the door people were talking about where they were going to take them. As Audrey drifted off to sleep, she thought about where they would end up. She imagined it would be an orphanage, and just like Pollyanna they would be scrubbing floors.

CHAPTER
THIRTY

Circling the Monster

At the same time they were raiding Fouke, law enforcement agents were entering the Alamo compound in Saugus, California. Unfortunately, they were five minutes too late. Someone had already tipped off church members, and Alamo had left. The agents conducted a thorough search of the compound to gather any evidence pertinent to their case against him.

Five days later, FBI agents tracked down Tony Alamo in Flagstaff, Arizona. Tony had what he considered was his secret cell phone. Unfortunately for him, his secret got out, and someone gave Randall Harris the number. Law enforcement trailed him for about a day and a half, saw which way he was headed, and finally arrested him at The Little America Hotel, a luxury retreat near the Grand Canyon. Among those with Alamo was Audrey's father. Also, Andrea and her daughter, Bella, had somehow already reunited with him. Alamo was arrested and charged with violating the Mann Act, which prohibits transporting children across state lines for illegal purposes.

The hurry-up nature of the operation meant that more evidence needed to be collected. Agents knew that more children were living under the abusive conditions of the cult. Although incarcerated, Alamo wielded complete

TONY ALAMO, NOVEMBER 23,
2008. COURTESY OF AP.

power over his followers. Randall Harris and John Bishop were relentless in their determination to dismantle the Alamo organization. In November 2008 they gained custody of more children by intercepting two large church vans on the Arkansas interstate, raiding Fouke and Fort Smith properties, and securing the children who were brought to the DHS court hearings to show support for Tony Alamo.

In the meantime, they had to get Alamo indicted. They had not found child pornography in the raid, but they had found Polaroid cameras and items that went along with the production of child pornography just as Monique and Shadow had described. At this point they had enough evidence to indict Alamo initially on charges related to only one child bride, Shadow. The US Attorney's Office was a little nervous about having evidence to pinpoint only one victim even though Alamo's history included five cases. They also knew that he could count on everybody in the church to testify on his behalf.

Testimony of Tony's child brides was critical to the case. So far they could rely on Monique and Shadow. Other corroborating information was provided to Randall via Brenda, who served as a middle person between him and some of the child brides. The girls' fear of Alamo was real. At some point, though, they all had to talk. Randall knew about Lynn, Gail, and Nora from his discussions with Brenda, Monique, and Shadow. Monique and Shadow had been trying to convince Gail to talk with Randall. Law enforcement was walking a careful line because they never knew where the girls' loyalties really were. Finally, Randall sent two agents to Florida and two to Oklahoma City to talk with Lynn and Gail. Both of them came around and agreed to travel to Fort Smith to provide additional grand jury testimony against Alamo.

Just by coincidence, a female FBI agent on the Texas side was going to San Antonio for a week of in-service training. The mother of Nora, an-

HOUSING IN FOUKE, ARKANSAS, COMPOUND AFTER RAID.

other child bride, lived in San Antonio, and the state police had been in touch with her. Randall called his agent and asked, "While you're in San Antonio, if we can set up an interview with this girl, would you be willing to break off and do it?" She said, "Of course!" Sure enough, Nora showed up with her mother and said she was willing to cooperate.

Now five underage brides were providing testimony against Alamo: Monique, Shadow, Gail, Lynn, and Nora. Along with the information provided by Brenda and other former members, their statements corroborated the dates when Alamo traveled across state lines with his child brides and conducted sexual activities with minors. The documented evidence against Alamo was mounting from several different directions.

TONY ALAMO'S HOUSE AFTER RAID, FOUKE, ARKANSAS.

CHURCH BUILDING AFTER SEIZURE
OF LAND AT FOUKE, ARKANSAS.

CHURCH BUILDING AFTER SEIZURE
OF LAND AT FOUKE, ARKANSAS.

FOLLOWERS PROTEST ALAMO'S ARREST, SEPTEMBER 25, 2008.

FOLLOWERS AT CUSTODY HEARINGS PROTEST THE REMOVAL
OF THEIR CHILDREN, SEPTEMBER–NOVEMBER, 2008.

CHAPTER THIRTY-ONE

CULTure Shock

It was nearly midnight, and most houses on the street were dark. As Ruth flipped on the porch light, she caught her reflection in the mirror by the door. Usually she was asleep by now. A dog barked a few houses away. Ruth anxiously looked out the window. Her husband Jay was away on business. She went back to the kitchen, sat down, and thought about the recent turn of events.

Ruth and Jay both had grown children from their first marriages. They loved their family and felt the need to open their home to children who needed a stable, loving environment, so they volunteered to be foster parents. After the home study and extensive training, they took an adolescent boy into their home. Sadly, the match wasn't a good fit. After about nine months, the child was moved to another place. Ruth and Jay had been devastated. They continued to pray that God would send them a child they could help.

On September 21, 2008, Ruth had just gotten home from dinner with friends when she noticed the telephone message light blinking. A person from DHS was calling to say that they needed to place a couple of teenage girls. Ruth immediately called and learned that those girls had already been placed in foster care, but they needed a home for one more girl. The caseworker said, "I know you've seen it all over the news, and we really don't want you talking about this." Ruth had not seen the news and had no idea what she was talking about. The caseworker explained that they had raided the Tony Alamo Christian Ministries compounds. She said, "This girl is fourteen years old, and the children have been raised on a strict diet. They eat no dairy products, no red meat, and are used to organic bread, fruits, and vegetables." They were driving from Texarkana, so they would arrive in a couple of hours. Ruth raced to the grocery store and bought sliced turkey, grain bread, and apples. She put the shiny red apples in a bowl on the kitchen counter.

Now Ruth was pacing the hallway. She usually had her pajamas on at this time of night, but she was still in her dress with a little make-up. She wanted to be welcoming and comforting to this girl. She searched her mind for what she knew about Tony Alamo. Over the years she had found tracts on her car window at the mall. She knew he was a cult leader and that he had been in prison for tax evasion at some point. She had heard that a child had been beaten in California some years ago, and that Alamo had been on the run before they finally caught up with him. She also knew that Tony's followers made denim jackets with lots of bling on them.

The ringing doorbell brought Ruth to her feet. As she opened the door, her eyes fell on a little fourteen-year-old girl with dark hair. A woman with short brown hair greeted Ruth with a weary smile and introduced Victoria. With a warm smile, Ruth invited them in, gave the girl a hug and said, "I'm so glad to have you at our home. My husband is out of town, so it will just be the two of us for a little bit." Ruth's stepson still lived with them, but he was gone for the evening. The DHS caseworker asked Ruth to sign a few papers and left a little bit of paperwork to be completed the next day.

After the caseworker drove away, Ruth and Victoria sat on the couch and visited for a few minutes. Ruth offered her an apple, and she ate it right away. It was late, and Ruth took Victoria upstairs to the bedroom that once belonged to her son who was away at college. Her son was an avid hunter and mounted on the wall was a stuffed duck that he had shot. So Victoria lay down on the bed and stared at that duck. She was so tired and alone. At last she fell asleep.

The next day Ruth took Victoria to get some clothes. She had arrived with the clothes on her back and a little bag with one more outfit. Ruth bought her sunglasses and told Victoria that they could get her whatever she needed. They went to the grocery store where Victoria could pick out what she liked. All the while Ruth was reassuring Victoria that she was safe and no one would harm her. Ruth told Victoria that she didn't know anything about her circumstances and understood that she was upset about being taken. Victoria was angry. She missed her friends.

Victoria was not going to say anything negative about the church. Instead she expressed dismay that they were kidnapped by DHS and held at gunpoint by the FBI. She said that she didn't know what foster care was, but they couldn't just take children away from their parents. She knew that this happened in Waco, and Tony had warned them of the same fate. Victoria was also very upset that she didn't have her books. She was home-schooled with the A Beka curriculum. Victoria ranted, "How dare they do that? Does the government not care about our education?" She wanted her books.

Ruth called DHS to find her books, and finally someone from the church found them and brought them to DHS. Ruth looked at the books and came up with a lesson plan according to the curriculum. Victoria did not complete anything Ruth asked of her. That is when Ruth realized how much Victoria loved to read. She really didn't want to do the lessons. She just wanted to have her books to read.

Ruth was determined to help Victoria feel safe. She decided to redecorate her son's room so she could personalize it for Victoria, and she gathered princess-looking draperies, a comforter, and pillows. She added stuffed animals and other items that she thought Victoria would like, which brought a smile to Victoria's face. She was so excited to have her own room.

At the grocery store, Victoria asked about foods that she was afraid to eat because of what she had been taught. Ruth told her that God says we can eat all of the things that they prepared in her home. Victoria confided that she really didn't like apples but ate the one Ruth had offered her the first night because she knew that Ruth had specifically put them there for her. When Ruth took Victoria to her first non-Biblical movie, Victoria jumped up in the middle of the feature and shouted, "Adulterer!" at a kissing scene. Ruth calmed her down, saying, "Shh. Sit down. You have to be quiet in a movie. This is only a story. It's not real." Victoria had a lot to learn about the outside world.

When Jay returned home, he greeted Ruth with a hug and looked around for their new foster child. Victoria was standing still with her head down. She would not make eye contact with him. She had been taught her entire life not to look or speak to men. Jay's heart broke, and he knew it would take a long time to show Victoria that she could trust him. At that moment he loved her even more.

When children are taken into temporary custody in the state of Arkansas, they have to go to court and appear before the judge within a week. The judge then decides if the child should remain in custody or return to the family. So Ruth and Victoria went to court in Texarkana. Victoria sat next to Ruth with her head down. Sitting next to his lawyer, Victoria's father stared at them from the other side of the room. When the state presented their case and said that she needed to stay in custody, the judge agreed, "Yes, she will stay in custody for now." Victoria broke down and cried hysterically in the courtroom. Ruth kept patting her and hugging her. Victoria's father just glared at the judge. The case would be reevaluated at specific time intervals, and going to court became a regular routine in their lives, as were court-supervised parental visitations.

On one of the occasions when Ruth was taking Victoria to DHS for a supervised visit, they ran into Irene, one of the girls who had been taken in the raid with Victoria. The girls were hugging and crying because they missed each other. Ruth asked the caseworker if Irene could come home with them to visit for the weekend. At first they had been intent on keeping the children separated. When they took them into custody, the girls were telling each other to be quiet and to stand their ground and to be a servant of God. They were also afraid that the children would run away.

As weeks passed and foster life was getting a little bit more comfortable, caseworkers believed that these children weren't going to run away, so they allowed Irene to go home with Ruth. After a few days, Ruth called DHS and said, "Irene is such a good kid and the girls are having so much fun together; can she just stay with us?" Irene wasn't really happy with her foster family because they lived way out in the country and had no one close to her age in the family. The caseworker approved the move.

The next month when Ruth, Victoria, and Irene were in court, another girl found her way into Ruth's heart. Victoria and Irene squealed in delight when they saw Audrey in the hallway of the courthouse. Audrey's foster placement was in a home with twenty cats and three dogs. She was unhappy there, and Ruth went home with yet another child in her fold.

Now with three children who had regular court appearances and supervised parent meetings in Texarkana, Ruth was making regular two-hour drives between her home and Texarkana. She was involved. Her heart broke for the suffering these children had endured. She was angered by the control Tony Alamo held over his followers, and she was determined to do what she could to make a positive difference in the children's lives. One day she called Jay and said, "We need to buy two more beds. Victoria's brothers, Ian and Stefan, are coming to live with us." The DHS staff regularly called Ruth for referrals to possible families for placement. Ruth understood the fears and challenges of these children. An added bonus—she worked with The CALL, an interdenominational Christian organization whose mission is to find a home for every foster child in Arkansas. Ruth generated excitement and willingness among families to step up and respond to this growing need.

Court visits were not easy. As time went on, testimony came from children, former cult members, and others who had witnessed Alamo's treatment of children. The court proceedings became quite lengthy. Sessions felt oppressive. Ruth would take the girls separately on long walks so they could feel free to talk. It took a while for them to be willing to talk in front of each other, because each feared that the other one would tell on her. They had grown up in an environment where brothers, sisters, husbands, wives, parents, and children were taught to report to Tony about what they were doing. Then they could be beaten. They could trust no one. Depending on his mood, Tony might ask to see all the reports. Other times there were so many reports that he would ask the girls working in the office to sort them and give him the most important ones. Victoria worked in his office and remembered a report on a woman who ran through a stop sign. Even the most trivial actions could be punished severely. Tony's control depended on this driving fear.

The children had supervised visits at DHS with their family for one hour each week. Sometimes their parents would give them notes warning them against talking to anyone outside the church. They had such a strong hold on their children that even if the children had told Ruth something, they would often backtrack and deny that they had said anything when questioned by an attorney or DHS caseworker. It took months before Victoria started to tell Ruth anything. But every time she went to court, Ruth would meet other children and learn a little bit more about Tony Alamo. For about two months the focus was on the girls, but with the second raid came the boys.

Ruth and the girls were in court on that November day. Something was different. The atmosphere was charged. More security officers were present, and Ruth could sense that something was beginning to happen. Since the end of September, the findings that were coming out in court proceedings made it clear: it was time to protect the rest of the children. So law enforcement coordinated a raid to bring in the children from Tony Alamo's properties at Fort Smith and Fouke, along with those in the courtroom—all at exactly the same time.

When the officers began to take the children into the courtroom, Alamo's followers pulled out their phones to warn people at the properties. Even a short two-minute warning could possibly be enough time for some to get away. The news spread like wildfire throughout Alamo's compound. Followers with vans filled with children trying to leave were intercepted on the highway. Victoria's little brother, Stefan, was taken into custody at Fouke. Her other brother, Ian, was in the courtroom that day with their father. Ian held his head high, casting a look of disdain at the officers. As the children were escorted out of the room, a few women cried out, "How can you do this? How can you kidnap our children?"

Ruth and Jay were doing their best to create a home with a regular routine for the children. When Irene came to live with them, Victoria had perked up considerably. Irene was eager for adventure. Later she would remember the day of the raid as a time that was scary but also exciting. She had always thought that if they were going to be raided as Tony had said, she wanted to be in the thick of it. She didn't want to miss anything. So given her sense of adventure, it was no surprise when Irene insisted that she and Victoria go to public school. She began to push for new experiences: "Victoria, let's do this! Let's go to school! Let's ride the school bus! I always wanted to ride a school bus!" Ruth registered Victoria, Irene, and Audrey for school.

Public school with six hundred students in the ninth grade alone was a big step.

The school year had already started. Gayle, the guidance counselor, had very little specific information about the children's history. She understood that they were coming into an environment vastly different from what they had known, and their foster mother had requested that they be placed together in classes whenever possible. It would take at least a week of testing and getting acquainted with the girls' previous work before they really knew where to place them academically. Gayle thought about the teachers and knew right away that her veteran teacher Gina would be a great fit for English. She called Gina into her office and said, "I just want you to know that you are going to get some kids who are going to need a lot of love. They will have to miss class every Thursday morning to go to a meeting at DHS." Gina seated the girls on the same side of the room so she could look at them all at the same time.

Gina was conscious of how frightened the girls must have been, but she had no similar experience to know how she could best help them. So she made herself available and encouraging. Early on they stuck together, not relating to the other kids, particularly boys. They had not been allowed to look or speak to boys their entire lives. Having boys in their classes was a big change.

Gina and Gayle understood that what the girls needed most was an adult they could trust. After about a month, the girls began to talk more. The support of their teacher gave them confidence to speak up in class. The girls popped into Gina's room even during other class periods if they needed a retreat. Gina herself had experienced a hard upbringing, and she regularly taught her students that what happens to them would mold them into their own special person but would not determine what they are going to do with their lives. She stressed that it was up to them to choose their futures.

The girls had a strong work ethic and performed well academically. They helped each other with homework and were avid readers. Ruth and Gayle spoke on the phone every day to be sure the girls were okay. Socially, the girls stuck together. They would go into class together in a line. If they got separated, they would wait and come together. They all had strength and determination to do something with their lives. And they liked the ways they were different. When they struggled, they never gave up; they just tried harder. Some days Victoria felt herself shaking so much from fear that she found it a challenge just to sit still at her desk. She didn't want anyone to look at her. Similarly, Audrey wished that she could be little and disappear so no one would look at her. When boys commented that they were cute, the girls didn't understand what they meant. Tony had taught them that they were fat and ugly. The girls cringed at the thought of a boy talking to them. What would they do? One day a girl commented to Audrey, "I bet you never saw a bad day in your life." To that Audrey thought, "Well, you go on thinking that."

Even when the girls were in different classes, the teachers made sure to schedule them for the same lunch period. The girls didn't talk to boys and stuck together as much as they could. Victoria had her head in a book when she wasn't in class. Coming from an environment where breaking rules carried serious and scary consequences, the children were more obedient than their peers. Victoria would remark to Ruth, "Those children are so disrespectful to their teachers! I just cannot believe the way they treat their teachers!" Victoria didn't understand why others didn't love teachers. She was appalled when they were rude and didn't want to participate.

Ruth always packed lunches for school because she didn't think the children would eat what the cafeteria served. In the cult they were not allowed to eat dairy. After a while, though, Irene wanted to try dairy products. Then all the kids tried macaroni and cheese. Anything with milk, butter, or cheese was new to them. They had eaten ice cream in the past. No one had really known the basis for certain food restrictions. Tony would get on a tangent, take away what they were used to eating, and set other dietary rules. Dietary rules were whimsical and a feature of his control.

Ruth and Jay also started taking the children to church. Ruth found out within a few weeks that there was going to be a youth sleepover for the girls in their early teens. So she packed them each a little backpack with a pillow and blanket. There they stood in front of the kitchen island with their arms around each other, and their pillows in their hands, bound for their first overnight outing. They were a little scared, but they were excited at the same time. And Irene kept saying, "Oh, Victoria! Oh, Victoria!"

Caring for the children extended far beyond trying out different foods, enrolling in school, and becoming involved in a church youth group. Victoria, Irene, Audrey, Ian, and Stefan easily could have lived on another planet. Everything that they had been taught was now being tested. They were pulled away from everyone familiar, everyone they had loved. They had no frame of reference for this new life they found themselves in. They didn't share the same socio-cultural history as the other kids their ages, and they really couldn't relate to current activities and trends. All they knew of the world had been told to them. Some children were third-generation cult members, meaning that even their parents had not seen the world outside of Alamo's. They had no concept of themselves outside of the cult. Their self-identities were created and defined by Tony Alamo. This new outside world was bombarding them with information that conflicted sharply with what they had learned. It wouldn't be easy to ignore the lens through which they'd learned to see the world.

The children were respectful of adults, but they were quick to defend their faith and lifestyle. They all knew the King James Version of the Bible, and they readily quoted by heart scriptures to underscore their opinions and beliefs. Tony had taught them that he was a prophet from God and that all of the people living outside the church were out of God's favor. They believed Tony's stories of the conspiracies between the pope and the United States government. They believed that Tony Alamo was the World Pastor with thousands of followers. They believed that they were right and that everyone else outside the church was wrong. The children were quite certain of the authority of the Bible as it was taught to them.

Ruth and Jay grew up in churches that used the Bible, but they knew that the children had studied the Bible more than they had. So Ruth and Jay began studying the Bible in earnest and reading the passages that the children used to support their belief system. They refreshed their minds and gained new perspectives about parts that they had forgotten or not seen as relevant in previous readings. When the children quoted scripture to defend a belief, Ruth would respond by saying, "So, you're reading the same Bible I'm reading. Where does it say that? It's time to speak the truth." Ruth put sticky notes around the mirror in the bathroom to prompt them to consider a reality different from the one they had been taught. She posted scriptures, and phrases such as "the truth will set you free." When the kids were brushing their teeth, they would read Ruth's reminder notes, "Lying is never acceptable."

Ruth and Jay started studying what Tony Alamo taught as well. How could they teach the children the truth if they didn't know what they had been taught to believe? Alamo had indoctrinated his followers with lies. They had to understand Alamo's line of thinking so that they could counteract it with the truth. Ruth and Jay prayed for God to show them what truths the children could see. Not everything the children were taught was based on a lie. Alamo took pieces of truth and twisted them to suit his doctrine. If there were no truth at all, then his teaching would be totally unbelievable.

All false religions have pieces of truth in them. Citing Matthew 7:6, Alamo taught his followers that it is okay to lie to outsiders: "Give not that which is holy unto the dogs, neither cast ye your pearls before swine, lest they trample them under their feet, and turn again and rend you." Tony declared his church followers' acts on the "inside" to be like the pearls, and the people and the US government on the "outside" to be the swine. And so he justified lying to outsiders about what really happens behind the closed doors of his ministry. Alamo also taught that there are two different sets of rules in the world: church law and government law. Their real beliefs supported church law, which included severe physical punishments, polygamy, and the marriage of girls once they reach puberty.

The more Ruth and Jay learned, the more they realized that the adults in Tony Alamo's cult were deceived just as the children were. They too were abused mentally, physically, spiritually, and emotionally. But as adults, they had more choices than their children did. Ruth learned to consider each parent and family individually. They weren't all unlovable, and they weren't all horrible. She just tried to be nice to them, caring, and when opportunities arose, she said what she thought they needed to hear. Ruth could say what the court officials couldn't say. She was not afraid to ask, "How can you do this to your children?"

Creating a safe place for the Alamo children was especially challenging on the days they went to court. Court appearances were required for ongoing custody hearings, and the children were also called upon as potential witnesses for the criminal trial of Tony Alamo. The case was drawing national attention. Law enforcement officials from the FBI and state police were present, the media had helicopters over the courthouse, and reporters were everywhere. On the sidewalks Tony Alamo's followers were picketing with signs: "Give us back our children!" "We serve the Lord!" "The US government kidnapped our children!" When the girls arrived, they were hustled through a back entrance under a canopy. Court officials hovered over them with umbrellas to prevent the media from taking photographs. Ruth had to enter through the front entrance and meet the girls inside.

The girls' nerves were revved up. Eager to see the happenings, Irene was charged with nervous energy and excitement. Meanwhile, Victoria was annoyed by everything. Both were excited that they would see others they had known in the church. They saw people they hadn't seen in years—people who had left the church and who were now willing to testify against Tony Alamo. Every time they went to court, they would have a supervised visit with their parents, so they were happy about that. They liked to visit their families. Sometimes their parents would bring some of their siblings with them so they would get to see them, too.

Every family had different dynamics during the visitations. Victoria, Ian, and Stefan were more of an audience to their overbearing father, who commanded their attention. After a number of visits, Victoria ignored her father, plugged buds into her ears, and listened to music while reading a book. Irene's mother was also aggressive but to a lesser degree. Her father was gentle and quiet. Irene was the only child in this group who had a mom that was still in the church. All the other moms had run away. Irene was extremely proud that she had two parents who were together and present in her life. She always tried to make it clear that her family was different from others in the church. She stood her ground in defense of the church longer than the other youngsters.

As time passed, Irene's mother started treating Irene differently, accusing her of being a backslider and a whore. The church taught that women who left the faith became whores. Children were taught to hate their mothers who had abandoned the church. They had to degrade their mothers

TONY ALAMO LED FROM THE FEDERAL COURTHOUSE, MONDAY, JULY 13, 2009. TEXARKANA, ARKANSAS. COURTESY OF AP.

in front of other people. If they did have any kind thoughts toward their mothers, they were afraid to express them.

When Ian referred to his biological mother as a whore, Ruth confronted him: "Don't you ever say that again in my house," she said. "You really don't know anything about her. You haven't lived with her for eight years. You only know what your dad tells you—that anyone who's not in that church is a whore, a drug addict, an alcoholic, a thief, and a liar. The Bible doesn't teach us to speak that way about our mothers."

The fear of Tony Alamo ran deep. Even when the children were in foster care, they were still reluctant to talk even among themselves about their past. Victoria started to tell Ruth little things after about five months after the raid. She talked about the rules, the work they did, and the places she lived.

On July 24, 2009, after a two-week trial that included emotional testimony by the five child brides, Tony Alamo was convicted on ten counts of taking underage girls across state lines for sex. A few months later, US District Judge Harry F. Barnes sentenced Alamo to prison for 175 years with no possibility of parole.

On that day, Irene started talking about her life in the cult. Victoria and Audrey joined her. They described the beatings, living in constant fear, and being forced to labor long hours without respite. Stefan talked later that November, one year after his father's appeal of parental rights was rejected—three years following the raid. Ian began talking two weeks later. That's how afraid they were.

At last they were free.

2009

January—Judge rules that the parents of twenty-one children must move from church property and find jobs outside the ministry if they hope to regain custody of their children.

Judge upholds the removal of eighteen children from Tony Alamo Christian Ministries, saying the children were endangered by the ministry's history of punishing misbehavior with beatings and allowing underage marriages.

The number of jailed Tony Alamo Christian Ministries followers rises when authorities in California jail a man on a twenty-year-old warrant alleging child abuse. Douglas Christopher is accused of beating an eleven-year-old-boy at the Alamo compound in Saugus, California.

A state Board of Health panel with clearly defined subpoena powers will investigate an illegal mattress-selling operation connected to Tony Alamo. Tempur-Pedic discovers the mattresses they donated to the Alamo Ministry for charitable distribution were being sold for profit.

February 10—A watchdog blog publishes "An Open Letter to the Children and Parents of the Alamo Foundation from Christhiaon Coie":

> I would like to introduce myself to you. My name is Christhiaon Coie. My Mother was Susan Alamo, the actual founder of the Tony and Susan Alamo Christian Foundation. Some of my earliest memories and things that my late brother Charlie told me are of Momma leaving him, a teenage boy, to care for me. With no food, milk, or cash and with landlords banging on doors for their rent, Charlie couldn't stand it any more and ran away and joined the Navy.
>
> From that day on it was Momma and me. One day my Mother would drag me to a church. I would sing and she would preach and we would leave with a LOVE offering. When the unmarked cans would be almost gone and the beer supply would dwindle the beatings would escalate; some so bad that school was out of the question. She finally took me out of school in the eighth grade.
>
> I was a teenager when Momma met Tony Alamo. Momma and I were sitting in a bar in the back of a restaurant. I sat there listening to them conning each other over a pitcher of beer, wondering who was going to have the cash to pay for it. She moved him in and that's how this "Foundation" started. I will never forgive myself for helping them put this together. All it was supposed to do was give them an income—not elect them king and queen of the world.
>
> So why would I say what I'm saying now? Because you are about to give up your children for a huge lie. I thank God that finally the courts have stepped in to stop this shell game. How far will you allow Tony to take you and your families down? I know what it's like to be raped by

him (literally) and I know what it's like to be beaten by
him (again, literally). I know what it's like to leave the
Foundation with two small babies, with nothing and no
one to help me.

Little girls ages 9, 10, 11, and up are not brides. They
are babies being raped by perverted thugs hiding behind
the Bible. Little boys are not men who have committed
crimes, to be held down and beaten bloody. I, and a great
many people, have heard Tony sing his putrid little song
on the airwaves. "I LIKE IT, I LOVE IT, I WANT SOME
MORE OF IT."

I know some of you Mothers and Fathers feel trapped.
He's made sure that escape is almost impossible in your
minds. You have no real money after all the years of slavery. Then there is the real big one. How do you look at
your children and say "I was duped for 5, 15, 30 years?"
Sometimes doing the right thing is the hardest thing you
will ever do. You owe your children that. If you won't or
can't do the right thing now for them, then let the court
find them good homes.

I do have some questions I hope you would ask yourself:

How many wives did Tony have when Momma (SUSIE)
was alive?

How many times have you heard him say one thing
publicly and do and say something completely different
in the church? Why didn't Jesus have a harem of former
wives in tow? Where in the Bible do you find Jesus taking 9, 10, 11 year olds to bed, or holding kids down and
beating them?

If you are one of the kids and you read this, I know
you think nobody cares about what's happening to you.
That's not true. I know you think that you are all alone,
at their mercy, and no one will find you. That's not true,

either. I know that you think that you must have done
something to deserve this. That also is not true. The
truth is that you will be found and there are people who
care about you. There are a great many people ready and
waiting to help you and I'm one of them. Though we have
never met, I know you. I KNOW YOU and I'm so very
sorry. Remember, "When you know the truth, the truth
shall set you free."[1]

April—Lawyers for Tony Alamo ask a federal judge to release the minister
pending his trial on charges he took young girls across state lines for sex.

The Tony Alamo Christian Ministries file a lawsuit accusing Arkansas
child welfare officials of persecuting the jailed evangelist's followers as he
awaits trial on child sex charges.

July 13—Alamo trial begins in Texarkana, Arkansas. Among those tes-
tifying is a young woman who says that at the age of fourteen she ex-
changed wedding vows with Tony Alamo in the Federal Correctional
Institution waiting area while he was an inmate at the federal prison in
Texarkana, Texas, for tax violations. The witness says her marriage with
Alamo was consummated on July 17, 1998, a date she wrote down in her
Bible afterwards.

July 24—A jury of nine men and three women deliberate for eleven hours
and find Tony Alamo guilty on ten counts of taking girls as young as nine
years old across state lines for sex. The five Jane Does and other victims
who testified against self-proclaimed evangelist Tony Alamo hold hands,
weep, and hug as a federal judge proclaims him guilty ten times. As he is
escorted to a waiting US marshal's vehicle, Alamo calls to reporters, "I'm
just another one of the prophets that went to jail for the Gospel."

---

1. Tonylamonews.com, February 10, 2009.

October 23—Still a fugitive, John Kolbek is ordered to pay three million dollars in restitution to two men he beat when they were children with a six-foot wooden board at Alamo's bidding.

November 13—Tony Alamo's sentencing. Before the judge issues his sentence, Alamo offers a brief statement to the court, praising God and saying, "I'm glad I'm me and not the deceived people in the world."

Tony Alamo is sentenced to 175 years in prison with no parole as a result of his abuse of young girls, crucifying Jesus again in their flesh through sexual degradation and humiliation. He shamed them in private, violating their bodies, and in public, where they were paraded before the congregation as his "brides." One of them addresses Alamo in court: "You preyed on innocent children. You have the audacity to ask for mercy. What mercy did you show us? What kind of a man of God does what you have done?" As he issues the sentence, trial Judge Harry F. Barnes says to Alamo, "Mr. Alamo, one day you will face a higher, a greater judge than me; may He have mercy on your soul."

The state court of appeals rules that human services officials were justified in removing children living at the Tony Alamo Christian Ministries compounds. The children faced "a clear picture of danger" from beatings and forced fasts ordered by the evangelist while the parents witnessed and did nothing.

2010

April—Court rules against Alamo's followers' appeal for custody, affirming that Alamo parents failed to protect their children from Tony Alamo's sexual abuse, beatings, ordered fasts, and underage marriages.

August—Businesses owned and run by members of Tony Alamo Christian Ministries and Tony's wife, Sharon, are among defendants named in a civil lawsuit filed by victims of Tony Alamo. The suit claims that the ministry, related organizations, and certain high-ranking members of Alamo's enterprise knew, or should have known, that Alamo was sexually abusing children. The complaint alleges violations of federal law concerning human trafficking that gives victims the right to recover damages in a federal case.

Maintaining his innocence, Tony Alamo files an appeal of the 175-year jail sentence for ten counts of transporting minors across state lines for sex. Alamo was also ordered to pay $2.5 million in restitution, $500,000 each to five Jane Does with whom he had sex, plus a $250,000 fine.

Christhiaon Coie, daughter of deceased Susan Alamo, issues the statement: "I'm sorry the appeals court has to even be bothered with this, but I have no doubt that they will rule appropriately because justice trumps madness. He's where he deserves to be and should serve his entire term."

September—Convicted Tony Alamo seeks new trial.

The Oprah Winfrey Show airs a story (repeat episode) of survivors who were victims of Tony Alamo's physical and sexual abuse.

Tony Alamo is placed in isolation in prison after a fight.

Tempur-Pedic Mattress Company is told it needs a court order to recover thirty-five hundred mattresses sold by Tony Alamo. The company donated mattresses to Hurricane Katrina victims but discovered that Tony Alamo intended to resell them for profit. Alamo claims that he bought the mattresses from Waste to Charity, Inc.

October—An Internet blog publishes "A Letter to John Kolbek from Canton, Texas, flea market vendor":

> John,
>   Turn yourself in. It's not worth all of this. I know you
> are tired of running and hiding. My concern is how is

Benjamin and the rest of the kids are. John, if you really
believe in Jesus Christ as you told me and as we spoke
about on several months of you coming to the market
then you know the Lord will take care of you. And you
will trust in him for the right thing to do. I know you're
not scared and I know that you meant no harm to any of
the kids. You were just doing your job within the church
as Tony told you to. It's not your fault that he corrupted
your mind as his. John, go do it my friend. Turn yourself
in and let's get on with life. . . . Shame is hard to deal with
but pray it will be OK. I promise that's what you told me
to do and it works.

Trust me, John, it really does.

Hope 2 CYA soon, Buddy. Take care and tell Jennifer
and the kids they are thought of daily.[2]

December—Federal appeals court upholds sex-related convictions for jailed
Tony Alamo. Alamo's attorney vows to take appeal to the Supreme Court.

FBI offers a reward of up to ten thousand dollars for information leading
directly to the arrest of John Erwin Kolbek.

December 11—*America's Most Wanted* television show features John Kolbek,
fugitive wanted for his alleged involvement in the 2008 beating of a teenage
boy who was a member of Tony Alamo Christian Ministries.

Another child bride victim of Tony Alamo departs group and is added as a
plaintiff in a civil lawsuit that names the ministry, church-run businesses,
and high-ranking individuals in the organization as defendants.

---

2. tonyalamonews.com October 15, 2010.

December 14—Media reports indicate that in spite of legal actions, Alamo's cult continues to function: "Tony Alamo was sentenced to 175 years in prison during July of 2009. His history in Santa Clarita extends over 40 years. In spite of his incarceration, this past weekend a flyer for his Tony Alamo Christian Ministries was placed on the windshield of my car. Heads up parents, his easiest converts are teenagers" (*News Blogs & Forums*, December 14, 2010).

2011

January 13—John Kolbek, age fifty-one, dies of heart failure in rural Lawrence County, Kentucky. Kolbek; his wife, Jennifer; his two sons; Jennifer Kolbek's sister Misheal (former wife of Tony Alamo); and six children are living in hiding. All children were among those listed to take into custody from the Alamo property in 2008. The removal orders have now expired.

Attorneys for two boys seeking damages from Kolbek for battery, false imprisonment, conspiracy, and outrage file a petition seeking to invalidate property transfers from John and Jennifer Kolbek to other members. They ask the court to declare those deeds void and to order Kolbek's interests in the Alamo properties sold. The proceeds from those sales are to be applied against the judgment in favor of the two boys.

Alamo followers including Jennifer, Kolbek's wife, keep Kolbek's daughter, Monique, from attending his funeral. Monique was taken to be Alamo's wife when she was eight years old. She testified against Alamo at his trial.

Tony Alamo seeks to advise Presidents Obama, Bush, and Clinton in exchange for a pardon. Excerpt from Alamo letter to President Obama:

> Therefore, as time is running out, I am asking your majesty to grant me immediate pardon so I can work out the different tactics, strategies, and ideas that God revealed to me and put them into immediate action, since

we wasted so much time by not taking immediate drastic steps to end this conflict. It will not only be beneficial to the disputing parties, but to all Americans, to our homeland security and values, the freedom, justice, and equality that we stand for as the land of the free and the home of the brave. Our integrity needs to be an example for the entire world. The whole world is looking at us to resolve their problems, and we can't afford to fail them. Let the needy, the hopeless, and the helpless know that America is there to listen, defend, and act on their behalf. We have become the hope of many nations and people, and we can't let this conflict drag on any longer, putting our integrity and reputation into question. For the sake of peace, I ask you, President Obama, to act courageously by freeing me from my prison cell so I can help you deliver an end to this conflict. I am a man of truth, and I mean every word I say. I would welcome you visiting me in person, or, if for some reason you can't come in person, I am willing to share the strategy that God revealed to me to any of your trusted representatives and to contact my lawyers to prepare the pardon papers. I am 76 years old. I am willing to direct all my influences, resources, and everything I have to help you end this conflict. I know and understand this conflict, and I know how to resolve it, as I know myself and I know how to get things done. Trust in me.[3]

April—Multiple Alamo followers file custody appeals for the return of their children to their families.

April 28—Arkansas Supreme Court upholds a lower court's termination of parental rights of five families who had refused to live independently

---

3. http://www.alamoministries.com/content/english/letters/obama.htm.

of Tony Alamo Christian Ministries, ruling that such an action does not violate the parents' First Amendment right to religious freedom.

Multiple former Alamo followers sue security companies that once patrolled the grounds and perimeter of Tony Alamo Christian Ministries in Fouke, Arkansas, and ministry-controlled businesses. Plaintiffs say guards allowed abuses at Alamo ministry.

May—Alamo changes attorneys a number of times.

May 31—Civil trial begins for Tony Alamo, charged with ordering the beating of two of his former ministry members.

June—Mother of a former Alamo follower calls Alamo and Kolbek "heroes" for spanking the children. Another woman testifies that her son getting slapped in the face and struck with a wooden paddle when he was fourteen by a member of the church was "the best thing that ever happened to him" and that later he told her he deserved it.

A former Tony Alamo Christian Ministries member testifies that he considered suicide when he learned he was to be beaten for a third time with a wooden board.

June 2—Jury awards two former members sixty-six million dollars in damages in response to charges that Alamo ordered them to be beaten, placed them on fasts, and verbally abused them while they were members of his ministry.

Plaintiffs' attorneys hunt Alamo assets to seize for payment of damages. Alamo's attorneys' appeals are unsuccessful.

Insurance companies seek exemption from responsibility to pay monetary damages arising from abuse allegations against Tony Alamo Christian Ministries.

August—Attorneys for Alamo follower and church property business owner file that the parents of women Tony Alamo took as his "wives" when they were young girls should be held responsible for any abuse the women suffered.

Attorneys for the plaintiffs scrutinize Alamo's practice of placing ownership of property in the names of multiple church members in fraudulent attempts to protect properties from being seized to satisfy federal court judgments. As an example, Alamo directed members to sign undated quit claim deeds. Later, if followers left the ministry, the deeds would be dated so that those leaving no longer had rights to the property.

Miller County Judge Joe Griffin clears the way for Alamo properties to be auctioned when he voids deeds that had transferred partial ownership of the properties from John Kolbek to other church members. Griffin's order directs the Miller County Circuit Clerk to auction Kolbek's twenty percent stake in the properties if the three million dollar judgment in a lawsuit by two former ministry members is not paid within ten days.

September—Alamo's attorneys file appeals and are unsuccessful. Judgments against Alamo mount.

October—Alamo followers continue to file appeals to regain custody of their children. The US Supreme Court declines to hear arguments because the parents would not agree to keep their children from exposure to the Alamo ministry.

Former Alamo member posts note on Internet blog:

> I am so thankful to the Lord for getting me out of Alamo's cult. Jesus is so good and loving. I am very grateful for his love. While I was in the cult, the Holy Spirit started showing me how demonized everyone there was and He got me out of there. Thank You God!

> I forgive Tony Alamo for mind control, fear, manipu-
> lation and witchcraft that he did on me. I pray for those
> poor young girls that had to give him massages every day
> for hours. I pray that God heals their broken hearts/
> souls and I pray for Tony to somehow come to his senses
> before he goes to meet the God who avenges. (August 25,
> 2011, comment on Andy Davis, "Path Clear for Auction
> of Alamo Properties," tonyalamonews.com.)

November—A federal judge refuses to halt a civil suit filed against Alamo by his former "wives."

December—The trial and law enforcement teams that investigated and prosecuted Bernie Hoffman (a.k.a Tony Alamo) are recognized and praised by Attorney General Eric Holder and Executive Office for US Attorneys Director Marshall Jarrett at the Twenty-Eighth Annual Director's Awards Ceremony in Washington, DC.

Media reports indicate that Alamo continues his influence over followers from prison: "Cult Leader Alamo Still Ministering from Prison. Threats, Rumors and 24-Hour Security Raise Suspicions About Local Church" (headline in *Santa Clarita Valley News*, December 12, 2011).

2012

January—Alamo's attorneys continue to file appeals of damages levied against him, and all appeals are denied.

February—Alamo parents file responses protesting that the parents should bear some of the blame and so be held responsible for the physical, sexual, and spiritual abuses suffered by the plaintiffs as children in Alamo Ministries.

June—In a civil lawsuit seeking damages for former child brides of Tony Alamo, defendants (Tony Alamo and his followers) accuse the women of willingly practicing polygamy and participating in the production of child pornography.

Tony Alamo seeks to vacate his 175-year sentence based on claims that the lawyers who represented him at trial and on appeal were ineffective.

Appeals judges question the size of a sixty-six million dollar verdict awarded to two men who said they were beaten and forced to fast while they were children and members of Tony Alamo Christian Ministries.

August—A federal appeals court orders punitive damages against Tony Alamo, who ordered two boys to be beaten, to be reduced from sixty million dollars to twenty-four million dollars. The Eighth US Circuit Court of Appeals upholds an additional three million dollar award for each of the abuses they suffered.

September–November—Attorneys for Alamo continue unsuccessfully to seek appeals and reviews of judgments against him.

December—Tempur-Pedic Mattress Company asks a judge to reopen a lawsuit over claims that thousands of Tempur-Pedic mattresses meant for Hurricane Katrina victims and other people in need were illegally diverted to a company affiliated with Tony Alamo Christian Ministries.

2013

Judge reopens Tempur-Pedic mattress lawsuit.

Attorneys for Alamo continue to file appeals of judgments with unsuccessful results.

Alamo's properties are key to remuneration for the judgments.

Attorneys battle to prove that all church properties belong to Tony Alamo regardless of his practice of deeding businesses and properties to church members.

Judges rule that Alamo properties can be sold to help satisfy judgments.

Former Tony Alamo follower described as "a man engaged in horrendous conduct involving sexual abuse of a minor child" pleads guilty in federal court.

Alamo is ordered to pay five hundred thousand dollars in restitution for each of five child abuse victims, a total of $2.5 million. As of May 8, 2013, Alamo had not made any restitution payments. In an effort to collect restitution for the victims, prosecutors file an action in district court that requests writs of execution against twenty-seven parcels of real estate property. Prosecutors also file six separate lawsuits seeking the forfeiture of property that facilitated the abuse of the five victims.

Nearly one hundred Tony Alamo followers fill the courtroom at a hearing to address claims to church properties.

A federal judge rules that most claims of followers to Alamo properties can be thrown out.

A federal judge rules that Tony Alamo and wife Sharon Alamo must reveal the source of money they use to pay their lawyers. Lawyers believe Alamo is concealing a "large sum of money," some of which is being used for legal fees.

A federal judge rules that Tony Alamo is the true owner of properties associated with his group. "The U.S. Marshal is directed to sell the properties at issue . . . to satisfy the final judgment in this matter," US Magistrate Judge Barry Bryant's October 31 opinion states. "The court finds the ownership claims made to the properties (by Alamo followers) are not valid, and further finds Bernie Lazar Hoffman, a.k.a Tony Alamo, is the true owner of the properties."

Video testimony recorded in 2012 and 2013 shows Alamo still in control of the ministry from jail. Members read all emails from Alamo and act on his orders. When he is dissatisfied with followers, Alamo says, "If they don't like it here, get out. Don't tangle with me. If they act like the antichrist and don't serve the Lord, get them out."

November 8—Media reports are critical of Alamo's continuing to operate businesses from prison:

> It remains shocking that someone convicted of crimes as heinous as Mr. Alamo's should find himself still able to run his businesses and maintain control over the ministries' members. The crimes of which he is convicted and the actions that led to the civil settlement against him are not financial, white-collar or minor crimes. They are crimes against the bodies and persons of young girls and boys.
>
> We do not imagine that a 175-year sentence given to someone of Mr. Alamo's age is meant as an opportunity for rehabilitation; it is rather designed to protect society from his influence. If he continues to run his sleazy empire from jail, we cannot see that the sentence is effective or that justice is served.[4]

Motion accuses Alamo followers of gutting property for auction. Federal marshals are asked to step in.

---

4. "Tony Alamo's Punishment Seems Inadequate," *Times Record* online edition, November 8, 2013.

2014

January—Hearing for Alamo properties case is set for February.

Judge dismisses federal civil lawsuit filed in 2010 by Alamo's former wives but declines to rule on violations of state law. Plaintiffs can file the suit again in state court.

Tony Alamo Christian Ministries member Douglas Christopher is sentenced to life in federal prison for sexual misconduct with three young girls.

Five women, the Jane Doe child brides, file a civil suit from the 2009 criminal case, and two other women seek damages in state court. The suit alleges negligence, negligent entrustment, negligent hiring, false imprisonment, and invasion of privacy, defamation, joint venture/enterprise liability, battery, and outrage.

Alamo members file liens, stalling property sales.

February—Alamo followers testify in a hearing over the property sales of Tony Alamo and the church.

The court awards a stunning $525 million to seven women physically and sexually abused by evangelist Tony Alamo, pushing the total owed by the imprisoned preacher and an affiliated church to more than one billion dollars.

March—A judge rules that the Tony Alamo Christian Ministries church in Fouke, Arkansas, and other properties may be sold to partially satisfy a thirty million dollar judgment that Tony Alamo owes to two men raised in his ministry.

April—Attorneys for two men who are owed thirty million dollars from a civil judgment against Tony Alamo say Alamo's followers may have stripped the properties since a federal judge ordered that the properties be sold to help pay the debt. "Plaintiffs have learned that certain fixtures such as air conditioning units, ceiling tiles, doors, sinks, commodes, and insulation are being removed from the properties," states a motion on behalf of the two men.

Twelve former members of Tony Alamo Christian Ministries file a federal lawsuit seeking damages for alleged abuses they suffered as children raised in the controversial group.

May—Followers of convicted Tony Alamo fail to show for a hearing on ministry properties. One man sends a letter to say that the proceedings are doing nothing "more than leaving us homeless."[5]

June—The church, three other properties in Fouke, and another property in Texarkana, Arkansas, are sold in auctions.

August—A Texarkana lawyer seeking compensation for the victims of Tony Alamo said he would likely be seeking Tony Alamo's Santa Clarita Valley, California, properties.

November—A federal judge in Texarkana denies a motion to vacate Tony Alamo's conviction involving the sexual abuse of young girls.

December—Tony Alamo files objections to a federal magistrate judge's recommendations that a motion to vacate his convictions be denied.

2015

April—Farm Bureau Mutual Insurance Company of Arkansas files a request to declare that it has no responsibility to pay court judgments against

---

5. Lynn LaRowe, *Texarkana Gazette*, May 1, 2014.

the homeowner's policy of Sanford Carl White, a follower of Tony Alamo. Judgments are based on allegations that seventy-one-year-old White of Fouke, Arkansas, participated in the abuse of children under the direction of Alamo's ministry. The insurance company contends that the Whites lied on their application when promising that no one in the household had been arrested on a felony charge and that they would be the only residents.

2016

Former members continue to file civil suits against Alamo, their parents still remaining in the cult, and insurance companies for restitution of damages brought to them as children living in the cult.

Alamo's attorneys continue to oppose civil claims.

2017

Alamo's followers post a petition to US President Trump on the Internet for the release of Tony Alamo. Followers write open letters and testimonials in their pleas for his freedom.

May 2—Tony Alamo dies in a prison hospital in Butner, North Carolina. Until his death he continued to operate his church and businesses from federal prison. Followers vow to continue "winning the lost and preaching the full truth to the world as [Alamo] taught so well by example" (tony alamochristianministries.com).

May 7—Tony Alamo's ashes are deposited in a crypt in Memorial Park Cemetery in Tulsa, Oklahoma, where his wife Susan Alamo was put to rest years earlier.

Sources: *Times Record* (Fort Smith), *Texarkana Gazette*, TonyAlamoNews.com, Southern Poverty Law Center, KNWA (Northwest Arkansas NBC television affiliate), Associate Press, WXTV Delta (Mississippi Delta CBS television affiliate), WREG (Memphis CBS television affiliate), Arkansas News Bureau, Beliefnet.com, Arkansas court documents, *Arkansas Democratic Gazette*.

CRYPTS OF SUSAN ALAMO AND TONY ALAMO,
MEMORIAL PARK CEMETERY, TULSA, OKLAHOMA.

THE
CHILDREN

IN
THEIR
OWN
VOICES

CHAPTER THIRTY-TWO

Audrey

Sometimes when I talk, I go away. It gets vivid.

The most depressing, unhappy period of my life occurred when I was put into foster care. I was seventeen. It was a very hard time for me because I wasn't allowed to see or talk to my family and friends until a month later. I didn't eat for the first two days until my foster parents threatened to insert a feeding tube into me. I just sat in my room and listened to the song "Sound the Bugle" by Bryan Adams. The song is about a soldier who was wounded in battle and is too tired to continue fighting. The beginning words sing, "Sound the bugle now, play it just for me, as the seasons change I remember how I used to be." Another part of the song laments, "Now I can't go on. I can't even start. I've got nothing left—just an empty heart." Toward the end of the song the words change from the soldier giving up to having courage again. One of the last lines talks about a voice in the distance telling the singer to remember who you are and "if you lose yourself, your courage soon will follow." I took these words to heart. I had to realize that I wouldn't get anywhere if I stayed depressed and felt sorry for myself. I tried to make the best of my situation and to forget everything. I became a stronger person than I was before the raid. Everything happens for a reason.

I was born in the cult in Tampa, Florida. We later moved to Dallas,
Texas, where my brother was born, and then moved to a large pink house
in Fort Smith, Arkansas, that was owned by the church. I was about six
years old, and my parents and their four children lived all together. I remember that Christmas. All of us three girls had Dalmatian earrings. I
remember going to the park and having good times there. From there we
moved to Moffett, Oklahoma, and we were together as a family for only a
short while.

My dad was mostly gone on work assignments that Tony gave him. My
mother would leave and then return to the church again and again. When
that happened, we just stayed with friends. When my family was together,
my mom and dad fought a lot. My mom had a really hard life growing up.
She wasn't loved as a child. She probably could have been kinder to us. Dad
was very stern, very strict, and even now he frightens me. So we were in and
out of different homes. When she was thirteen, my oldest sister, Tatum,
moved into Tony's house in Fouke. I was so sad—I cried and cried for her.
Tony let us visit her at the church. When my next older sister turned sixteen, she married and eventually left the church after a few years. She had
four children, and three are still living with Jennifer Kolbek in the church.

The summer I turned twelve, Tony let all the girls who were celebrating their birthdays have a pool party. It was a fun, long day. By the time I
reached our home in Moffett, it was dark. One of the sisters walking with
me said, "Audrey, the office needs to talk to you." I grabbed the phone and
was told that my dad had been kicked out of the church. He had taken my
little brother and sister with him. I was given no reason. This shocked me.
I was only a few feet from home. What had happened? I thought my dad
was so good. What could he have done to get kicked out of the church? I
was totally alone. My oldest sister was living with Tony. I gave the phone
back to the sister, and she said I could get what I needed from home and
go to the sisters' dorm where all the single sisters who didn't have families lived. I went into my small house where someone had already started
packing things. There were boxes everywhere. It was a shock for me; I got
a few of my things and went to stay at the sisters' dorm.

The next day I heard one of the sisters talking on the phone. She said that Tony wanted to know if I wanted to go with my dad. I told her no. I didn't want to leave the church. I knew what people said about those who left the church. I didn't want to be a backslider. I stayed by myself doing what I was supposed to do. A few weeks later, someone moved all the stuff out of my house to the warehouse without letting me know. They took a lot of things that were precious to me. I was pretty upset about that. A sister saw that I was alone and wanted to take me in, so I moved in with her. I stayed with her for a few months until my dad was allowed back in the church. I was ecstatic that my dad came back and moved to live with him, my brother, and my sister in Texarkana.

The instability of our family continued, though. My dad was again told to leave the church. When he returned to Fouke, I stayed with him again. Less than a year later I moved into Tony's house, where my oldest sister still lived. My younger sister, Charlene, resided there, but when Tony accused her of being mean to his daughter, Bella, she was moved to The House of Scorn. My little sister was not allowed to be anywhere near Bella. When Bella was outside, Charlene had to go inside. My oldest sister moved to The House of Scorn to watch over Charlene. She also worked in the office, so when needed, I went over to the green house to watch Charlene.

Secrecy always blanketed the church. There were so many rules and inconsistencies that we never knew when we were going to get into trouble. And we never knew who was watching to report a misstep. Girls couldn't hold baby boys—not even a nephew. No one could drive a vehicle without a rider. We had to go to church every night and twice on Sundays. Females couldn't wear tight clothes or anything low. No one could wear makeup until they were fourteen years old. But when a girl began menstruation, she was ready to be a wife.

When we broke rules, the consequences were severe, and being put on a fast was a common punishment. When I was eleven years old, I was living in Fort Smith. Our class had a prayer room. We weren't allowed to go into the prayer room wearing shoes, capris, or shorts. Our bodies had to be covered. Six of us girls were wearing capris, so our teacher told us to sit outside the prayer room door to pray. We prayed for about an hour. A little bit later when we went back to our classroom, we were told that our teacher reported to Tony that we hadn't gone into the prayer room to pray. When we heard this news, we were confused, because our teacher had told us not to go into the prayer room, and we did pray outside where she instructed us to be. We were all put on a four-day fast. We could only drink lemon water.

When I got home, my parents had already learned that I got into trouble at school. That evening as I was helping my mom prepare dinner, my father came in and told me that it wasn't a good idea to be in the kitchen because I might get tempted to eat the food. I remember sneaking a little piece of chicken into my mouth. I felt guilty. As the days went on, I would secretly sneak bits of food. But I felt guilty, and I feared God would know. We just sat on the stairs when food came. On the fourth day at the exact hour when we had been put on the fast, we weren't supposed to appear eager to want food. I remember eating spaghetti that night. One of my friends threw up because her stomach couldn't manage since she had been on the fast. We didn't know until we saw the bathroom floor the next day. She had been too scared to tell that she had gotten sick.

We were not allowed to cry for someone who was being disciplined. If we did, they would ask, "Do you want to be next?" So we would cry silently. When Tony hit us, we would not dare cry. It was different with the parents. I remember a time when he hit my little sister and she just stood there. And she was really little. If we started crying, then he would just feed off of it and threaten us with other punishments. Tony had different styles. To discipline girls and the sisters living in his house, he typically hit them with his hand. With his wives he would use something to throw at them in front of us. When he hit the other girls and me, he used his fist, and then he would kick us in the shins.

On the day John Kolbek beat Paige, we were working in the warehouse. We saw Jennifer Kolbek and another sister dragging Paige to the back of the room where there was a door that entered a bigger space in the warehouse. Paige got scared and said that she had to use the bathroom. She stayed in there for a long time. They were knocking on the door and telling her that she needed to come out. And then she said that she wanted to call her mom. Her mom was not in the church. They said that she could call her later. They got her out of the bathroom and with one sister on each side, struggled to pull her to the back room. When Paige saw John standing there, she knew she was going to get beaten by John and not Jennifer. So she sat on the floor. And then I remember Jennifer just turning her head as John came rushing through the other room. He said, "Do you want to come with me? Do you want to come with me?" He grabbed Paige by her feet, and she was screaming the whole time. And then we heard her scream. And of course we all were crying, and Victoria, Paige's little sister, was really upset, saying that she wanted to go home or she wanted to leave. When they dragged Paige away, they slammed the door, and we could not see in the room. But we could hear her screams all the way up in our other room.

I don't know how long the beating lasted, but it was probably a good twenty minutes. It seemed like she was back there for a long time. I remember her walking out: her face was pale, and she didn't say one word. She walked into the next room. She had her clothes on. We were not really close to her, but I did not see any blood. She had to go back to work. They were making rhinestone jackets in the other room. So she went into the other room and continued working. I was in the mailroom part. I remember her later saying that her bruise was huge on her leg. I could just imagine how huge it was.

Our daily schedule followed a regular routine. Morning school or chores started at 8:00 a.m. We went to school—boys and girls separately. Tony pulled girls—some at the early age of eight or nine—out of school to live in his house, where they would mingle and become a little community among themselves.

We girls were competitive at school. We didn't learn math, but our reading lessons were good. Sisters taught school, and the quality of our education depended on who our friends and parents were. Favoritism definitely existed. Overall, kids whose mothers were gone were left more vulnerable to being picked on and punished. We ate our meals separately from the boys. We had recess, and I loved playing kickball in front of the church. We played hide and go seek, soccer, volleyball, and Bible charades. At one point a rule was passed that we couldn't touch each other when we were playing, so we would use a toy to touch each other for tag. Just one of many crazy rules. Mostly we girls got along. We were together. It was traumatic when we all got taken away, because that was all we knew.

We attended church service every night. On Sunday we went twice. I loved singing in the church choir, and we also had practice times. That was the only time we were actually doing something with boys. Still, we weren't allowed to look at them or talk to them.

We all had assigned jobs. Girls would help in the kitchen, preparing meals and also putting together meals for people who weren't able to come to dinner. Sometimes I could feel a lot of tension among the younger sisters working in the kitchen. We worked in warehouses to sort and box up donated goods for resale. These were all kinds of things, including candy, clothing, toys, canned foods, and juices. We had to remove price tags, expiration dates on foods, and organize the goods on big wooden pallets. Bedding was commonly donated. We used sticky tape to remove hair and brushed pillows and mattresses to look like new. It was definitely hard labor in dark, dirty warehouses. We started working when we were as young as seven.

We also collated the literature that Tony printed and went on tracting trips to spread the word of God. On these trips we got very little sleep and often became sick and dehydrated while putting pamphlets on cars in parking lots. Sometimes we younger girls had to sleep on chairs in the hotel rooms with limited space. It was exhausting work but could be fun depending on the sisters leading the crew. We had to distribute thousands of tracts on these ventures.

Other jobs included working in the mailroom packing boxes of literature and recordings sent to people throughout the world. We sent boxes to Africa, South America, Asia, and many other places. I remember a time working here when a sister refused to take me to the bathroom because mailing Tony's literature was more important.

Tony recorded his messages for everyone to hear. We listened to them in church and at home. We sent them to people the world over. He always had some tapes that needed to be redone, and one of our jobs was to break his bad tapes in half and burn them in the backyard. I still have a scar from cutting myself on the sharp edge of a broken CD. Other work included babysitting, cleaning the church, weeding the properties, and making rhinestone jackets that Tony sold for thousands of dollars.

When we turned ten, we were given more responsibilities. I remember being excited—it meant that I was growing up. This was our life, what I wanted to do when I grew up. Get married and have babies, do God's work. I never dreamed of actually leaving Tony's church, never dreamed of ever going to college, never imagined joining the military.

When I went to my first public school, I once asked, "Who is Rihanna?" And the other students said, "Oh my gosh, have you lived under a rock?" So I said, "Well, I listen to Elton John." Oh my goodness! I still don't know how people could like me. I was just different. I didn't know what "boobies" or "booty" or anything meant. I did not know any music when I got out. I didn't know any of the new artists—all the famous people and all that stuff. I had never been to a movie theatre until I went to see *High School Musical 3*. I went with my counselor from Hope, Arkansas. She had blond, curly hair. She wore glasses. I sneaked a piece of pizza because I did not want people to see me and think I had gone over to the "other side."

I remember the first time my foster parents bought me gum. I felt so big getting my own pack of gum. I remember the first time I went to church and it was not the cult. It was one of those churches where they speak in tongues, and the pastor was saying some things that disturbed me. I thought, "I am going to go talk to him," but I didn't. My foster parents said that it might have been too early to send me to church. We thought we knew the Bible and that no one else really knew it. Then when we went to court, and I was talking with others, I started to realize that everything we had been taught was a lie. It was really shocking. The cult was all that we ever knew. We thought that everything else was evil. My world turned upside down.

Today, the little things still get to me. I'm in Walmart getting my oil changed. It's funny. I never thought I would be in Walmart with my own car getting oil changed. This was not possible in our world. Moving forward with our lives is a huge accomplishment.

When I see people that are kind of different, I look after them and make sure that they are okay, because you never know what someone has been through. It is hard to imagine that parents can actually watch their children get beaten and bloodied and then tell that child to thank the man who beat them. I am still learning, and sometimes I sound mature, and then other times I am like a child still trying to figure out how everything is supposed to be. I feel I am very behind in some things and far ahead in others.

I'm still nervous about telling people about my past. There are people I care about, and I want them to know about me. And I have told a lot of my friends, and they respect me, and we are still just as close as ever. But I'm not sure how some people will react. I'm still processing my past, and I'm still learning. Sometimes it can be pretty overwhelming. I grew up with one mindset, then was placed into a world with totally new ways of being. And then I served in the army, where I encountered yet another cultural shift.

Trusting people is very difficult for me. I always have my guard up, and I can't be just totally vulnerable. But everything is making me stronger. And I am steadily learning that I deserve what I accomplish.

CHAPTER THIRTY-THREE

Irene

When the judge spoke, I remember putting my head in my hands. I was inconsolable at that point. I saw my parents on the other side of the room across from me. I had been certain that they would take me home. They had said, "Yes, we're going to get you back." I had so much faith in them and in God and in Tony. My ears began to ring, and the air was sucked out of me. I collapsed into myself.

"Why can't she come home if we put her in a private Christian school, and she works and puts her money in her own savings account?" my mom protested. "Tony is in prison for the rest of his life, and he is not allowed to run anything now."

"Because you are still financially dependent on Tony, who is a registered sex offender." The blow comes like a stinging smack in the face from the DHS prosecuting attorney. I wish she hadn't said it even though it's true. The moment the words are spoken, I can see the pent-up hurt that my mom feels displayed on her face. And I feel the pain she feels. I know the dismay and agonizing pain of betrayal as someone you hardly know so easily points out the lifelong mistake that you were just barely aware that you made. The betrayed feeling is not directed toward the stranger but toward yourself, your life, and in this case, God's prophet, Tony Alamo. It is the feeling that tells you what he does is wrong, but you don't believe it, because you have always believed everything he told you. I pull my legs up onto my chair and lean on my dad's shoulder, wondering if he will always be there to hold me and soothe my nerves. I am a foster child. I am used to conflict.

I don't know if I ever really asked my mother about her feelings that day. I don't even know if she asked for me after that. I think it may have been harder after the second raid because then both of her babies were gone, and she had nobody. Her boys weren't able to speak to her. They were cut off from her life. And then she lost her two babies. All she had were my sisters Kay and Avril, and they were married. She lost them all in two months. I can't remember exactly what she said, but she told me that every day was filled with despair.

Then again, I think she should have left and tried to get us back right away. It's sad that they had faith in Tony. Tony told them, "Don't leave because the Lord's going to bring your children back to us." And all he did was make them lose all their young people. People commented how sad it was for these mothers to lose their young children. And I'm thinking it is sad because some of them were really great mothers, and some of the children were still just babies. My mom was saying, "It's so horrible." Yeah, it is, but mom—you shouldn't have listened to Tony. You should have gone with your motherly instinct and saved your children.

On the night of the raid we slept on iron cots in the National Guard armory. The next day word spread that we were going to go to foster homes. We all hoped they wouldn't be bad foster homes. We just thought that if we were not good children, then they would not take care of us. That was scary. At this point, my adventuresome spirit probably died down a little, because I was ready to go home. We learned that they would split up all the kids. We couldn't believe it. That day they took us to the CASA (Court Appointed Special Advocates) house where they conducted individual interviews with each of us. They asked me questions that put me on the spot. I didn't know how to answer them. I didn't want to make the church look bad. I didn't want to get in trouble with Tony. We had been taught that what happens in Tony's house stays in his house. Once I was kicked out of his house for accidentally saying something that the outside world could use against him. Tony had taught us that he was married to all his wives in God's eyes. He based that on the Biblical story of Isaac, who took his wife into the tent and consummated their marriage; they were married in God's eyes. I didn't know that we weren't supposed to say this. They asked us so many questions that day.

I was placed with a family that lived out in the country. They were nice, sweet people. They had four little foster children between the ages of three and six. The children had to be on the school bus at 6:00 a.m., because it took an hour to get anywhere. You could walk outside at night and see the entire galaxy, but I like to be around people. I felt a little lonely. Tony had told us that we would be raided one day, and oddly enough, my sense of adventure was piqued by the thought. I had always wanted to go to public school. I hoped that if we were raided, it would happen before I turned 18. Now at age sixteen I had a whole life ahead of me. I wanted to be in a city, in the thick of things.

One day when the DHS caseworker took me to court, I asked if I could go somewhere else to live. These people were wonderful, but I just wanted to be around the girls. I wanted to be around someone I knew. Up to this point, we weren't allowed to hear about or talk to each other. We were becoming accustomed to foster care, and none of us tried to run away. As luck would have it, Victoria was also at court that day, and her foster mother asked if I could spend a few days with them. We became one happy family.

I think of my life in two parts: birth to age sixteen and life after the raid. I need to come to terms with my past to figure out who I really am apart from anyone else. There is really no room for the positives until I let go of the negatives. As a child, I remember hearing the song "Born Free." I think it was featured in a National Geographic film that I saw when I was young before our TV was confiscated. The tune has stuck with me all these years, but I did not remember all the words. On Facebook a girl that I grew up with recently posted a link to this song saying that it always made her cry. I replied that it made me cry too and I never understood why. Listening to it now, it's so ironic that we both were drawn to the same song. Maybe our tears were escaping because somewhere deep inside we knew we weren't free.

Just like all the kids, I worked at a lot of different jobs. I spent many hours at a little resale shop Tony owned in Texarkana called Junkin' For Joy. We used to get a lot of clothes donated from Walmart, Cato, Ralph Lauren, Nautica, Guess, and Gap. Those clothes were sometimes just out of season, returns, or damaged goods. I spent many hours in Tony's backyard (he had a large cinder block building used for storage) sorting out what clothes could be used by us church members, what could be sold at the shop, and what needed to be tossed out. Those who donated clothes intended them for charity, not to be sold for profit. But Tony had a thriving business selling donations of all kinds. I hated doing this work. Even though I could pick clothes for myself, the store was dirty and customers weren't friendly.

I also worked in the kitchen for lengthy periods. I helped prepare food, washed dishes, and cleaned. The sisters supervised kitchen work, and I had little interaction there with other kids. We weren't allowed much time to play.

I spent some time working in what we called the tape department. This was the place where we made hundreds of copies of cassette tapes or CDs containing Tony's messages and sent them all over the world to people who requested to be on our mailing list.

At the age of seven I moved into Tony's house where several other young girls lived. Tony enforced strict cleaning schedules in his house, and housework was broken down and divided among the girls. With no purposeful explanation, we were to complete our assigned tasks one to three times each day, depending on the task. For example, another girl and I cleaned all the bathrooms in the house twice each day. At first there were five bathrooms, and later Tony expanded these to nine. If we didn't do our jobs perfectly— if a single thing was out of place—we were forced to fast for a day or two.

One summer day Tony decided that there were too many weeds growing on the properties. He made a rule that everyone over a certain age, ten to my best recollection, had to be pulling weeds at 7:00 a.m. Tony made sure that everyone was pulling weeds. Those who weren't had to fast for a day.

We girls also had to clean the sanctuary once a week. Vacuuming the huge room with pews would have been impossible without the help of the other girls. When we were working together, we almost always found ways to have fun.

We worked in warehouses as well. Donated goods needed to be sorted. I remember sorting socks that were mismatched. We rubbed expiration dates off of food cans with acetone. One year we had little porcelain dolls, each with a birthstone for the month, and we had hundreds of Little Mermaid and Barbie dolls. We sorted through them all and made sure the boxes were the rigid ones.

One of the jobs I had just before the raid was responding to ministry email. We got emails from Africa and all over the world asking for Tony's materials, and we would have to send the requests for literature or recordings to each department. People also emailed asking for charity items such as televisions, clothing, or other items. We sent our refusals directly to the petitioners.

Tony was quick to penalize us with beatings, fasts, removing privileges such as swimming, and "house arrest" to segregate us from friends. I cannot count the number of times I was sent to The House of Scorn, a holding place for girls and sisters who offended him. We girls also saw Tony abuse his wives on a regular basis. He yelled, threw things at them, chased them through the house, and hit and punched them. When he wasn't angry with them, I'd watch him sit in his cushioned office chair while his wives (some my age in their early teens, my friends, and even my own sister) rubbed him down. It was disgusting to watch, but an everyday occurrence, from the first time I moved into his house (age seven) until the day I last saw him (age fifteen).

We really didn't have a sense of well-being. We all were on edge. At any given moment, I could be on report, and it could be something minimal like spilling water on the floor and not wiping it up or something big like telling a lie. If you hear that you're on report, you try to figure out why if you don't know. "What did I do? What did I do?" You don't want to talk to anyone about it, because if you were wrong, then you would be adding more fuel to the fire. You would try to forget about it. Then a few days later you're told, "Tony's on the phone for you," and your stomach would drop.

I am still affected with these feelings. I can hear messages like "Tony's on the phone, you're in trouble, or he wants to see you." I was always living on the edge with that fear of getting a beating.

I do have happy memories, too. I loved summer activities, swimming, and picnics. Some really fun times for us happened when I lived in Texarkana. Tony sometimes gave families monthly allowances called "bucks." We could save that money and use it for things that weren't banned. At some point Tony let us go on field trips, and I loved going to Magic Springs, a theme park. We went to the zoo and the county fair. These events were huge deals because we would go with the kids from Fort Smith, too. They gave us something to look forward to. In fact, I went to the fair three days before the raid. At the time when my family lived in Fort Smith, everyone had a little more freedom. My family took my sister's mother-in-law to a hospital in New Orleans, and while we were there we went to the aquarium. Tony probably never even knew about it because we went there to see a doctor. That was my first trip going to a place like that. I was aware of the people on the outside, and they scared me. I felt different.

I remember sometimes I would feel happy or excited, like looking forward to going to the fair or just having a good time with friends. Almost every time, someone would tell us we shouldn't be happy because Tony said we needed to focus on praying that we had enough funds to carry out his mission and to be on guard for the devil lurking about and trying to take over the world. Sensing when we felt good about how we were doing, Tony would deliver a very depressing message and say that we were wrongfully happy when there was so much evil going on. His point was to keep us miserable and fearful. Happiness leads to self-confidence, which leads to individual questioning, and that inevitably could lead to Tony's demise. He truly was a smart guy.

Tony's system kept us full of fear and low self-esteem. I believe this is where the figure of Jesus comes in, a perfect God-being who would share His peace and perfection with everyone. Tony used to quote Jesus as saying, "Be ye perfect as I am perfect." To make us think that Christ's perfection was attainable to us sinful humans, Tony knew he would have to show us a modern-day saint who had achieved such perfection. He set himself as the example. Since he put himself in such a position of power, this meant that he also had the power to tell us what we were doing wrong in order to teach us which path to take. Tony set himself as a perfect model (Jesus) for us to follow so that we could hope to become like Jesus. The catch was that Tony never let any of us attain our goal. He degraded us and let us wallow in misery and never forget our mistakes as a way to keep us unfulfilled. By never meeting our goals, we always "needed" him to show us the way. He crippled us and made himself our crutch. We were all too scared to see it.

When you're under the discipline of a sociopath, there is no such thing as a simple right or wrong answer. There isn't even an "almost right" answer. If what you say doesn't line up one hundred percent with what the sociopath wants to hear, then you are not just wrong. Ninety-five percent of the time you are in for a random punishment that he sees fit. In my personal experience, it ranged from losing driving privileges to being starved for days on end or even beaten with a two-by-four. If you're lucky to avoid punishment (about five percent of the time), you will be corrected and told not to contradict or question the said sociopath.

There are several things that can happen to victims of such abuse. Obviously they will not be too confident after being repeatedly told that they are wrong. In severe cases, victims no longer know how to think for themselves. The sociopath can effectively drive his or her own opinions on another through fear and over time so that the victims don't even realize they are no longer thinking for themselves and can only regurgitate the despicable thoughts that have been hardwired into them through repeated degradation.

Another result of this kind of abuse is that even when a victim has been separated from such a situation for a significant amount of time, some self-preservation behaviors will stick around for the long haul. These tend to be pretty difficult to get rid of, depending on the degree of abuse one has suffered. Speaking from my own experience, after living dangerously close to a sociopath who was always changing his words to suit his own benefit, and realizing there was almost never a correct answer for him, I learned how to float by being invisible. The only time I was in the spotlight was when someone else brought me into it. I tried to stay out of trouble. Even though I knew that I could earn "brownie points" by telling my friends' dirty secrets, I chose not to. I knew I could become a target for revenge. This invisible strategy of mine worked fairly well in the world of the sociopath. I only got beaten about twenty times and starved for no more than three days at a time. (Trust me, that wasn't too bad.) But now I am in the real world, and being invisible doesn't work quite so well.

In my new life, my real life, the one that is free of sociopaths, I have a tendency to make a special effort to be out of trouble. It is not something I do on purpose or because I do not want to take responsibility for my actions. I am coming to realize that my problem is in the anticipation of what the consequences for my actions will be. In my case, most of my life experiences have conditioned me to feel fear. I'm realizing that in the real world, while there are consequences to be avoided, like getting fired or disappointing a parent, these consequences need not be feared. My problem is that before I think rationally about the possible consequences of my actions, I automatically start to fear the outcome, whatever it may be, which in turn causes me to avoid getting involved.

An example of this illogical thought and conditioned response follows: When I was 18 years old, in high school and living with my foster parents, I found out I was pregnant. They didn't even know that I was sexually active, and now I was going to have to drop two bombs on them. I was terrified and, of course, decided not to tell them for as long as I could. Eventually someone talked my foster mom into getting us girls birth control as a precaution. Not until we were halfway to the hospital, I realized she was about to find out the truth when I told her I already knew I was pregnant. I was so scared. I had no idea how she would react, but I knew that I should brace for the storm that I was sure would come. But the storm never did come. She was disappointed, yes, but she didn't call me a slut or a whore. She simply sat incredulously and demanded that I pee on a stick for her. I asked her if she was angry, and she replied that what was done was done, and there was no use in being angry about something that she couldn't change. She said that having a baby at my age would be enough trouble for me, and that she may as well provide the emotional support that she knew I would need. I was shocked and in awe. Even though what she said made perfect sense to me, I couldn't believe she had said that. It seemed too good to be true—my impending fear was completely pointless.

In reflection, that day was the first memorable lesson I had in overcoming my fear. At the time I didn't know where my fear was coming from or realize that if I thought rationally about my possible consequences, the weight of the fear that I carried would drop considerably. I know I have many other psychological issues caused by my sociopath ex-"prophet." But now I'm always trying to spot the cause and effect of what happened then and what I do now and how to solve the difference. They always say that the first step to improvement is acknowledgement, so I guess I'm on the right track.

During the days in court I remember turning to Victoria and asking, "What if everything Tony taught us is a lie?" It was unthinkable. Everything we believed was a lie? How could that possibly be? The very idea was too much to bear. So I got up every morning and engaged in the day's activities without really thinking about it. Every now and then I felt a kind of foreboding, a sense that something too overwhelming was lurking nearby.

For a while, I straddled a ledge between this new life and the one I had always known. I kept quiet. I was protecting my family. I couldn't accept that Tony was wrong because I was afraid to. I was just kind of stuck. During the trial, the facts started to reveal some truth. And on that final day, Tony was convicted on all ten counts. He was going to prison for 175 years. In one moment, all that I knew was gone. He was a false prophet. If he was a false prophet, then everything he told me was a lie. If everything he told me was a lie, then where was God? What about our sacrifices? What about our rules? What about the wives? What about the beatings? With one thought came another and then another, an avalanche of thoughts mixed with incredulity, fear, and grief.

I started talking to my foster mother, Ruth. I had to explore the possibilities. I had to deal with this revelation, to figure out where to go from here. Everything I had learned so obediently was false? What did that mean about me? Who am I? I remember being so relieved to go to sleep, and though my nights were plagued with vivid dreams of terror, I was able to sleep. And in the first brief seconds of opening my eyes, I would have that clear-headed emptiness before thoughts came rushing forward again to bring me to this impossible reality. At times I didn't think I could stand the pain and anguish. But it was impossible for me to turn away from the truth.

I couldn't talk to my parents about this because I was afraid that they would cut me off as they did my brothers who had left the church. I loved them. I walked that fine line and told myself to act a certain way around my family. In doing that, I began to act differently on the outside from how I felt on the inside. Eventually I did tell my parents that I couldn't believe anything they would tell me. I love my mom, but that doesn't mean she is right. For the first time, I was considering that everything—or at least ninety percent of what I had known—was untrue. I thought that maybe I should just discount everything that I had learned in the cult, but I realize that some of what I learned there was true.

I was born a 1990s child, but my experience of the outside world began in 2008. Sometimes I'm embarrassed by what I don't know. So many times I've wished that my family had been kicked out of the church when I was little. When I was five years old, we lived in a house in Fort Smith. So many times I've wished that we had stayed there on our own. But when I was eight, Tony told us to move back to the compound, and we went back. I imagine what it would have been like to be a normal family. We all would have been tight knit, and I would have gone to school and made friends from my childhood and wouldn't have had to split up with them and start over. I never felt that I was good enough for my family. I always wanted to be as special as my sister, Avril. Tony picked her to be his wife.

I worried about my brothers who left. I had mini-funerals for them in my head, trying to close off the hurt I felt. When Frank left, I knew that was hard for my parents, because they had lost two boys already. My mom said, "Irene, please don't ever leave. That would just break my heart. I just couldn't take it." I promised that I wouldn't leave. At the time I didn't have that kind of courage. I couldn't imagine where I would go. I didn't ever want to leave, but I did want something to happen to me. I wanted to explore, to have an adventure. When Tony warned us about the raids, I would think, "I want to see what happens. I hope I'm here when that happens."

Sometimes I think that if I had died in the cult, no one would know that I existed. We didn't have birth certificates. People never stayed in one place. Families broke apart, and we never knew what really happened to those who left. Tony denigrated them and used them as examples of the fate that awaited any of us who left the cult. I have lost half of my family. But I am different because of what I experienced growing up, and I like being different. I'm coming to terms with my past.

Trying to get used to the real world is an exhilarating experience. It's scary yet exciting. You don't really know what to expect. Probably the most important thing a person in this transition can have is someone (or even better, a few people) who understands that while you were raised in the same country and possibly state as they were, you really aren't from the same place at all. In all the places I have lived during my life in the cult (from birth until I was sixteen years old), I never had been to a movie theater, gone bowling, attended one of the community churches, or stepped foot in a public school. My life was totally different, and to adjust to the real world comfortably, it is important to have a support system of people who make you comfortable with being different, people who understand you aren't weird, just sort of foreign. My foster family was a tour guide through the real world for me, showing me the good, bad, and ugly, but most importantly they showed me what was real.

I can't imagine all the psychological issues we are experiencing without even realizing it. I feel that we only know a fraction of what happened and how it affected our lives. I suppose I will spend the rest of my life decoding those formative years so that I may truly understand, and that will be my journey.

CHAPTER
THIRTY-FOUR

Victoria

It felt worse than being an orphan, having parents who couldn't take care of me. The drive was taking forever, and each mile took me further away from my home—my reality. I looked out the window and tried to ignore the caseworker's constant chattering. I didn't want to talk. The past two days had been overwhelming. I didn't know if I would ever see my family and friends again. In a matter of minutes, my entire life had been turned upside down. I'd been asked so many questions that I didn't care if I ever spoke again.

The chattering suddenly stopped. I peeked over the car seat and realized the caseworker was asking me a question. On a normal day, I would have been polite and asked her to repeat her question, but this was not a normal day. I felt like screaming at her for ruining my life. Instead, I quietly whispered, "I don't want to talk." I turned back to face the window and watched the world blur by.

I felt unwanted and tossed aside. Everyone who was supposed to take care of me had betrayed me. Tonight I would be in a home with people I'd never met. I'd sleep in a different bed. What if this family didn't like me? I missed home. Even though home wasn't the best, at least it was something familiar. Being thrust into the great unknown with absolutely nothing of my past life was more terrifying than I could have ever imagined. The strong urge to cry nearly knocked me over, but I bit my lip to hold back the flood.

I was so deep in thought that I jumped when I realized the car had stopped. Grabbing my small bag with pajamas and toiletries I got out of the car and followed the caseworker up the pathway to the house. My heart was pounding and my mind racing. The door opened almost at the same time the caseworker rang the bell. I held my breath, cringing at the thought of another awful parent. Without hesitation the woman opened her arms and said, "Victoria, it's good to finally meet you." She clasped me in a firm, warm hug.

After a moment I looked up and was surprised to be greeted by a petite woman with fiery red hair, compassionate blue eyes, and a radiant smile. She introduced herself as Ruth, my foster mother. I barely smiled a response, but my frayed nerves settled some. We went into the house, and the two women talked for a bit. Ruth talked to me for a little while, but I don't really remember what she said. All I could think was that maybe I was finally home.

I have been in a lot of different places that were called home.

I was born in Fort Smith, Arkansas, where I lived with my mother, Quinn; father, Glen; big sister, Paige; and little brother, Ian. From there the family moved to Los Angeles, and my little brother Stefan was born. Quinn, with baby, left the church and moved to Vermont. Then all the kids lived with Quinn in Vermont until Glen took us back to California. After that, Glen moved us to Muldrow, Oklahoma. As Tony assigned Glen to jobs that took him out of state for long periods of time, we were farmed out to various sisters for care. I really liked the time we spent with Sonia and her kids. The kids with absent parents tended to be easier targets for hard labor and punishments. It wasn't that the other kids were spared the rod, but those with no parents had no buffer. Sometimes I sensed that we were a bother to sisters who already had their own children to handle. We were singled out as troublemakers.

Life became more difficult as time went on, and when we moved to Fouke, the rules were especially rigid. We were taught that our mother was a whore and a drug addict because she left the church. We learned to hate her. Our family was torn apart by Tony Alamo. But some good memories of happy times with our dad before the move to Fouke stayed with me. I knew that the outside world wasn't completely bad. I saw some clues just in the way my dad used to talk about his own childhood.

In Fouke my sister, Paige, and I lived in Tony's house. Paige was often in trouble with Tony and spent time living in The House of Scorn with the other banished girls. Sometimes I went with her so that she could take care of me. Paige was as close to a mother as I knew.

Living in Tony's house came with privileges. We could order food from restaurants, watch movies or TV, and had access to the Internet. There was always tension in Tony's house, though. The sisters sometimes resented having to take care of us girls who didn't have our mothers in the house. Tony's two boys lived there, and they were always blaming things on us. Tony expected us to stay in the house, and the shades and heavy draperies on the windows kept us hidden. I worked in Tony's office and was responsible for keeping track of behavior reports. Sometimes there were so many that Tony wanted us to show him only the most serious. Other times he personally wanted to handle every one.

Beginning when I was thirteen, older men in the church began asking Tony if they could marry me. Tony always declined with a remark that suggested he was saving me. Other times Tony confused me with one of his wives. He made suggestive comments about my figure and wanted me to wear tight-fitting clothes. I believe that he was saving me to be his bride. Fortunately, the raid occurred before he acted on that.

Like all the kids, I worked. I would go out with a group to hand out flyers to raise money for the church. We would do this from very early in the morning to late in the night in bad downtown areas and often in extreme weather conditions. We were taught to evade the police and had to run sometimes to get away from them. I cleaned the cafeteria, prepared food, took care of children my same age and younger, weeded gardens, and cleaned bathrooms, the church sanctuary, and many other rooms throughout the property.

I also worked in the warehouse, where I was required to prepare merchandise to be sold. This ranged from removing expiration dates from items with acetone (which resulted in my fingers becoming blistered) to sorting pallets of candy into specific boxes. We were also required to sort through clothing, and many items that came through the warehouse were quite unsanitary. We were not allowed more than a few small breaks and were required to be on task the entire time. We also went through the stock of items to retrieve things for church members. These items ranged from personal hygiene products to food items. The warehouse was not kept clean and put us in an extremely dirty environment.

The most fun place to work in my opinion was the rhinestone room. Tony Alamo had a line of denim jackets that were extremely popular. He sold them in stores and personalized some for stars and well-known public figures. The jackets were big-ticket items and sold as quickly as we could make them. I was always envious of the older girls who got to work in the rhinestone room.

Punishment was a regular part of life. When I was ten years old, I was put on a fast for seven days. Beatings were the most common and frequent form of punishment that I suffered. There was always a paddle, belt, or switch involved, and punching and slapping were not uncommon. Humiliation was always part of the process. Such punishments began when I was born, starting out with my being paddled with a brush to being beaten with a two-by-four wooden board. Holes were drilled in the board to allow for bigger impact.

Given all that we endured, we were happy kids. Our lives were normal to us. We found the simplest ways to have fun. We were so close. We ate well, learned, and excelled in school. As often as Tony told us we were ugly pigs and humiliated us, we still found ways to be happy. I think that says something important about the human spirit. We've been through a lot, so we have been able to contain a lot.

I have something that I carry with me everywhere I go. It never goes away. It is always on my mind, be it on an unconscious or conscious level. When I think about it, I feel as if my mind is closing in on itself, and I am paralyzed. I avoid going to that dark place in my mind, but sometimes I can't avoid it. After all, these experiences did happen, and I will always remember. You might wonder why I continue to carry this weight. Well, mostly because it is impossible not to, and no one can run away from their past experiences. They must learn to live with them.

Most people are not even aware that I bear such a heavy burden because I plaster on a smile and pretend everything is okay. It can still hurt. Though I have gotten past the hard part, the pain and memories are still there. And the culprit for placing this thing I carry on my shoulders? Well, that's a long story. It is the stuff that comes from living in an abusive environment and prison-like life. It's watching my friends get hurt and being forever afraid that I would be next. I came through the worst, and I came out strong. I'm pretty sure that everything's not all bad. I am learning to love and to accept the support of people who show me that I am lovable and can love.

It took me a long time to trust. People need to do a lot to earn my trust. Even now I don't talk to just anybody. I waited a long time before I was willing to talk. I want people to know that I am not a victim. I am a person who can do anything I set my mind to. I'm very goal-oriented, and I'm excited about life and all the opportunities we have to embrace a new and different day.

On the doorstep of my new home that day, I was afraid of the unknown. That isn't all I felt, though. I also felt a thrill. At the moment I was so overwhelmed that I didn't give it much notice. But as time went on, I realized that I was thrilled at the prospect of a new life and a chance to start over. Losing everything that had defined me and being thrust into a new environment gave me a different outlook on life. I was given a blank canvas and began to paint myself as the person I am today. The image is getting clearer, but I know it will never be truly done. That's the journey. My message is about hope and believing in myself. I'm strong because of my past. I embrace that. Where we come from isn't as relevant as what we do with who we are.

CHAPTER
THIRTY-FIVE

Ian

It was March 2013, five years after the raid and four years since Tony's sentencing. I stood at the edge of the church property in Fort Smith. It appeared to be deserted, but I knew better. I quickly walked through the barbed-wire gates and turned into the first building on my right. Though it was pitch dark, the familiar smell and echoing sound told me this was the gym. I nearly tripped on a basketball. I picked it up, thinking, "Wow! This is my ball! I played here!" Turning it over in my hands, I realized it wasn't my ball at all. I had written my name on the ball I used, and this was not it.

Leaving the gym, I walked into the sanctuary, and memories flooded my mind. I went up to the stage, and there my eyes were drawn to my dad's guitar. It was right there on a chair. I picked it up and strummed a note. It was in perfect tune. I knew my dad was there. In the hall, a brother intercepted me. I greeted him with a handshake and my name. He knew who I was, of course, and flipped out a phone to call my father. Grabbing the phone from his hands, I closed it saying, "Oh, don't call him. I want to surprise him." I got in the car to drive to the apartment complex where I knew I would find my dad. I also knew that he would get a warning call from the brother.

Just a few blocks away I spotted a group of about ten brothers standing in the parking lot of the apartments where my dad lived. I noticed John Kolbek's son among them. I got out, shook a few hands, and responded to a few nods. They were careful, and so was I. I think they probably thought that I had decided to return to the church. My dad emerged from an apartment. We greeted each other with nods. He motioned for me to follow him into his apartment. I met more men inside.

This was the moment I had pictured ever since the raid. I never doubted that my dad loved us. I believed he would leave the church to get his children back. But he did not attempt to do that, which left me angry and confused. I needed to hear his reasoning. I asked him why he never tried to get us back. He spouted Bible passages to me and assured me that I was on the devil's track. He called me a backslider, reprobate, blasphemer, and bastard. He said since I was living outside the church I was no longer a son to him.

I shouted through my tears, "Dad, you were my hero. All this time I have thought you would come for me. I thought your children were the most important part of your life. No one has ever replaced you. Now you are gone for good. I'm done. Now I'm going to be my own hero. Tony misled you. Now you mislead others. I believed in you. You aren't the man I thought you were."

Now I know my dad doesn't care about me at all. I always believed that he would come after us to bring us back. Other parents did that. If they promised to leave the cult, they could get their kids back. I didn't understand why my dad didn't do that.

I defended Tony Alamo in the courtroom because I was defending my dad. Now I have no respect for my dad. He had the option to take back his kids if he would just get a job outside the church. But he wouldn't do it. Tony told him not to, and he didn't. He could have kept his family together. The court literally gave him an opportunity that he didn't deserve to have his kids, and he blew it off. How could he do that to me when I raised my shield and stood under it by myself for years as a child, and he wasn't there to defend me? The dude should feel awful. I wanted to be the one to break his heart and for him to take that heartbreak to his grave. He should know that he had the perfect opportunity to save me from pain, and he didn't. He could have spared me so much hurt. It was my father's job to protect me. He didn't do his job. He should know that.

I believed in what I was taught. I tried so hard to be the man my father would be proud of. Our father was in town much less than half the time. The task of raising my brother often fell to me. When our father was in town, he would beat my brother or me to a bloody pulp. It happened every time an adult said we did something wrong. My brother has always been a rebel, and he was punished more times than I can count. I became Stefan's father. I disciplined him, taught him, and protected him—all the while not knowing where the real evil was. My sisters Victoria and Paige were the only girls I was ever allowed to interact with.

My mother has been gone for as long as I can remember. I remember meeting her when I was four or five when my dad got my brother back from her. We didn't hear from her again until I was thirteen, and she came to Bryant. That wasn't fun—it was a weird feeling. She was coming around, and I thought, "I don't know that lady." It hurts. What can I say? If I were my mother, I would have left my dad too. I know her leaving wasn't about me. I used to be indignant because I figured she should have put up with him. There is no real right answer to that question. You hurt your kids by leaving and hurt yourself by staying. So I really can't blame her.

When I was growing up, we lived in different homes. I spent the most time in Muldrow, Oklahoma, where we lived in a trailer park owned by Tony Alamo. None of us had our own room. Stefan and I had a bunk bed that was in the living room. The girls stayed together in a bedroom. When I was ten, we moved to Fouke, where my brother and I lived in a dormitory with all the men or brothers who had no wives or family. My sisters lived in Tony Alamo's house, which, at the time, I considered to be a great honor. I never questioned the fact that only females were allowed to live in his house.

It was clear how we should live. We were to fear God. Before my dad would beat us, he always said, "You may not fear God, but I promise you: you will fear me." My brother Stefan feared our dad more than any of us did. He was in trouble all the time. When we sinned, we literally had the hell beaten out of us. Then we were to be thankful to the one who kept us on the straight and narrow by beating us. One of the Biblical references Tony used to condone the brutal beating of children was the scene where Jesus ran merchants out of the temple with a whip (Matthew 21:12).

I knew there was another world out there—people always referred to it as the "outside." Dad told stories to make the outside sound awful and our world seem like paradise. Adults would come to church services and testify about their sinful existence before they found salvation in Tony. The most I ever got outside of the church property was as a rider with my dad or as a member of tracting crews. We didn't interact with outsiders except to tell them about salvation if they asked.

They took my sister in the first raid. I was at the courthouse with my dad when they took me in the second raid. They put us kids in a little room and said we would be staying there for the next seventy-five hours. I sat in a chair at a table and cried my eyes out. I didn't know what to do. Then a caseworker came in. I was belligerent. "Shut up! You just took me from my dad. I may never see him again. I don't want to talk to you. Leave me alone." They took us from the courthouse to the National Guard armory where we slept on cots and watched movies.

I remember Ruth came on the second or third day. I knew she had my sister and she wanted to talk to my brother Stefan and me. I said, "I don't know you. Who do you think you are?" At that moment I hated her. I hated everyone. I couldn't help it. I had just lost my family. That was all I had. Now people were telling me that everything I had ever learned was wrong and that my dad couldn't be my parent anymore. My dad was my whole world. I stayed hateful for a long time. Even after most of the other kids were accepting what had happened, I wasn't. I stood my ground. I wasn't going to believe that my dad was bad just because these people said so. I held onto my beliefs until that day I returned to Fort Smith—seven years after the raid. That's why I had to go back to see my dad—one more time. Then I could let go of the past.

I like to think that my childhood experiences have forged my character in a positive manner. I certainly developed a strong work ethic. I have definitely learned not to hurt another human being. I am resolved to search for my own truth. I hate my story. I wish I could have been normal. It doesn't feel good to be exceptional. But my past has made me tough as nails. I know I don't have to like where I came from. But I do have to come to terms with it and figure out how to be happy with myself.

An overall lesson I've gotten from life is just to survive when you have no reason to. For a while I thought I was going to go back home with my dad. I thought, "Well, I will just sit this out. I will go back home and everything will go back to normal." That didn't happen. The thing is, I adapt not quickly but well. Back there in the past I was considered a good kid, I did what I was supposed to do, and I didn't get into trouble overly often. Whatever society you put me in—if you point me in the right direction, I can survive. One day I am going to grow up and be better than my dad.

It will take me a while. I'll learn from my own mistakes, but I'll be better. My past helps me to understand what drives my desires and why I'm passionate about certain things. I've been abandoned by literally everyone I have ever cared about—except for my brother and my sister. I lost them all. And it wasn't when I was three and didn't know them. I was thirteen, and I did know them. I knew who they were, and I knew why they were there. And so it tore me up; having lost all of that left a hole in my heart. And I need to know that someone cares about me. I need to know that I matter to someone.

I wanted to be a police officer for the longest time, because I did not want anyone to get hurt in my town. I wanted to be home every night to read bedtime stories to my kids and to be with my wife. I'm going to be there for my family. That's going to be my job.

I can't blame the world for what happened to me. There's no real target for my anger. But then being angry requires too much energy. My anger isn't going to impact Tony. I'll just fizzle out and won't have the energy to do what I want to do. So instead I think about why he and the people in his cult hurt me and how I can fix it. How can I use that energy to build myself up? Consider track, for instance. I hated running when I first did it. I had never participated in school athletics before. But once I got into it, I had to stay. I have never had the opportunity to build myself before—

just to make progress with myself. So when I'm upset, rather than go hit something, I can just run, and I get stronger rather than hurting myself and someone else.

I do believe in God. I did so excessively. I read the Bible every day and prayed for at least thirty minutes every day. I don't think believing in God means having my nose in a book, even the Bible. We have to go out and experience God. Obviously what I was taught was far different from outside world teachings. I have a lot to learn. I'm going to let life teach me—let God teach me.

I have made my peace with my dad. I let him know how I feel and gave him the opportunity to love me. And I may never speak to him again. It's painful. It hurts. But by seeing my dad one more time, I pulled a dagger out of my heart, and it does hurt. But I am closer to finding peace.

CHAPTER

THIRTY-SIX

Stefan

I thought they were going to kill us. They came after us on the highway with sirens and pulled us over. One of the brothers started videotaping everything. A sister shouted something about kidnapping, and then some of the little kids started crying. The police told us to get out of the vans. I thought we could run through the cornfield and get away. The officers had us surrounded. There was nowhere to go. I was ten years old.

Papa Tony had told us that we were dead, done for. He told us about Waco, and we had comic books about the Holocaust. He said they would come for us. They already had my sister. Tony said everyone outside the church was going to hell. Tony was so powerful. He got people off the streets, cleaned them up, and told them about religion. The older people in the church say it was Tony's wife, Susan, who was really the preacher. But when she died, Tony became the king.

Growing up, I couldn't talk with anyone. The whole place was based on lies, cheating, backstabbing, and tattling. Your best friend would turn on you on a dime. I really didn't have close friends. My brother was closest to me, but I couldn't trust him. He told on me for everything. He thought he was doing the right thing. My uncle caught me trying to escape one time, and I pretended I was sleepwalking. He didn't tell on me. He saved me a beating that time.

One of my happiest memories is my eighth birthday party. All of my friends were actually in one spot, and we went swimming. My friends were all spread out, so when we could all be together, it was really fun.

Overall, though, I was not really happy. I was beaten all the time for doing something wrong. I was always getting in trouble for something. Looking back now, I can see that I was just being a kid. I never did anything to harm anyone. I was always anxious. I think being treated badly as a child has made me stronger. I wouldn't want to relive it, though. I don't want to be like my parents.

I remember when I got in trouble for playing with action figures and falling asleep in church. I got called out in the middle of church. The pastor pointed to me in the back of the room. He pointed me out to Tony. For three or four weeks I couldn't go to church. I was an outcast and only eight years old. I felt horrible. Another time I got in trouble for singing "Take Me Out to the Ball Game," a song I had heard when we were in the outside world.

I lived in different places. When I was a baby, I lived with my mother at the sisters' dorm. Not long after I was born, my mom took me and left the church. Later Glen (what I call my biological dad) got me back. We kids lived with sister Sonia and her kids when Tony sent Glen to work away from home. I lived with Glen off and on. But my brother, Ian, was more of a dad to me. I always looked up to Ian. If it weren't for him, I would have made even worse decisions.

Just like the other kids, I worked. I went with the men to construction sites, and when we were too small to do big jobs, we would play around. I liked going out like that and being with friends. We also worked when the brothers thought we could handle the job. I did a lot of roofing and today could probably frame a house.

I also liked going tracting because we didn't have to sit behind and listen to every bit of Tony's words. I would be on crews with my brother, and we would make the best of it by racing each other. It was fun to stay in hotels and eat fast food. Some of the places I've tracted are Arkansas, Oklahoma,

Washington, California, Idaho, Montana, Utah, Oregon, Texas, Wisconsin, Michigan, Kentucky, Tennessee, New York, New Jersey, and Mexico. When we were on the outside, we didn't really know what to think of the people we saw. We just didn't focus on them.

When I was a kid, I always wanted that perfect family setting with a mom and dad. I used to think things would be better as I grew. But as I got older, I saw that things weren't better. Tony Alamo was in prison and now is dead. People are leaving. But Glen is still there. My brother, Ian, thought he could change Glen. He couldn't. Glen doesn't care. I don't think he loves us. I don't love him.

Adjusting to foster care took a little bit of time. We were first placed with people who weren't quite prepared for us. We were four teenage boys with all these beliefs set in our heads by false prophets. After a year we were moved to the foster home where our sister, Victoria, lived. Ruth and Jay helped us to gradually learn what to believe. Every experience was a life shock. We hadn't been allowed to talk with girls. Suddenly I was in public school, standing in front of a class of boys and girls. I just stuttered, and the teacher let me sit down. Girls came up and talked to me, but I didn't know what to say to them. I didn't even know that men talked with women.

I was trying to cope with the loss of another parent, my sisters taken from me, and the only world I knew being gone. It was scary and sad. I stayed close to my brother and leaned on him to get us through this new scary world. We went to school, the movies, and out to dinner, but we mostly stayed in with our new foster parents and the other kids they took in from the cult.

I know that Ruth and Jay aren't my biological parents, but they are there for me. Now I'm spending time with my biological mom and meeting family members I never knew I had. That helps me to feel like I am at home. I have learned not to take something as important as my beliefs from another person but to find out for myself what is true to me.

Do I trust people now? More than I did then. There are always people who will lie and turn on you. I don't talk about my life to others. If I try to base all my decisions on things that happened in the past, I will stay in the same spot forever. I try not to think about it. I will never go back to it. I want my past to stay there. I wish it didn't bother me to have missed what everyone on the outside experienced. It's as if I grew up in another country and era. I believe in God. I don't think you need to be in a church to worship God. Home is where your heart is, and God is wherever you are, under a bridge, at home, at work, anywhere.

A few years after the raid I talked with a boy who had just been taken from the church. He still thought Tony was the right way. I told him, "I understand that you believe in Tony's church. He told us this is true, but it's not. Some things you just have to trust me on." We have to spend time with these kids and nurture them. They have to see for themselves what to believe in. We have to listen, be there, take a step back, and look at life from their point of view.

CHAPTER
THIRTY-SEVEN

The Lawyer

The lawyer pulled his weary eyes away from the computer screen. Leaning forward and feeling the strain of an ongoing headache, he propped his head on his hands and massaged his brows. Through all the years David Carter had been practicing law, this was the case that held him hostage.

He was no stranger to the demands of being a trial lawyer. He tried his first death penalty murder case at age twenty-five. By the time he was forty, he had represented clients in some of the most celebrated, multi-billion-dollar cases in history. Eighteen- to twenty-hour work days were typical during trials. But what he felt after seven years of representing the Alamo victims was more than just pressure. It was more than fatigue. Day after day of graphic testimony about the abuse heaped on these kids in the name of religion was taking its toll—not so much on his body as his soul. It was almost impossible to compartmentalize this case and "leave it at the office." It was always on his mind at some level. At some point he had even begun to feel guilty. Guilty that he grew up surrounded by family and friends who cared for him and would protect him from danger. Guilty that he could always count on his parents to put his interests ahead of their own. Yet, here he was trying to speak for children whose own parents either turned their backs or, in some cases, actually encouraged their physical, mental, and sexual abuse. All because God's "prophet" commanded it. In some respects, he felt wholly unqualified to be these kids' advocate.

Five days after the 2008 raid on Tony Alamo Christian Ministries, the FBI tracked down and captured Alamo in Flagstaff, Arizona. One year later a jury found Alamo guilty of transporting girls as young as nine years old across state lines for sex. A sentence of 175 years in prison without possibility of parole assured that Alamo would never again be free. As he was escorted from the courthouse to a US marshal's vehicle, Alamo called to reporters, "I'm just another one of the prophets that went to jail for the Gospel."[1]

Some said that was punishment enough. The heinous leader was behind prison bars, and the remaining followers were free to do as they wished. Never mind that families had been torn apart and followers spiritually abused and enslaved as laborers to line Alamo's pockets in the name of God.

And then there were the children. Alamo had preyed on young girls who believed him to be God's prophet. "Papa Tony" had destroyed the innocence of these children, instilling in them values based on fear, anger, and dread. Five brave young women, ages seventeen to thirty-three at the time of the trial, testified that Alamo privately "married" them while they were minors and took them on trips outside Arkansas borders for his sexual gratification.[2]

David Carter lifted his head and caught a glimpse of the morning sun playing on the papers strewn across his desk. It was not enough to put Alamo in prison for life. Alamo needed to pay for his despicable actions. The children whose fractured lives might never heal deserved justice. With the grit and fortitude of a hound tracking its prey, Carter returned his eyes to the computer screen to review a deposition he had taken with Tony Alamo. He was laying the groundwork to resolve that Tony Alamo's wealth was in fact his own and not the property of the followers. During

---

1. *Texarkana Times*, (AP), July 24, 2009.

2. Ibid.

this deposition, Carter had played a tape recording of Alamo's bantering to remind him of his claims to ownership of the church.

> CARTER: Why is your name on the Church?
>
> ALAMO: They wanted to put my name on their Church because I'm famous.
>
> CARTER: That of course was you. Was it not? Speaking?
>
> ALAMO: Yes.
>
> CARTER: And you said right in the beginning, "This is my Church."
>
> ALAMO: It is. It's my Church from God to take care of.
>
> CARTER: And if you want to stay in it, you better abide by my—
>
> ALAMO: No. God's rules.
>
> CARTER: No, you said "my" first. Didn't you?
>
> ALAMO: My rules that I follow from God! You creep!
>
> CARTER: Are you denying that you said, "This is my Church"? "And if you want to stay in it you abide by my—"
>
> ALAMO: That's your interpretation of what I was saying, but what I'm really saying is—
>
> CARTER: We'll play it again if that's what you want us to do.
>
> ALAMO: No! I know what it said, Jerkwater!
>
> CARTER: You also said in that tape—
>
> ALAMO: I don't want to hear it again!
>
> [CARTER plays the tape]
>
> ALAMO: Yeah, by my rules which is the Lord's rule.
>
> CARTER: Yeah and you also said if you're deciding to do something like open a school, no "damn judge" will stop you.
>
> ALAMO: That's right. When God tells me to do it, I do it. And we did open a school and it's still open all over the world.
>
> CARTER: Did any of these members hire you to be their pastor?
>
> ALAMO: Hire me? I'm not out for hire!
>
> CARTER: Did any of these members have the right to fire you?
>
> ALAMO: No. Yeah but see nobody hired me. God did. Nobody hired me. Therefore no one can fire me except God. I'm a moneymaking dude, and if you don't do what I'm telling

you in your business, you could very well go out of business. If you don't like it here, then leave.

CARTER: Because this is your Church.

ALAMO: This is our country and if people don't like it, you should
just get 'em out of here.

CARTER: And you tell them, "It's my Church! Don't tangle with me."

ALAMO: I didn't say that. Like I said, I'm the Pastor so don't tangle
with me. They didn't come to me; nobody would dare
come to me and say we're going to remove you. Except
that kid that I had his butt beat.

CARTER: [name]?

ALAMO: If you try to remove me, well I'll beat your butt!

CARTER: Let's try it this way.

ALAMO: And do it again, I'll do the same thing! I'm a dangerous
dude, man. And I say "you want to fight somebody?" I
said, "John [Kolbek], this guy wants to beat the hell"—if
there was any hell left in me—"out of a blind man that's
82 years old or 76 years old." What do you think about
that? Let's make a decision here. Okay so the Bible says
that if any kid does that, you are supposed to actually kill
him. Okay? So instead of that, what we do is we made a
decision to whip his butt for him and because of that I
got sued. And the judge put in an order to make me have
to pay them $66 million! Now, do you think that's fair?

CARTER: You're not supposed to ask the questions around here,
Mr. Alamo.

ALAMO: I know what you are leading up to.

CARTER: I'm just asking the questions.

ALAMO: You are such a clever man.

CARTER: Why do we need adults holding down any of these girls
if it was just a spanking?

ALAMO: So that they wouldn't get struck on their stomach or anywhere else.

CARTER: To protect them?

ALAMO: Yes. You can never strike anybody more than 39 stripes. That's the most you can give them. That's what the Bible says.[3]

With one quick click Carter closed the file. *That's what the Bible says.* The lawyer pondered Alamo's use of the Bible to justify his egregious behaviors. Alamo wielded control over his followers by misusing words in the Bible and pronouncing himself as God's prophet. He used fear, guilt, threats, and corporal punishment to enforce complete allegiance and threatened that non-compliance by followers would result in eternal damnation.

The children he represented were second- and third-generation cult members. In some cases, their parents were still members of Alamo's church. The children were at once strong and fragile—they had been taken from a home that assured blessed eternal life and entered a world they had learned was lost. They had learned to distrust "outsiders," including law enforcement and attorneys. In fact, Alamo's system of reporting rule breakers taught the children to trust no one. Even their sisters, brothers, and parents tattled on behaviors construed as violations of the church. These children have been shunned by all remaining in the church. They have lost their families and friends.

Carter had been working diligently to earn the trust of the children. He knew that his was the first voice to represent them in the system. Never before had anyone, not even their own parents, spoken up for them against Tony Alamo. He knew that the children likely felt overwhelming guilt, shame, and a sense that what had happened was somehow their own fault. Those who abused them as well as those who continued to follow Alamo's teachings have told them this. Even though Tony Alamo would be behind bars for the rest of his life, facing the past and Alamo's authoritative followers was a daunting task. The children had no wealth, birth certificates,

3. Deposition of Bernie Hoffman a.k.a Tony Alamo, taken by David Carter, Esq., February 29, 2012.

or social security numbers. Civil action could at least provide monetary restitution to help them move forward with their lives.

The lawyer was restless. A glance at the clock told him that it was nearly noon. He grabbed his keys, left the office, and jumped into his truck. His Texarkana office was less than a thirty-minute drive to Fouke, Arkansas. Almost without thinking, he wove through the familiar turns of highways until he found himself on I-49 south. Ten miles took him to the North Fouke Road exit where he turned left onto County Highway 88, North Fouke Road, and then turned right onto US-71 south. On this desolate highway, Carter felt his attention sharpen. Coming into view was a yellow brick structure with a sign proclaiming it "Tony Alamo Christian Ministries." Except for a single white van parked in front of the building, the church appeared to be deserted. Carter made a sharp right turn onto a dirt drive that ran alongside Tony Alamo's house. Across from Alamo's house was the infamous green house that contained girls being punished for displeasing the preacher. As two men emerged from a small gatehouse, Carter made a fast sharp turn and gunned his truck back out to the highway. He steered around the perimeter of the compound of shuttered homes and multi-purpose buildings and wondered how many eyes were watching his movements. He would likely get a call from Alamo's legal team complaining of harassment. With renewed resolve, the lawyer turned back onto the highway and headed for his office.

Thirty minutes later, Carter was back at his desk and scrolling for a file on his computer. This time he wanted to review a segment of his deposition where he questioned Tony Alamo's philosophy and role in doling out punishments. This session had also given Carter an opportunity to address ownership of church property and underscore the complete authority Alamo wielded over his followers.

> CARTER: You all had a reporting system within the church down at Fouke, did you not?
> ALAMO: A recording system?
> CARTER: Reporting system.

ALAMO: Reporting?

CARTER: Yes, sir.

ALAMO: What do you mean? What do you mean by that?

CARTER: Where you encouraged members to write written reports on each other if they were seen violating rules.

ALAMO: You better believe it. That goes on in every church. It goes on in this prison. It goes on in any successful business. You'd better have people that will report to you if anything is being done that's not right.

CARTER: And you also required, or at least asked anybody who had an infraction reported against them to write a counter report?

ALAMO: Absolutely. That's fairness.

CARTER: And then you would review those materials and then you would make a decision as to who to believe?

ALAMO: I would take—yes.

CARTER: Okay. You also—before we move on, if punishment was to be meted out to one or more persons based on a report, you were the one who decided what the punishment would be?

ALAMO: I'd pray about it.

CARTER: And then you would say what, after prayer, the punishment would be?

ALAMO: I know what you're leading up to.

CARTER: I'm just asking if that's true.

ALAMO: You're acting so clever. You are such a clever man. Well, we know what the punishment is in the Bible.

CARTER: And you would be the person who said this will be the punishment for this infraction?

ALAMO: Well, no. I tell them—the mothers and dads, I say, "Now, look, if your kid comes up to you and smacks you, you whip his butt. Okay? Now, don't abuse them, but give them a good swat." Give them some swats, yes. That's what the Bible says. And—but so the parents are the ones that decide if their kid was so out of line. "Don't go by Dr. Spock," I tell them. "Give them a swat."

CARTER: And you on occasion would tell—after prayer or consultation with the Lord, what punishment would be in a given situation?

ALAMO: No. Because I don't know if the—what the kids are doing with their—to their parents or doing around the house.

CARTER: Okay. You're ahead of me. You're saying why. I just want to know were you the one—

ALAMO: No, I'm not. Okay? Now, that's final. I'm not the one. The parents do that.

CARTER: Okay. Now, what about the adults?

ALAMO: What about the adults?

CARTER: When it came time for them to be punished based on—

ALAMO: Well, okay, I'll give you for instance, and that happens to be one of these lawsuits here. Is this kid is—he's not a kid anymore. He's 18 years old. And he's—he says, "Can I get together with this 15-year-old girl over at your house?" And I say, "No. You can't marry young girls." Okay? It's approved in the Bible, and you can ask any Muslim— there's one billion one hundred million Muslims, and they all say that, and Webster's Dictionary says, that it is ab- solutely—a childhood ends at puberty. When a woman starts menstruating she's not a child anymore. She's a woman. That's absolutely in the Bible and in the—in the Qur'an. And the Qur'an tells us that Mohammed married a girl that was six years old. And if you ask any Muslim, "Do you believe that Mohammed is right and that it was okay to do that," and they'll say, "Well, we don't want to say because we're afraid we're going to get thrown in prison." But they'll say, "We won't throw you in prison, just tell us the truth." "Yes. It's all right if she's—but he didn't have sex with her until she was nine years old."

CARTER: Mr. Alamo, I didn't ask you about—

ALAMO: No, but I'm trying—

CARTER: —having sex with children. I asked you who made the decision as to what punishment was meted out to adults?

ALAMO: I say they take it out of the Bible. That's—

CARTER: I didn't ask where it comes from. I said who makes the decision who's going to punish adult members of Tony Alamo Christian Ministries when they are found to have infracted a rule?

ALAMO: The parents.

CARTER: It was you, was it not?

ALAMO: I was just building up to this. Now, the kid comes up to me and says, "I'm going to beat you up, Mr. Alamo." It's an 18-year-old, real strapping guy. I says, "Oh, you want to do that, huh?" I says, "Let's go over to the gym then." So we walked across the street. And John Kolbek was in there. And I say, "You want to fight somebody, huh?" I said, "John, this guy wants to beat the hell," if there was any hell left in me, "out of a blind man that's 82 years old." Or 76 years old. "What do you think about that? Let's make a decision here." Okay. The Bible says if any kid does that, that you're supposed to actually kill them. Okay? So instead of that, what we do is we made a decision to whip his butt for him. And because of that, I got sued and the judge gave them the order to pay me—I have to pay them $66 million. Now, do you think that's fair?

CARTER: You're not supposed to ask the questions here, Mr. Alamo. I'm going to go back to my original question.

ALAMO: And that's my decision. That was my decision. Now, if somebody come up and smacked you across the face, or wanted to kick your butt, who would make the decision as to what to do with that person? It would be you, wouldn't it?

CARTER: In my case, yes. But let's go back to my original question.

ALAMO: Okay. Well, then, that's my answer, too.

CARTER: You were the person who declared what punishment, if any, would be meted out to adult members if you determined they had violated the rules based on the reporting system?

ALAMO: If I knew for sure that they were doing that to me, you better believe I'd do it.

CARTER: And you sometimes utilized Mr. Kolbek on those occasions where you determined someone needed to be struck?

ALAMO: Not necessarily. If Kolbek was around I'd say, "Here, fight somebody your own age."

CARTER: Well, Kolbek was in Fort Smith, was he not?

ALAMO: No. He was in the gym.

CARTER: I'm talking about in general. He lived in Fort Smith?

ALAMO: Yes, he did.

CARTER: And when he showed up at Fouke, it was because somebody was going to get a beating, wasn't it?

ALAMO: No. No. Because his daughter lived there.

CARTER: You're going to deny under oath that you have called John Kolbek in Fort Smith, Arkansas and told him to come to Texarkana because—

ALAMO: You asked—

CARTER: —someone needs to be administered a punishment?

ALAMO: No, I didn't have to call John Kolbek.

CARTER: Never did that?

ALAMO: No.

CARTER: Okay.

ALAMO: I mean, you're trying to make it look like John Kolbek is my lieutenant and all this kind of buzzwords that you guys use. Okay, but go ahead. What's the next question?

CARTER: There was a needs list—

ALAMO: Yes, there is. Yeah, uh-huh.

CARTER: —because a great number of the church members lived in property that was owned by other church members?

ALAMO: Yeah. Everybody owns their own property.

CARTER: And they—those same people would work in some of the church operations and businesses?

ALAMO: They would volunteer their services unto the Lord, yeah.

CARTER: They would spend their days, sometimes nights working?

ALAMO: Sometimes, yes.

CARTER: Landscaping?

ALAMO: Yeah.

CARTER: Helping get the tapes out?

ALAMO: Yes.

ALAMO: A number of jobs?

ALAMO: Whatever they do, yes. I'm not aware of everything they do.

CARTER: And those people had no other source of money, they spent their time working for you, did they not? They didn't have outside jobs?

ALAMO: Why do you keep saying they are working for me? They are working for the Lord. We're volunteering our services to the Lord.

CARTER: Working in—

ALAMO: Which you don't believe exists, otherwise you wouldn't keep saying they are working for me. I don't need anybody to work for me.

CARTER: They were working for the Tony Alamo Christian Ministries?

ALAMO: No, they are not. They are working for themselves. They are volunteering, not working. They are volunteering their services to the Tony Alamo Christian Ministries.

CARTER: But these volunteers would have to submit lists of what they felt they needed in terms of clothing, school items and things?

ALAMO: Yeah, they have people that work at the warehouse and people turn their requests in to them, and the people at the warehouse give them to them. I don't even know it's going on, but I know it goes on, but I—

CARTER: You didn't approve the needs list?

ALAMO: I don't approve it.

CARTER: You didn't approve the needs list back in 1999, 2000, up to 2008?

ALAMO: No. Because I don't want to know about people that need toilet paper and Kleenex and cleaning powder. I don't have time for that.

CARTER: Who did approve it?

ALAMO: Huh?

CARTER: Who did approve it?

ALAMO: The people that work at the warehouse. I just got through telling you.

CARTER: So if folks testified that they couldn't get items of clothing purchased or things they needed for school without your approval, that's just wrong?

ALAMO: That's wrong. Absolutely wrong. Because I don't—I'm not interested in it. I just want to make sure that the people get everything that they are supposed to have.

CARTER: Okay. Let's focus, Mr. Alamo, on the years after you were released from prison in 1999 up until the properties were raided in September of 2008. You follow me so far?

ALAMO: Yeah.

CARTER: Okay. During that time, who was the church leadership?

ALAMO: I told you that the Lord is our leader and everybody knows what to do. And there's nobody—you're trying to make a cult leader out of me. First of all, we're not a cult. We're a church. A very holy church. And we all are led by the spirit. And that's what we are supposed to be. And every church is supposed to—every member of every church is supposed to be led by the spirit and not by some cult leader. That's another one of your buzzwords.

CARTER: Okay. Well, I didn't use the word "cult," you did.

ALAMO: Well, no, the paper do, and you attorneys do also, and that's what I'm—I know by your line of questioning what you think. Because this isn't the first time to be going through these depositions. I've gone through them for years now, my friend. I've probably been in as many as you have.

CARTER: Oh, and I'm sure you're going to know where you think I'm going, and that's fine.

ALAMO: I know where you're going.

CARTER: But, really, your job is to answer the question I ask.

ALAMO: Well, I'm answering.

CARTER: If you'll do that, this will go so much quicker.

ALAMO: Yes, sir.

CARTER: And what I asked you was—

ALAMO: I can't wait to get back to my cell.

CARTER: What I asked you was—

ALAMO: Let's hurry this up.

CARTER: If we'll have fewer references to country western singers—

ALAMO: What's that?

CARTER: If we'll have fewer references in the answers to the country music business and Hollywood, we'll get through quicker. Again, we're focusing on '99 to 2008 while operations were in Fouke. Okay?

ALAMO: No, the operations are all over. Los Angeles, Fouke and—

CARTER: I understand. But you were operating Tony Alamo Christian Ministries primarily from Fouke?

ALAMO: I was not operating it. The people operate it. All I do is write. I don't have anything to do with the toilet paper, the cleaning solvents, and stuff like that. I don't do that. I have to stop you every time you say things that are wrong. Sorry. I mean, I'd like to get through with this.

CARTER: Let's go back to my question. It had to do with—

ALAMO: —me running everything.

CARTER: No, it didn't. The question was—thanks for helping, but the question was, what was the leadership structure of the church? We have God. We know that. Who was the pastor?

ALAMO: I'm the pastor insomuch as I write.

CARTER: Okay.

ALAMO: But they run the services. I haven't been in one of those church services for years.

CARTER: Okay.

ALAMO: They run the services. They preach, they teach, they do everything.

CARTER: But you will agree with me that you, Tony Alamo, were the pastor of Tony Alamo Christian Ministries from '98 through 2008?

ALAMO: Oh, no—well, I'm the pastor, yeah, but that doesn't—that doesn't mean—not your version of what "pastor" means. Your version means that I'm in there, you know, "How many rolls of toilet paper do you need? No, you can only have two. If you need more than two, you're in trouble."

CARTER: So we have God and we have Pastor Tony Alamo.

ALAMO: No, it's not like that, man.

CARTER: Well, in my example God is over all.

ALAMO: Yeah. Yeah.

CARTER: Would you agree with that?

ALAMO: Yes, I do.

CARTER: Okay. So He's the ultimate leader of Tony Alamo Christian Ministries?[4]

Carter scrolled to another section of his deposition. Alamo preached a conspiracy theory not uncommon among leaders of high-demand groups. His particular brand focused on the United States government and the Vatican. In that session, Carter brought the discussion around to Alamo's views of women, polygamy, and the age when a young lady could marry.

---

4. Deposition of Bernie Hoffman a.k.a Tony Alamo, taken by David Carter, Esq., February 28, 2012.

CARTER: Oh, okay. Give me, if you would, just a snapshot version of how the Vatican conspired with the government here, at least as it applies to you.

ALAMO: Well, okay. A snapshot. It's kind of hard to do a snapshot, other than murdering Christians for centuries. But apart from that they—Cardinal Spellman took Franco and others to form the United Nations. The law that the government is operating under now are not United States constitutional laws, they are Roman Catholic laws. The Bible said that the antichrist or the seat of Satan is in the city of the seven hills—or seven mountains. This is Rome. The seat of Rome is the Vatican. Satan's seat is the Vatican. And the Bible says that every abomination that's happening in the world today is coming from the Vatican, Mystery Babylon, the Great Harlot. And so I mean, you know, that's a snapshot of it. But I could go into a lot of detail. I've had—every judge that's ever convicted me was Catholic. I've gone into a lot of study on it, and it's—there's no question about it.

CARTER: And if I'm following you—

ALAMO: I don't think you have the capacity up here to follow me.

CARTER: Well, you know, I appreciate that, Pastor Alamo, but I'm trying as best I can.

ALAMO: I don't really think you do.

CARTER: As I understand what you just said, the constitutional government that we set up in America—

ALAMO: —is no longer.

CARTER: —is—that our government at this point today is simply an arm of the Catholic church?

ALAMO: This is not our government. This is not our government. This is Roman canon, the U.N. government. As a matter of fact, they have thrown people in prison for saying they were in the United States Navy. They said, "You have to say it's the U.N. Navy, the U.N. Marines." The U.N. this, the U.N. That's why instead of saying, "Well, we're the world's bodyguards," that's why the U.N. is using us up by sending our troops over to all these different countries and fighting the battles. That's why we're in debt now.

CARTER: Okay. We're going to play another excerpt from your—

ALAMO: Yeah.

(AUDIO recording played.)

MALE VOICE: They are saying that homosexuality is evil—it's good and that polygamy, which the Bible doesn't condemn at all, is evil. And that women are—become women when they are—when they reach puberty, and these bastards are saying that that's wrong. I mean, who the hell do they think they are to come against God. You know?"

(AUDIO recording ended.)

ALAMO: That's true. That's what I said.

CARTER: That sort of recaps, I think, some of the things you told us yesterday.

ALAMO: Absolutely. That's the way I believe. I believe God is right and everybody else is wrong unless they agree with him.

CARTER: And that polygamy for certain godly men is acceptable?

ALAMO: Well, Abraham was a polygamist and he married young teenage girls when he was a hundred years old.

CARTER: And I think you reiterated—

ALAMO: Moses had three wives, and he was the lawgiver. He's the one that brought the law. The law came by Moses, but grace and truth came by Jesus Christ. And Moses had three wives. And it's—

CARTER: And it would be okay today for certain men to have three wives?

ALAMO: For people that would choose to, and if their wives wanted to be married to them, yes.

CARTER: Six wives?

ALAMO: A hundred wives.

CARTER: Hundred wives?

ALAMO: Yeah.

CARTER: You also made brief mention—

ALAMO: If they could support them.

CARTER: —in that visit to puberty being the age at which a young lady can marry.

ALAMO: Yeah. See, I don't agree with today's consensus of that, but Webster Dictionary says it, the Bible says it, the Qur'an says it, and a bunch of ignorant people such as yourself don't believe it. You're trying to make mock of it.

CARTER: Well, and your writings—

ALAMO: You're mocking God.

CARTER: Your writings—

ALAMO: Yeah, I write what the Bible says.

CARTER: —say, among other things, that girls reach puberty as young as nine?

ALAMO: Well, the record will bear me out on that.

CARTER: Sure.

ALAMO: But I don't believe in marrying a nine-year-old.

CARTER: Just so we're clear, you think it's acceptable Biblically for a woman to be married when she reaches puberty?

ALAMO: That's what the Bible says.

CARTER: And that can be as young as nine?

ALAMO: But that doesn't mean that I did it.

CARTER: I'm just talking about what you preached.

ALAMO: I believe it. Yeah, I believe it.

CARTER: That's what you preach?

ALAMO: Yes, that's right. I don't preach just that. That's one little small segment of the Bible that I preach.

CARTER: That's part of your message?

ALAMO: Well, I had to preach that because you arrested me, you people, on that premise.

CARTER: Well, I can assure you, Mr. Alamo, that no one in this room is a member of law enforcement, save and except the folks here from the prison who are watching us.

ALAMO: Well, are you a lawyer?

CARTER: I am, but I—

ALAMO: Well, you're part of the law then.

CARTER: Oh, I'm part of the conspiracy?

ALAMO: You are.

CARTER: With the Vatican?

ALAMO: Yes.

CARTER: And with the federal government?

ALAMO: With Satan.

CARTER: And with Satan?

ALAMO: Yes.[5]

Carter glanced at the clock and was surprised to see that it was after six o'clock. Shifting in his chair, he paused, considering whether he should call it a day. Maybe he was obsessed with this case. Maybe he should listen to his friends who said that it was enough to have Alamo in prison. Maybe he was caught up in a vendetta to crush all things Alamo. Were the followers innocent? Was he pressing too far? Shaking his head, the lawyer turned his eyes to the computer screen and settled in for a few more hours' work.

---

5. Deposition of Bernie Hoffman a.k.a. Tony Alamo, taken by David Carter, Esq., February 29, 2012.

Afterword

Like all true stories, this one doesn't have an ending.

Audrey went to college and joined the army, where she trained to be a military police officer. "Putting men in compliance" was her job. Her confidence has grown in leaps and bounds. Her service duty is completed, and she is moving forward in her life. She continues to encounter surprises in the world outside and embraces new experiences. Still, the past can be haunting, and Audrey uses her art to discover and express her innermost feelings. Once those feelings emerge, so do her thoughts. She is closer to joining her past with her present. Audrey's oldest sister, Tatum, is still in the cult. Her younger sister and brothers are no longer in the cult. She has no contact with her father and mother.

Irene devours every day as a new adventure. She is a thinker and is determined to understand her past experiences and the ways they impact her now. She is a writer, a painter, and most of all, a mother. What she does is helping her to discover who she really is. She is quick to embrace experience, examine it from every angle, try it on, and see herself from the inside out. Irene completed college and is excited to embark on adventures of the global kind. Her contemplative nature brings delight and wonder to her every day. She is not afraid to confront her demons, though sometimes she is taken aback by the force they can muster. Irene's mother is still in the cult, and Irene struggles with an emotional array of anger, hurt, and love that she feels for her mom. Occasional email communication can be disturbing. Irene grieves for her sister, Avril, who married Tony, and her sister, Kay, who are still in the cult. Happily her father left the cult, and along with her brothers, he is a joyful constant in her life.

Victoria graduated from college, is gainfully employed, and has stepped up to opportunities for travel and study abroad. Always ready for a challenge, she thrives on pushing herself to the next level, whether it is in physical exercise or in professional endeavors. Victoria has been private about her past life in the cult mostly because she doesn't want that to be what defines her to others. That being said, she is not hesitant to speak when she feels called to do so. In her freshman year she was in a session to learn about a club's philanthropy, Court Appointed Special Advocates (CASA). Noticing that others in the room might not be appreciating the critical role that CASA has in the community, Victoria stood up and told her story. She told it so well that she was asked to share her experiences as an advocate for CASA at conferences. Victoria has no contact with her biological father, who remains in the cult, but has a little bit with her biological mother, who left the cult many years ago. Along with her brothers and sisters, she is moving on.

Ian graduated from high school, entered the armed services and having completed service is exploring career options. Confronting his father helped Ian to gain some closure with that relationship. He has visited with his biological mother, Quinn. Ian sees his brother and sisters regularly and is moving forward with positive expectations for his life. He is fiercely protective of and loyal to those he loves. Ian is creative, and when monsters from the past bubble just under the surface, his emotions find an outlet in his writing. Ian grew up with adult-size responsibilities. The upside of that is his strong sense of responsibility, his determination to overcome barriers, and his quick-minded intelligence.

After difficulty adjusting, Stefan is thriving. He has a deep desire to be connected to his family and spends quality time with his biological mother, Quinn, and his oldest sister, Paige, when he isn't with his adoptive family. He has closed the door on his father, who remains in the cult. He is now active in sports, has good friends among his peers, and graduated from high school. He has a good relationship with his sister, Victoria, and feels deeply loyal to his brother, Ian, who served as a father figure for him in the cult. Like the other children, Stefan carries emotional scars from his life in the cult. Also like the others, Stefan is looking at life with new eyes. He is having positive experiences that are helping him build a new set of values and beliefs.

Paige is studying to be a nurse. She remembers the day she ran away when she accepted help from Drucker and Wilma, and recalls thinking, "I'm going to be so mad at myself for getting in this car." Paige was the only one in her sibling group who testified at the custody hearings. She understood that the others were too scared to say anything. She had escaped, reunited with her mother, and felt safe. But Paige still has bad dreams. A repeating nightmare has her back in the cult, unable to get away. It's always a comfort to wake up.

Frank works at a local business and owns a home not far from where he grew up. After running away and joining his brother, he agreed to talk with the FBI. His testimony went a long way to build a case for restitution for the physical and emotional injuries that Tony Alamo inflicted on him. Frank is an accomplished musician and enjoys close relationships with his father and siblings who have left the cult. He grieves for his two sisters who are still living in the cult.

Avril and Kay both remain in the cult.

John Kolbek died of a heart attack on January 6, 2011, while on the run from the FBI.

Bella lives in hiding with her mother, Andrea, and they are shunned by the cult.

Allison left the cult.

Monique, Gail, Allison, Nora, Shadow, and Lynn were awarded $525 million for punitive damages in a lawsuit charging Tony Alamo with physical and sexual abuse when they were children.

Ruth and Jay adopted Victoria, Ian, and Stefan. Though Audrey and Irene aged out of the foster care system, Ruth and Jay consider them permanent members of their family. After learning more about the growing need for stable foster families, Ruth and Jay became advocates. They actively recruited foster parents, became certified trainers, and were significant in growing collaboration between the State of Arkansas Department of Human Services and THE CALL, a Christian organization that strives to ensure that every foster child has a safe home.

Quinn is excelling at college, supporting her family, and rebuilding her relationships with her children. She volunteers at a community mission.

Sonia left the cult, is gainfully employed, and contributes much of her time to her family and friends who are also in the ranks of former cult members.

Glen continues to remain staunch in his faith in Tony Alamo.

Wilma and Drucker still keep a good eye on things in Fouke.

Randall Harris retired from the FBI at the conclusion of this case and is in private practice. His steadfast determination and genuine commitment pushed the momentum of justice forward. Even after the children were in foster homes, Randall continued to meet their many needs. His reach also extended to the children who were not in foster care. Because Paige had escaped the cult and found her home with relatives, she was one who did not have the benefit of immediate DHS assistance. Harris followed through to be sure all the children had every opportunity to be safe and to thrive. Among the many hurdles he cleared was in helping Paige begin public school—a process that, without the required birth certificate, would have been impeded.

John Bishop also continued to extend his commitment to the children. The age-ready children especially remember his clearing the way for them to obtain driver's learning permits when they had no birth certificates. The permits were significant documentation to affirm that they belong in the world outside the cult. Driving gave them some means to learn independence and forge their way through a new world of school, work, and friendships.

Attorney David Carter entered the scene in 2009 to represent former followers in civil lawsuits against Alamo for restitution. His efforts have resulted in awards of $66 million for punitive damages to Frank and another boy and $525 million to seven child brides, the largest monetary judgments ever adjudicated by the State of Arkansas. Judgments against Alamo and the church total just over $1.2 billion. Carter is dedicated to the quest to dismantle Alamo's property and financial resources. His work has put a gash in Alamo's power, and each finding of restitution affirms the means for new beginnings. Carter acknowledges that as they secured judgments, sold off Alamo's assets, and opened doors financially for these young people, some of the fatigue and weight of the cases was lifted. But these cases forever changed him professionally and personally. His work representing victims of horrendous abuse as minors continues. He is moving forward better equipped to accept the fact that sometimes people act in ways we can never wrap our brains around. They simply defy logic and compassion. And trying to fully understand it, as opposed to simply stopping it, can exact a heavy toll on anyone.

Tony Alamo died on May 2, 2017, in the federal prison facility in Butner, North Carolina, after serving eight of his 175-year sentence with no possibility of parole. Throughout his incarceration he was moved multiple times after building a network of followers in each prison. Wherever he was incarcerated, wives lived nearby to visit Tony and report on the followers. Alamo continued to run "church" businesses and control an estimated three hundred followers, despite being behind the bars of a federal penitentiary.

The church in Saugus, California, is still operating. Tracts papering cars advertise nightly services followed by a nutritious meal and an additional service on Sunday afternoons. Free transportation to and from the service is available at 6:30 p.m. at Hollywood and Highland Boulevard.

Alamo's followers hold services in numerous locations throughout the United States and continue to live according to the tenets of Alamo's teachings.

A story like this one has a number of heroes. Ruth and Jay are two of them. They did more than provide respite care. Up to this point they had not felt successful as foster parents. They were searching for a compass.

Theoretically, the foster system is based on the intention of providing a temporary haven for children whose homes, through no fault of the children, are not safe. The number-one permanency plan is always to reunite the child with parents or family. During this time, DHS staff and the court establish the goals that need to be accomplished to complete the permanency plan. Typically the parents are given a year (this may vary among states) to accomplish their goals with monitoring by DHS and the court.

The permanency plan can be changed when circumstances clearly show that parents will not be able to accomplish the goals. Even at this point, to terminate parental rights can be a lengthy process. So when children enter foster care, they are likely to be there for at least one year—and typically longer. They have been removed from their home, and regardless of the conditions, the children are upset. Thus, many children in the foster care system have emotional and physical issues, trouble interacting appropriately with others, and difficulty expressing their thoughts and emotions. The best scenario has a child in a foster home that is a great match for developmental needs. Custodial parents complete the permanency plan within the given time period, and the family is reunited.

The foster care system is a kind of paradox. Its intention is to be temporary, but the return of children to their parents or custodial guardians takes time. And often return is unlikely. Children need permanent love. They need permanent safety. They need stability to have friends, to learn, and to thrive. Parenting is the most difficult and most rewarding job that exists. Foster parents are willing to give permanent love temporarily to a child needing a home. That is magnificent.

Successful foster care depends on a number of key variables: adequate number of foster parents; background checks, screening, and monitoring to assure safety of children; training for foster families; reasonable caseload for caseworkers to provide monitoring and support to parents working on their permanency plan goals; and community resources to meet the physical, psychological, and emotional needs of children in foster families. In the US alone, more than four hundred thousand children are living in the foster care system without permanent families. Of these, 101,840 are eligible for adoption, and nearly thirty-two percent of eligible children will wait for more than three years before being adopted.

These figures have significant implications. In 2014 a disturbing 22,392 youth aged out of the foster care system without the emotional and financial support necessary to succeed. Of these, one in five became homeless; one in four experienced post traumatic stress disorder; only half became employed by age twenty-four; fewer than three percent earned a college degree; and fifty percent of all youth who aged out of the system were involved in substance abuse. Of the women, seventy-one percent became pregnant by age twenty-one.[6]

The statistics can be even worse for children who, prior to living in foster care, were isolated from the general population.

Without specialized help, the children of Tony Alamo Christian Ministries face even worse odds for success. On the positive side, in the cult they did not suffer from malnutrition or homelessness. They developed some skills through their "employment" and were taught basic academic subjects. They even learned some effective survival skills. But human beings need more than food and housing. Once basic needs are met, we need to know that we belong on emotional, psychological, and intellectual levels. Once we know we belong, we are ready to embrace all that is unique about us and strive for the self-actualization that Maslow teaches in his Hierarchy of Human Needs.

The harm imposed on these children was somewhat invisible when the children came into state custody. The children were clothed, seemed healthy, and were smart. They were defensive of their teachings and behaved perfectly according to Alamo's training. After all, Papa Tony had warned of this takeover. The children had no strong sense of self identity and knew only a world defined by the cult.

Foster children come into the system not because they did something wrong. They are taken because their home is not safe for them and because their basic needs are not being met. These children will likely have emotional and behavioral issues. The longer they have lived in an unsafe environment, the more troubling their behaviors may be. When children don't understand what is happening in their families and homes, they supply their own answers, often blaming themselves. Guilt, anger, sadness, fear—all of these are emotions that typically result from their beliefs and then drive actions.

Alamo children didn't exist in this world. They entered with a completely different world paradigm and have no contextual history for the outside

---

6. Adoption and Foster Care Analysis and Reporting System (AFCARS) FY 2014 data.

world. They have no knowledge of even the simplest things—movies, music, sports, and significant public events. The way they lived discouraged the development of trust and attachments to family and friends. Their single authority figure, Tony Alamo, taught them to fear him and especially not to trust anyone outside the cult. Then, after all of this, they were taken from the only world they ever knew and dropped into a completely different society. They spoke the same language but had no shared experience to develop relationships. They had to unlearn a rigid belief system before they could even begin to function on the outside. The development of a sense of belonging is a huge challenge for these children. Even more daunting is the ability to embrace their uniqueness and self-actualize.

The Alamo children who came under the care of Ruth and Jay are moving forward because of this strong family that fostered and adopted them. Ruth and Jay worked diligently to learn what Alamo had taught the children. They studied the Bible to understand the children's perspectives of God. No training prepared them for the needs specific to children who have been kept in a high-demand cult for their entire lives. No training prepared them for the interactions they would witness between the children and their parents still in the cult. No training prepared them for the shame, guilt, and embarrassment they would witness in adults who broke free from the cult.

September 20, 2008, was a day of the first in a long series of traumas for the children who lived under Tony Alamo Christian Ministries. These children were born in the cult; some had parents who were also born in the cult. They had no birth certificates. They were brutalized and frightened all the time. They were taught to fear a God who promised destruction. A leader thought to be as powerful as God Himself controlled them. Trust was not a part of their character. They learned not to form close attachments. People disappeared. There was no limit to the terror they knew their leader would create—in the name of God. Even when Tony Alamo was sentenced to prison for 175 years, followers worshipped and obeyed him. Alamo's wives visited him in prison; they even circled to form a privacy shield so he could fondle young girls on their visits. They complied with every command in fear of being beaten, starved, banished, and humiliated. The reporting system always worked. Tony Alamo always had a way of knowing. And Tony Alamo knew how to break people.

How do children thrive after such a hideous imprinting? How do their broken parts heal? The truth is they will likely always have experiences that take them back to their beginnings. Just a slight movement, a familiar smell, a song, or a loud noise can trigger a response so deep that we aren't even conscious of the origin. The children are filled with all they learned, and this is not their fault. They did what they were supposed to do as children. They listened, learned, and obeyed. They all have that remarkable human spirit of survival. And in spite of it all, they also found ways to have fun. They learned to play and laugh and sing and love. As they run in this outside world, they are trying on ordinary experiences and integrating them in extraordinary ways. We can't ever escape the past, but we can look it in the eye and decide how we want to remember. The resiliency of these children—Audrey, Irene, Victoria, Ian, and Stefan—is possible for others. Triggers can unexpectedly summon memories of the past, but new experiences can offer balance as additional significant pieces of their emotional, psychological, intellectual, and spiritual makeup.

Unfortunately, though, too many cult survivors do not thrive. Emotional, psychological, and spiritual shackles display as guilt, fear, and shame. Whoever they were before the cult is deeply buried by the person they become, molded by the leader. They learn to fear the outside world and are told that leaving the cult will assure divine retribution and punishment. The cult leader dictates every aspect of living, including what to eat, what to wear, what to think, who can be friends, and family structure. Behavior is modified through methods including sleep deprivation, extensive fasts, poor nutrition, and punishment. Their sense of self is destroyed; and yet, somewhere inside, they do have a pre-cult identity. Finding that central core can be difficult if not impossible.

The children, second-generation adults (SGAs) and third-generation adults, have no life history before the cult. Their exit from the cult and entry into the outside world can be laden with anxiety. They are "aliens" to general society and have no understanding of the context of their new environment. Separation from their parents still in the cult stirs emotional

alienation and a deep sense of betrayal. Fear, lack of trust, and detachment
from others are at the central core of children taken from a cult. Their basic
human needs to fit in and to belong play out in behaviors of hiding their
true feelings, keeping their thoughts to themselves, and trying to "look
good" on the outside. Troubles run deep in SGAs whose entire childhood,
adolescence, and early adult years were spent entirely in a cult intent on
controlling them and crushing their individuality. They can be destroyed
emotionally, physically, and sexually. They don't even know what they have
in common with everyone in the general human experience. They just know
they feel different and frightened, so they try to cover up their past and
manage on their own. SGAs who were forced to exit have special issues
that are distinct from those who willingly left the cult. Every survivor has
a unique set of psychological, emotional, and cognitive needs.

Research to forge new ways to help SGA cult survivors is becoming more
possible as survivors self identify and tell their experiences.

The story of Tony Alamo is one of greed, corruption, and sociopathy.
Why would anyone join a cult? Why would everyone not leave? The hunter
and his prey are intertwined by opposites—power and insecurity, strength
and vulnerability, self-sufficiency and helplessness. Once he indoctrinated
them, Tony Alamo held his prey by every means available to him. His rules
for eternal salvation deny all aspects of the world outside his "church." He
destroyed natural family structure by separating children from their parents, spouses from spouses, and banishing the "backsliders" from their
homes. He took all money earned in wages, sent by families, inherited,
and paid by the government, such as social security and disability. His
rules are inconsistent, so punishments seemed to come out of nowhere.
Alamo's influence over his followers was so strong that he maintained his
power even from his residence at the federal penitentiary. His death has
done nothing more than add an exclamation point to the determination
of his followers.

It is possible to break the lifeline of this cult. Although they have demons from their past, with nurturing support, survivors can be physically,
spiritually, and psychologically safe. Experts estimate that more than five
thousand high-demand cults exist in the United States today, and the

number is growing. It's time to join forces to develop the special services needed to assure healthy and successful lives for all survivors.

DOES A CULT DIE WITH THE LEADER?

On Tuesday, May 2, 2017, Tony Alamo died. Initial news of his death stirred conflicting reports. Tony was first believed to be dead but then thought to be alive and moved to a different hospital unit. Some of his followers claimed that the US government stole and hid Tony's body. When his death was indeed verified, news flew throughout the Internet. Major newspapers carried the story with a few paragraphs reminding the public of Alamo's sordid past.

Former followers expressed mixed emotions, joy, and relief. Rebecca Gay who spent the first fourteen years of her life at the compound on Georgia Ridge wrote on Facebook: "Last night Tony Alamo, the leader of the religious cult where I was born and raised, a man who was an annihilator of lives, the fracturer of families, and a thief of innocence took his last breath. It feels strange—like someone cut the invisible tie that bound me for so long. I'm still processing. So many thoughts." Another former follower, Dorothy Curry of Fort Smith, posted: "I don't rejoice, but I'm kind of glad. I don't want to celebrate somebody's death. I'm not jumping up and down. We were all hurt by that ministry—spiritual abuse is what you call it. Some people have gotten over it, and some haven't." A posting on the Tony Alamo Christian Ministries Worldwide website gave tribute to the leader as a devotee to the Lord, exposing "the satanic world government and the very seat of Satan in a world-wide and effective way, when no one else dared." Followers vowed to "continue in winning the lost and preaching the full truth to the world as [Alamo] taught so well by example." On May 7, 2017, Tony Alamo's ashes were deposited in Memorial Park Cemetery in Tulsa, Oklahoma, where Susan Alamo was put to rest years earlier.

The impact of Tony Alamo's death is a double-edged sword. While Tony is no longer present to preach his destructive messages, his damage remains. Tony injected twisted beliefs and values into the minds of his followers. Those who willingly joined the church believed that they were finding a happy, God-centered community. Stepping into Alamo's world took them away from life as they knew it. Their pre-cult identity faded into the memory vaults of their minds, and new beliefs and regimens became their norm.

Children born to parents already in the cult grew up knowing only the singular world created by Tony Alamo. Their minds have no comparison set of tenets. The irony that both generations share is that Tony Alamo's death will not free them. They are imprisoned by the beliefs that Tony instilled in their minds and reinforced daily through abusive and denigrating treatment. Imbedded beliefs are the shackles that hold followers to obedience.

In *The Wizard of Oz* Dorothy discovered that she always had the power to go home. When she clicked her heels and returned to Kansas, she recognized that her brain, courage, and heart had been with her all along. The all-powerful wizard behind the curtain was really a somewhat inadequate person who hid behind illusions of grandeur. Fortunately for Dorothy, she returned safely to her home where her fundamental values were planted before she went to Oz. Had she been born in Oz, Kansas would have seemed scary and foreign to her. Even though Oz was built on deceptions, she would have believed and defended that as her reality.

The power to be free is and has always been held by the individual. We are the only ones who can release our beliefs and create new ones. Tony Alamo's death will not free anyone. Some will continue to preach Tony's teachings. Those who have left the cult may now face the realization that even though Tony has died, they still have some work to do. The triggers of past experiences and beliefs grounded in their psyches continue to pop up unexpectedly. The journey to freedom is a struggle through internal and external signals. While the willingness of the survivor generates the power to move forward, successful transition to life outside the cult depends upon steady, consistent, and reliable support and resources.

Acknowledgments

To the children: I am forever grateful that you entrusted your story to me. Your courage has brought us to this point today, through tears, fear, anger, and even laughter and joy. I am thankful beyond measure that you chose me to be your writer. You take my breath away. I will always treasure you as "my kids."

Ruth and Jay, you have shown us a model for parenting that embraces all children. Your love is safe, constant, and unconditional. Your fierce determination to stand tall for the rights of children and your compassion for the struggles of all former cult members set a high standard for the responsibility we all have to be difference makers. You have erased old boundaries and created a new definition of family.

To all the former members who have shared your stories with me: You opened yourselves from the inside out, and in so doing you changed me. I respect you especially for confronting your demons, fears, and regrets. I will never really know what your life feels like, but I hope that every day your guilt and shame diminish and at once disappear. I hope for you the time when your painful memories are powerless, and you feel the strength and joy of your true spirit.

Randall Harris, many thanks for being a supreme fact checker and teaching me the law enforcement side of this case. You are one of the heroes. A hero with a heart.

David Carter, as their legal advocate you give volume to the voices of these children. Your belief in them and fight for their rights have given them support to step into this world so foreign to them. You have signaled that we are not the world that Tony would have them believe.

To the many community people who talked with me—foster parents, adoptive parents, school counselors, teachers, pastors, psychologists, community agency representatives, judges, law enforcement officials—I am inspired by your commitment and genuine desire to help those in need.

You may be compensated for the hours you work, but you will never be compensated enough for your deep level of caring.

Lauri Currier, executive director of THE CALL, many thanks for helping me to appreciate the needs of our foster care system. I believe your passion will result in meeting your goal of having a thriving foster home for every child in every county of Arkansas. The next step is to meet this goal for every state in our country.

I am particularly grateful to the experts who gave this manuscript a thorough reading and advised ways to make it better. You all devoted much of your time to attend to all aspects of the book, to assure that it is accurate and pertinent. I hope you see the results of your efforts and know that I accept all responsibility for any missteps.

The University of Tennessee Press offers a stalwart group of professionals. I know that books published by this press will be edited, designed, and marketed by top-notch professionals. Scot Danforth, your encouragement and direction give me the confidence to keep growing as a writer. Thomas Wells, Tom Post, Linsey Perry, Lisa Davis, Jon Boggs, Kelly Gray, Stephanie Thompson, and Jake Sumner—I am grateful for all the ways you breathe life into a manuscript. To my copyeditor, Kathryn Little, special thanks for your sharp eyes and attention to source details.

Lorena Rostig, my marketing consultant in the early days of developing a plan for this story, thank you for giving me a jump start. Your direction connected me with Hillel Black (now deceased), an extraordinary editor whose sharp pencil performed magic on the manuscript.

Jill Knight, designer extraordinaire, you have created my presence on social media in spite of my limited expertise. Your guidance and direction give volume to this story. Thank you.

Another individual, taken too soon from this life, Cheryl Carson, was at once my cheerleader and sharp-witted critic. Reading my early drafts, Cheryl kept me going forward. She does still.

And to my friends, you all have helped in countless ways: by reading sections and responding, by understanding when I'm buried in my writing cubby for weeks at a time, and by spreading the messages of my work to your friends, families, and colleagues.

Finally, I am blessed with a wonderful family. My husband, Rob, is always here, encouraging me at every step. Kate, my daughter, inspires me every day with her ability to find joy even in a single daisy. And now she and her husband, Kenzie, are making me smile to see the love and happiness in their home. Our moms and dads, sister and husband, nieces, brother, and cousins—all have a part in giving character and life to this fabric—my family. I am grateful to have you all.

APPENDIX I
Dangerous Traits of Cult Leaders
Joe Navarro, MA, Former FBI Agent

1. Has a grandiose idea of who he is and what he can achieve.
2. Is preoccupied with fantasies of unlimited success, power, or brilliance.
3. Demands blind unquestioned obedience.
4. Requires excessive admiration from followers and outsiders.
5. Has a sense of entitlement, expecting to be treated special at all times.
6. Is exploitive of others by asking for their money or that of relatives putting others at financial risk.
7. Is arrogant and haughty in his behavior or attitude.
8. Has an exaggerated sense of power that allows him to bend rules and break laws.
9. Takes sexual advantage of members of his cult.
10. Sex is a requirement with adults and sub adults as part of a ritual or rite.
11. Is hypersensitive to how he is seen or perceived by others.
12. Publicly devalues others as being inferior, incapable, or not worthy.
13. Makes members confess their sins or faults publicly subjecting them to ridicule or humiliation while revealing exploitable weaknesses of the penitent.
14. Ignores the needs of others, including: biological, physical, emotional, and financial needs.
15. Frequently boasts of accomplishments.
16. Needs to be the center of attention and does things to distract others to insure that he or she is being noticed by arriving late, using exotic clothing, overdramatic speech, or by making theatrical entrances.
17. Has insisted in always having the best of anything (house, car, jewelry, clothes) even when others are relegated to lesser facilities, amenities, or clothing.
18. Doesn't seem to listen well to needs of others, communication is usually one-way in the form of dictates.
19. Haughtiness, grandiosity, and the need to be controlling are part of his personality.
20. Behaves as though people are objects to be used, manipulated, or exploited for personal gain.
21. When criticized he tends to lash out not just with anger but with rage.
22. Anyone who criticizes or questions him is called an "enemy."
23. Refers to non-members or non-believers in him as "the enemy."
24. Acts imperious at times, not wishing to know what others think or desire.

25. Believes himself to be omnipotent.

26. Has "magical" answers or solutions to problems.

27. Is superficially charming.

28. Habitually puts down others as inferior and only he is superior.

29. Has a certain coldness or aloofness about him that makes others worry about who this person really is and/or whether they really know him.

30. Is deeply offended when there are perceived signs of boredom, being ignored, or being slighted.

31. Treats others with contempt and arrogance.

32. Is constantly assessing for those who are a threat or those who revere him.

33. The word "I" dominates his conversations. He is oblivious to how often he references himself.

34. Hates to be embarrassed or fail publicly—when he does, he acts out with rage.

35. Doesn't seem to feel guilty for anything he has done wrong nor does he apologize for his actions.

36. Believes he possesses the answers and solutions to world problems.

37. Believes himself to be a deity or a chosen representative of a deity.

38. Rigid, unbending, or insensitive describes how this person thinks.

39. Tries to control others in what they do, read, view, or think.

40. Has isolated members of his cult from contact with family or outside world.

41. Monitors and/or restricts contact with family or outsiders.

42. Works the least but demands the most.

43. Has stated that he is "destined for greatness" or that he will be "martyred."

44. Seems to be highly dependent [on] tribute and adoration and will often fish for compliments.

45. Uses enforcers or sycophants to insure compliance from members or believers.

46. Sees self as "unstoppable" perhaps has even said so.

47. Conceals background or family which would disclose how plain or ordinary he is.

48. Doesn't think there is anything wrong with himself—in fact sees himself as perfection or "blessed."

49. Has taken away the freedom to leave, to travel, to pursue life, and liberty of followers.

50. Has isolated the group physically (moved to a remote area) so as to not be observed.

APPENDIX 2
The Author's Interviews with Tony Alamo

After many unanswered attempts to contact Tony Alamo directly, I sent a request for an interview by email to Tony Alamo Christian Ministries. I received an immediate response, and while Tony Alamo was not willing to meet me in person, he suggested that a member of his organization could read the questions to him and then he could dictate his responses to me. We communicated by email.

Alamo's responses reveal a great deal about how he viewed me and how he viewed the world. Keep in mind that in answering my questions he was writing to you, my readers. He was also writing to his own people in the ministry. His words are consistent with those of people who misuse power, manipulate doctrine to justify their actions, see themselves as superior and even God-like, and claim that all opponents are conspiring against them.

INTERVIEW ONE—APRIL 28, 2014

1. *How did you prepare your children to be ready for a governmental assault like what happened at Waco?*
   ALAMO: We just trust in the Lord.
2. *What management style is required of the leader of such a large following?*
   ALAMO: You just have to be anointed by the Lord.
3. *As Christ had disciples, what do you foresee for your church after you die?*
   ALAMO: Well, I'm not planning on dying.
4. *What criteria are necessary for you to be confident in authorizing the church leaders directly under you?*
   ALAMO: You're not qualified to write this book. You ought to just stop it because your questions are the most carnal I've ever heard.

5. *I can't imagine how painful it must have been for you to see children taken from their parents during the FBI raids. Looking back, what thoughts do you have about how the children were prepared for that?*

ALAMO: You just have to be prepared. I always tell people to trust in the Lord no matter what happens. God can either let it happen or not. And whatever is of the Lord is fine with all of us.

6. *What doesn't the world know about Tony Alamo that you want them to know?*

ALAMO: If the world doesn't know about it, why should I tell you? Then somebody would know, wouldn't they?

7. *Without the governmental interference, what might your ministry look like today with you at the helm?*

ALAMO: If I was at the helm, we'd really be in trouble. I always put Jesus at the helm and anybody that's going to be successful; they'll do the same.

8. *Just as Jesus was asked if He had been a prophet such as Elijah from the Old Testament, are you a prophet from the old time? If yes, do you have knowledge of who that would be?*

ALAMO: Some people think I'm a prophet.

9. *In the future can the world anticipate your return to continue prophesying?*

ALAMO: The world is going to Hell, and born-again Christians know how it really is. It's just a matter of trusting in the Lord and anyone who's of the Lord will trust in the Lord and not ask such stupid questions.

10. *What is your message for me?*

ALAMO: My message for you would be: don't write this book. It's going to be too carnal. You're full of carnality. I believe the Lord's coming back real soon, and that people who are alive in the Lord and doing His work will not be dying like you plan for me (Question #3).

INTERVIEW TWO — APRIL 30, 2014

ALAMO: Your questions are too carnal. It's true that we live in a carnal world, but there are some of us that are spiritual, and we don't like to respond to carnal questions.

AUTHOR: Thank you for responding to my questions. I hear what you say about my being carnal. I guess I am, and I believe this is by and large a carnal world. I want to convey the power of your ministry in a way that carnal ears can hear. In that vein, I have some additional questions that I hope you will answer.

1. *Describe how people who have left your church can find God and forgiveness.*

ALAMO: I'm not saying that they do. Why do you think they do? That's what I mean by you being so carnal. People like you would probably say that Judas Iscariot could be reconciled with the Lord and that he could be forgiven. That's not possible. It's impossible to restore them, as the Bible in many places says (Hebrews 6:4–6, 10:26–31).

2. *Many church communities claim to be Christian. Do you have pity for them in their ignorance?*

ALAMO: Those people are willingly ignorant. I'm not going to take part in a book like this. There's no value to it because you're just merely going along with the carnality of this world, and I don't go along with the carnality of this world. I'm spiritual, and you are carnal.

3. *I don't intend to be critical with my questions. I think I may be among the many people who believe they are Christians who believe in the Lord. What can I do?*

ALAMO: You don't intend to be critical? Well then you're not a Christian. If you're a Christian, you must be critical. All the things that the Lord says, He said you're either saved or you're lost. So that shows that He criticizes people. He rebukes and reproves them and tells us to do the same. And I'm not interested in your book.

4. I read in your materials a little about two witnesses, and I am fascinated and want to learn more. Would you please tell me more of the story?

ALAMO: Read the eleventh chapter of Revelation. And it's not my story; it's the Lord's story. Everything you say is repugnant. You are not qualified to write anything spiritual, and it's just going to be a big, stupid book.

5. I grew up having a minister's carnal interpretation and description of heaven and hell that depicted images of physical bodies suffering or angelic. When you think of heaven and hell, if you don't see physical bodies burning, what do you see instead?

ALAMO: I'm not your student and you're pretending that you want to be mine. I don't take on students like you because you ask all the wrong questions. I've seen Heaven and I've seen Hell. You have to believe the Word of God that says it's a place of eternal punishment. If you want to take that in a light way, well then you can do that if you want. But I can tell you as a person that's seen it, and have had many other people down through the fifty years that I've been saved and in the ministry, I've heard people give very excellent and spiritual explanations about what they've seen of Hell and of Heaven. It wouldn't do any good to tell you because you're opinionated in the wrong way.

AUTHOR: I am continuing to listen to your audio messages and appreciate your willingness to communicate with me.

ALAMO: I'm not that willing to communicate with you. I totally wish that you'd stop wasting my time. You're going to write whatever you want, and I'm keeping tapes of these questions of yours to show that I never encouraged you at all to write anything, and I have not asked you to write anything. As a matter of fact, I told you not to, because you don't know what you're doing. You're self-appointed. You're a self-appointed scribe.

INTERVIEW THREE — MAY 20, 2014

1. *My heart went out to the children who were taken in the 2008 governmental raid. Now that they have been taken, what do they need to hear from you?*

    ALAMO: I have no access to them. The problem is that they're hearing from homosexuals and people that are anti-Christ and pro anti-Christ government. I have no access to tell them anything. You're just fishing around to find out what my feelings are. I can't help it that they were picked up and that false charges have been brought against me. I've done nothing wrong. This seems to be a case of people persecuting Christians throughout the entire world. That's the game nowadays. The government feels that time has lapsed enough and that they've gotten enough satanic doctrine into the people of the world, that there's not going to be that much of an uprising against persecuting and lying about Christians. I've done nothing wrong, and I'm in prison, they say, for 175 years. And it looks like they have sent these people that are accusing me to the Cult Awareness Network, which has been renowned for lying and deprogramming people. We'll just see how this plays out with the Lord God. I believe that you're part of the whole thing, and there's nothing that you could say that would make me change my opinion, because everything you say more firmly establishes that in my mind.

2. *There has been mention of a "house of scorn" with a suggestion that sending girls to live there was inappropriate punishment. Why did you believe it was appropriate?*

    ALAMO: Why do you care? You have nothing to do with the house of God. There were people in the Bible that were banished from the general assembly of the saints because of their anti-Christ actions. This was done temporarily to people who were getting out of order. Instead of spanking them,

they were separated from the others because of their un-
godly ways. That happens to be the Lord's way of running
a church. You don't know anything about that and you
just keep asking stupid questions.

3. *You have been accused of excessive physical disciplinary tactics.*
   What is your response to that criticism?

   ALAMO: I already told you that it's all false. The Bible tells you to
   spank kids. I haven't spanked anybody, their parents did
   the spanking and other people have done it and I haven't.
   We just keep the commandments of the Lord. Is there
   something wrong with that, you reprobate?

4. *I was surprised to hear on your CD that you have ten children.*
   Would you please share what they are doing now?

   ALAMO: I don't know and I don't care what they're doing now.
   They're grown up and they're individuals themselves.
   You're just a nosy swine. Now you can gather that I am
   the kind of person that they've probably told you that I
   am. I'm very forward and very nasty to people who are
   trying to undermine the church.

5. *With the government seizing church properties, do you have a sense*
   of responsibility for your people who are losing their homes?

   ALAMO: That's none of your business. I have a sense of responsibility
   to the Lord. All the questions you're asking show me that
   you're working with the government. And if you think I'm
   so naïve that I don't know it, well, you're sick in your head.

6. *I talked with my best friend about your telling me of my carnal frame*
   of reference. She said that you're right about that, and she clearly
   recognized your description of being saved, and said that you "nailed"
   it. She asked if I knew how people living far and wide become members
   in your church. I told her that I don't know, but that I would ask you.

   ALAMO: It's a spiritual matter and the Bible says that carnal people
   cannot understand spiritual things. So if God says that
   you're unable to understand spiritual matters, why should
   I try to explain them to you?

APPENDIX 3
Tony Alamo's Wives

NAME/*PSEUDONYM	CHILD BRIDE	YEAR OF MARRIAGE	DIVORCE
Joann Dill	No	1950s	Yes
Helen Hagan	No	1961	Yes
Susan Lipowitz	No	1966	No
Birgitta Gyllenhammer	No	1984	Yes
Elizabeth Caldwell-Amrhein	No	1985	Yes
Diana Elana Williams	No	1987	Yes
Sharon Ast-Kroopf	No	1989	No
Lydia Willis	No	1993	No
Jody Fryer	No	1993	No
*Gail	Yes	1993/94	N/A
Misheal Jones	No	1993	No
*Marsha	No	1993	No
*Anne	No	1993	No
*Carla	No	1993	No
*Andrea	Yes	1994	N/A
*Ellen	No	1994	No
*Patsy	Yes	1994	N/A
*Christine	Yes	1994	N/A
*Lynn	Yes	1998	N/A
*Allison	Yes	1999	N/A
*Avril	Yes	1999/2000	N/A
*Monique	Yes	1999/2000	N/A
*Shadow	Yes	2003	N/A
*Nora	Yes	2003?	N/A

Reflections by Randall Harris,
Lead FBI Agent in Tony Alamo Case

First, I want to make it clear—the investigation which ultimately led to the conviction of Tony Alamo was a joint effort in every sense. John Bishop and the Arkansas State Police provided invaluable assistance during both the investigation and the trial. My partner, along with our Texas-side counterparts and our secretary, could always be counted on to drop their own work and jump in to assist. Other FBI agents and support professionals throughout the Little Rock Division as well as other offices such as Oklahoma City, Denver, and Los Angeles were also instrumental. And all of our work would have been in vain were it not for our lead federal prosecutor and her associates.

If any one person should be considered a "hero" in this case, it certainly has to be the former child bride identified in this book as Monique. She was the first child bride who was willing to come forward and tell her story, providing the most recent account of what was occurring in the Alamo compound with intricate details of the polygamy, child sex abuse, physical abuse, and Alamo's penchant for taking illicit photos of his child brides. Without her help, we likely would have never obtained the cooperation of Shadow, who detailed her interstate travels with Alamo. Early on in the investigation, before being contacted by Monique, John Bishop and I knew that Lynn was no longer living with Alamo. Brenda reported back that Lynn had corroborated all of our suspicions but that she refused to cooperate with law enforcement: she still feared that Alamo could actually be a prophet and that her soul would be sent to hell. John and I knew then and there that our work was cut out for us. How were we to overcome a person's fear of eternal damnation?

Throughout my FBI career, I served as the case agent on investigations involving children and teens as victims. I investigated cases involving teens dying from heroin overdoses, the interstate transportation of young girls for sexual purposes, kidnapping, Internet predators, and child pornography. None of these cases, however, were going to hold a candle to what I was about to experience during the Alamo investigation.

A number of people voiced complaints that law enforcement had not acted soon enough. When I got involved in the Alamo investigation in late 2006, the information coming in was primarily from former members who had been out of the group for several years. The allegations were of crimes that would be state violations, and the information was "stale." State statute of limitations had expired. Until a recent change in state law, even child sex abuse allegations would have been met with Arkansas statute of limitations problems. It was in about May 2008 when John and I first met with Monique. A couple of months later we met with Shadow. Now, with the allegations of child pornography and Mann Act violations, we could build a federal case. In the federal system, we weren't going to be hampered with statute of limitations issues for these types of crimes.

By late summer 2008, John and I felt our case was coming together. We had an October target date for raiding the Alamo compound. On that September Friday night when I learned of the errant email that disclosed our plans, my life was about to change in ways I had not imagined. It was about to be consumed by Alamo. I found myself not only responsible for preparing the federal case for trial, but also with a de facto responsibility to assist the State in their efforts to remove all the other children from Alamo's grasp. From that Friday night until the day Alamo was convicted at trial, I had worked seven days a week. I could almost count on only one hand the number of days I took off, including Saturdays, Sundays, and holidays. I immersed myself in learning all I could about Alamo's previous trial tactics. I ordered in FBI files from every office that had previously investigated him. I consulted with an IRS agent involved in his tax fraud trial. I enlisted the help of former and current Alamo members or associates. My intent was to be able to discredit anyone Alamo might call as a witness on his behalf. If we sniffed out a hint of anyone willing to cooperate with us, FBI agents were dispatched to conduct interviews and take statements.

During the course of this process, we located a number of witnesses who would not necessarily benefit our criminal case, but who certainly had information that would assist the State in their custody proceedings. In those instances, we referred those potential witnesses to the State. On top of all this, as a coincidental result of the child custody hearings in Arkansas, a fugitive Alamo member wanted in connection with the 1988 beating of Justin Miller was arrested. Now, Los Angeles County prosecutors seeking assistance with locating witnesses willing to testify in that case were also contacting me.

In retrospect, all of our efforts were successful. Alamo was convicted and would spend the rest of his life in prison. He would never be able to harm a child again.

In many of the cases I investigated involving children as victims, it was apparent that the reason they became vulnerable was due to a lack of parental oversight and/or the apathy of other adults who could have and should have taken steps to intervene. In the Alamo group, we found an entire culture of parents and other adults who willingly turned a blind eye to Alamo's abusive tactics. Ultimately, the downfall of Alamo was the result of the children themselves who mustered up the courage to report the abuse.

It is gratifying to know that many of those who were liberated from Alamo have found some success in life. I'm sure, however, that some still struggle to assimilate outside the cult. To those, I would offer the testimony of one of the child bride victims at Alamo's sentencing who stated to Alamo, "My bad days in the real world are better than my best days were in your house, your hell."

APPENDIX 5
Expressions

Human beings are at once emotional, physical, intellectual, and spiritual. As we develop and interact with others, these parts find expression. In the most healthy and safe environment, we achieve balance to become whole. Along the way we may fall off center, and the journey back to balance is an invaluable teacher that can even make us stronger.

When children are raised in a home that suppresses healthy development, their life paths inevitably have starts and stops. The true inner self may become seemingly paralyzed and overtaken by the adult controller, who exercises complete charge of what to think, feel, and do.

Even in this oppressive and frightening culture, the inner self never dies; it is lost. Those who look at us closely can see evidence of our true selves through behaviors and expressions. And the expressions, no matter how painful or dark, are beautiful. They show us stark truth.

The following pieces embody the voices of the children—voices that have been there all along and whose expressions now find strength and wholeness by speaking out loud. The poetry and letters of Ruth and Jay give us a glimpse of the brand of unconditional love that is essential for the true self to thrive.

ORIGINAL ARTWORK BY AUDREY.

ORIGINAL ARTWORK BY IRENE.

ORIGINAL ARTWORK BY IRENE.

EYE SURVIVED

By Irene
This piece was made with love and empathy in remembrance
of all the victims and survivors of domestic violence.

Hello warrior.

I see your tale in your eyes.
They read like a history:
Vulnerability, misplaced trust,
Disrespect, pain, shame.
But your story does not stop there, no.

Do read on to see:
The lessons learned, character forged,

Hope ignited, spirit emboldened.
They arise from destruction, and realization
　　that you never belonged
In those specious cages which bound you.

When I see your warrior eyes,
I know you are brave, tenacious,
Weathered, wary.

And yet, your capacity to love,
Ability to understand, and strength to bear
　　it when you want to let it overcome
you have only grown.
For as deeply as the words and wounds tore
　　into your mind and body, you now feel your triumph.

Wear your story proudly. Remember the battles
　　you have overcome and shine for those who need
　　to see you prevail. And when they ask why your
　　countenance is heavy and your eyes an enigma,
　　I hope you reply, "Eye survived."

Breathe.
Release.
We broke our cages.
We are free.

MEMORIES OF A FORGOTTEN ANGEL

By Victoria

I do not want to close my eyes for fear of your memory surfacing behind
my exhausted eyelids. For your memory pains me deep down in the depths
of my core. I cannot take another blow that you would strike at me, for
I am down to my lowest point. My heart weeps at the memory of happy
days wherein my entire being smiled. Your glow consumed me and now
I am left with nothing but the memory of it. I am as ashes—burnt and

hollowed out from your glory that once filled me. Your absence leaves a deep ingrained sorrow that cannot be undone. Your beauty plagued me with its presence. Your laughter poisoned my soul. For now that they are gone I am left desolate. The shrieking winds sing my song and the moaning waters mirror my dance. My sight is grayed and dim from the aftershock of your bright light. My soul continues to decay from the lack of your sun. I am battered. I am beaten. I am without you. Where can I go? What will I do? Live? I think not, for you have taken away the meaning of my life and without it I must surrender to the evil of death.

SOLITUDE

By Ian

Solitude? This concept is my best friend,
For I've never had anyone,
On which I could depend.

Bloodied and broken
By the one I called "Father;"
I've learned to trust no one,
For there's nothing they can offer.

Strengthened by anguish,
Hardened by grief,
Nothing now supports me,
Save my own two feet.

In this moment of solitude
To ask who I am,
Is to peer at a heart ever breaking
And a pair of empty hands.

IT WAS ALWAYS YOU

My heart yearned for you
Yet I did not know you.
My soul cried out for you
But I could not find you.
My eyes
Looked for you and I could not see you.
He made you, but I did not know it yet.
He placed in you and me a connection into the depths
   of our souls.
He bonded us together
As mother and daughter and waited
For that perfect moment to reveal us to each other.
And because of our openness to accept what He had done,
I knew it was always you!
Love,
Mom (Ruth)

DEAR VICTORIA,

I cannot believe this day is here. It has been a bit of a challenge to get to this point. But Wow, is it worth it. You have been my daughter in my heart since I met you. I truly feel blessed that we can now make it official and that we now share the same last name legally. I love you more than I know how to express. I am so happy that you are my daughter. So I wanted to say a few things to express what this great day means.

As you know, I am not always that kind of person that shows my emotions openly. For that I apologize. But I want you to know that the excitement inside of me right now is exploding even though I may not show it. You have lit up my life and have given me more joy than I can explain. You are just as beautiful on the inside as you are on the outside. I love to see you smile and hear you tell stories.

I promise you a life of unconditional love from me. As your dad, I want to always be there for you. I know I will make mistakes and have already, but I never intend to and will do my best to avoid them. I hope that you feel that you can trust my advice and that you will always try to do the right thing no matter the consequence.

I look forward to seeing you get married, have children (of course many years from now), and live a life of excellence. You have what it takes to live the life you want to live. You are capable of being whatever you want to be. I am excited to see what you decide and how you do it. Never forget that you are in charge of your future. Your thinking and your decision-making ability will determine where you go. So always improve your thinking and decision-making ability. You are a very intelligent and courageous young lady that can do many great things.

I want you to feel that you can talk to me about anything. Do not ever worry about what I may or may not get upset about. Never worry about hurting my feelings. Just be open and honest, and we can always have a great relationship. I want to be the best dad you could dream of. I want to be a part of your life for the rest of my life.

Always remember it is not what happens to you; it is how you handle it. I know that you were brought into my life for a reason. I know you have a purpose. I hope that I can help you discover that purpose and fulfill your destiny. Never settle for Good when Great is available. I am so happy to be in your life as you answer these questions for yourself: Who Am I? Why Am I Here? Where Am I Going? How Will I Get There? Always remember that "You Don't Know What You Don't Know." Meaning you need to constantly seek more knowledge throughout life.

I am so proud of you for all you have accomplished and gone through over the last few years. You are a very beautiful angel. I love you so very much.

Love, Dad (Jay)

DEAR IAN,
Wow, what a journey. And it is just beginning. What a great day. I am very proud to have you as a son. I just wanted to take a few minutes and tell you what is on my mind.

First, I think you are an incredible young man with a very awesome future. Watching you grow and achieve things is something that makes me feel blessed to be a part of. Seeing you for who you are and who you will become is an honor, and I thank our Lord for allowing me to be a part of that. I am truly sorry for what you have had to endure to get to this point in your life. I also hope that you keep your heart open and continue to move forward in life. You have and will serve a great purpose.

I know that I can come off as being hard to talk to or closed off. I truly do not mean to be. I want to be a person you can talk to about anything from God to morals, from girls to school, from honor to just everyday life, and of course to the future and anything else. I want to be someone you feel you can trust with anything. I want you to know that I would do anything for you and look forward to being a bigger part of your life.

I want you to know that you can talk to me about anything and not to ever worry about hurting my feelings. I know you have a big heart, and I just want to be part of it. I want you to know that I always mean well even when it does not seem like that is what comes out.

I will try harder to have some time with you and do some things that we can do together, like maybe go fishing, shooting, or something like that. I know we are about to get to spend some time together while you learn to drive. That will be fun. I will work on being more expressive to you and ask that you do the same. But know in my heart you are a big part of my life, and I am thankful that you are. You are a very smart young man. If you choose to apply yourself, you can do and go anywhere you want in life. You have the ability and you have the power to guide your future.

I am so happy to be in your life as you seek answers to these questions for yourself: Who Am I? Why Am I Here? Where Am I Going? How Will I Get There? I for one, cannot wait to see as you grow into the answers. God is great.

I love you as a son and am very blessed to have you in my life. I hope that this day means something special to you and that I can live up to your expectations. You are a very special young man, and I pray for you often. I look forward to your future.

Love, Dad (Jay)

DEAR STEFAN,

Here it is, the big day. I am so excited. I hope you are too. We have been together for a while now, but this is a new beginning. I am thankful that God chose me to be in your life. I am so sorry for what you went through to come to this point. I pray I can help you look forward and move forward and live a life of excellence. I am excited to be a part of it.

I know there will be some struggles in the future and that we may not always agree. But as we move forward, always know that I will do my best to provide for you and protect you. I know I do not always express my emotions to you. I will work on that and ask the same from you. You have taken a firm position in my heart, and I love you as my son. I do not want to be distant from you and hope that our relationship will continue to grow, as a real father/son relationship should. Anything I can help you with I will. Please do not hesitate to talk to me about anything. I will not express my reply in anger and will do my best to give you the best advice I can.

I am looking forward to helping you find your way and discover your purpose in this crazy world. I am looking forward to seeing you grow into the young man you are meant to be. You are a special young man and have experienced many trials in your short life so far. I pray that your life from this point forward will be full of love and happiness even through the normal struggles of life. You are a very smart young man, and if you choose to apply yourself, you can do and go anywhere you want in life. You have the ability, and you have the power to guide your future.

I am so happy to be in your life as you answer these questions for yourself: Who Am I? Why Am I Here? Where Am I Going? How Will I Get There? And I look forward to watching you develop and grow into the answers.

I love you as a son and want to always be there for you. I hope this day means a lot to you and that I can live up to your expectations. I am very proud of you for all you have endured and how you continue to grow as a young man.

Love, Dad (Jay)

Selected Bibliography

This bibliography is by no means a complete record of all the works I have consulted. I have chosen to offer a spectrum of resources for those who wish to pursue further study of cults. The International Cultic Studies Association (ICSA), in particular, provides a wealth of information on cults, cultic groups, psychological manipulation, psychological abuse, spiritual abuse, brainwashing, mind control, thought reform, abusive churches, high-demand groups, extremism, totalistic groups, new religious movements, alternative and mainstream religions, group dynamics, exit counseling, recovery, and practical suggestions for those affected by or interested in these subjects. ICSA sponsors annual conferences, regional workshops, and workshops focusing on Second Generation Adults (SGAs). Website: icsahome.com.

Armstrong, Karen. *The Spiral Staircase*. New York: Knopf, 2004.

Aron, Raphael. *Cults, Terror, and Mind Control*. Point Richmond, CA: Bay Tree Publishing, LLC, 2009.

Buchanan, Susy. "The Ravening Wolf." *Southern Poverty Law Center Intelligence Report* 127 (Fall 2007).

Carter, W. David. "Do It In the Name of Heaven: Handling Spiritual Abuse Cases." Unpublished paper presented to Arkansas Trial Lawyers Association, March 4, 2014.

Duncan, Wendy J. *I Can't Hear God Anymore: Life in a Dallas Cult*. Rowlett, TX: VM Life Resources, LLC, 2006.

Eichel, Steve K. D. "All God's Children: Another Tragedy." *Wilmington (DE) Sunday News Journal* (April 20, 2008). http://www.dreichel.com/Articles/FLDS_Texas.htm.

Erwin, Christie. *The Middle Mom: How To Grow Your Heart by Giving It Away . . . A Foster Mom's Journey*. Little Rock: Grayson Publications, 2009.

Furnari, L. "Born or Raised in High-Demand Groups: Developmental Considerations." *ICSA E-Newsletter* 4, no. 3 (2005). http://www.icsahome.com/articles/born-or-raised -furnari-en4-3.

Goldberg, Lorna. "Raised in Cultic Groups: The Impact on the Development of Certain Aspects of Character." *Cultic Studies Review* 5, no. 1 (2006): 1–27. http://www.icsa home.com/articles/raised-in-cultic-groups-goldberg.

———. "The Harsh Conscience of Second-Generation Former Cultists." Workshop session presented at the International Cultic Studies Association SGA Workshop, Cornwall, CT (April 2006).

Goldberg, Lorna and William Goldberg, Rosanne Henry, Michael Langone, editors. *Cult Recovery: A Clinician's Guide to Working with Former Members and Families*. International Cultic Studies Association, 2017.

Hasson, Steven. *Combatting Cult Mind Control*. Newton, MA: Freedom of Mind Press, 2016.

———. *Releasing the Bonds: Empowering People to Think for Themselves*. Somerville, MA: Freedom of Mind Press, 2000.

Huddle, John. *Locked In: My Imprisoned Years in a Destructive Cult*. Marion, NC: Survivor Publishing, LLC, 2015.

Kent, Stephen A. *From Slogans to Mantras: Social Protest and Religious Conversion in the Late Vietnam War Era*. Syracuse: Syracuse Univ. Press, 2001.

———. "House of Judah, the Northeast Kingdom Community, and 'the Jonestown Problem': Downplaying the Child Physical Abuses and Ignoring Serious Evidence." *International Journal of Cultic Studies* 1, no. 1 (2010): 27–48. http://www.icsahome .com/articles/house-of-judah-the-northeast-kingdom-community-and-the-jonestown -problem-kent-ijcs-2010.

Kocsis, Vennie. *Cult Child*. venniekocsis.com, 2014.

Lalich, Janja and Madeleine Tobias. *Take Back Your Life: Recovering from Cults and Abusive Relationships*. Berkeley: Bay Tree Publishing, 2006.

Langone, Michael D., ed. *Recovery From Cults: Help for Victims of Psychological and Spiritual Abuse*. New York: W.W. Norton & Company, 1993.

Lasch, Christopher. *The Culture of Narcissism: American Life in An Age of Diminishing Expectations*. New York: W.W. Norton & Company, 1979.

Lattin, Don. *Jesus Freaks: A True Story of Murder and Madness on the Evangelical Edge*. New York: Harper Collins Publishers, 2007.

Martin, Walter. *The Kingdom of the Cults*. Minneapolis: Bethany House Publishers, 2003.

Miscavige, Ron, with Dan Koon. *Ruthless: Scientology, My Son David Miscavige, and Me*. New York: St. Martin's Press, 2016.

Perlstein, Rick. *Before the Storm*. New York: Nation Books, 2001.

———. *The Invisible Bridge: The Fall of Nixon and the Rise of Reagan*. New York: Simon & Schuster, 2014.

———. *Nixonland: The Rise of a President and the Fracturing of America*. New York: Simon & Schuster, Inc., 2008.

Robertson, Irvine. *What the Cults Believe*. Chicago: The Moody Bible Institute of Chicago, 1991.

Rosendale, Herbert L., Michael D. Langone, Russell H. Bradshaw, and Steve K. D. Eichel. "The Challenge of Defining Cult." *ICSA Today* 6, no. 3 (2015): 2–13.

Singer, Margaret Thaler. *Cults in Our Midst: The Continuing Fight Against Their Hidden Menace*. San Francisco: Jossey-Bass, 2003.

Sire, James W. *Scripture Twisting: 20 Ways the Cults Misread the Bible*. Downers Grove, IL: InterVarsity Christian Fellowship Press, 1980.

Tucker, Maria Luisa. "The Barely Legal Empire of Tony Alamo." *Village Voice* (May 13, 2008).

West, Louis Jolyon and Michael D. Langone. "Cultism: A Conference for Scholars and Policy Makers." *Cultic Studies Journal* 3, no. 1 (1986): 85–96.

Wright, Lawrence. *Going Clear: Scientology, Hollywood, & the Prison of Belief*. New York: Knopf, 2013.

Index